Young Reni, a girl on the precipice of adolescence, takes us through the darkest days of the Holocaust and her budding understanding of the human spirit. What I found was heart, courage, tenderness, and hope. Not since the *Diary of Anne Frank*, have I been so touched by a book that grapples with the dark abyss of the human condition during the Holocaust. This book is a revelation about what sustains the human spirit, what is far stronger than hate.

JACQUELINE SHEEHAN
NYTimes bestselling author

In this striking memoir, Irene Butter gives us the sweep of catastrophic history through her child eyes. Taking the reader from "black zigzags" to cattle cars, from Berlin to Amsterdam to Westerbork to Bergen-Belsen to Algeria, and finally to the United States, young Reni shares the ordinary and the unimaginable with stunning detail, with generosity, with hope. Irene Butter's beliefs that one should never be an enemy and never be a bystander are important lessons for us to understand the past and to act in the world of today.

ELLEN MEEROPOL
Author of *Kinship of Clover*, named "One of the best books from Indie Publishers in 2017" by PBS

Irene Butter paints a gripping picture of a girl's sense of self in the Holocaust. German-Jewish through birth and heritage, stateless through persecution, and Dutch and American through refuge, Butter invites us to walk with her on the vulnerable journey of forging her young identity. In a time of resurging racism and xenophobia, the book forces the reader to consider what happens when adult dehumanization shapes the real life of a real child. The book bears witness to pre-war Germany, occupied Amsterdam, and the Bergen-Belsen of Anne Frank, and shares the warning of the *Diary of Anne Frank:* we lose our humanity when children are forced to normalize hatred.

ANNEMARIE TOEBOSCH
Director of Dutch and Flemish Studies, Lecturer of Anne Frank in Context
University of Michigan

As Holocaust memory moves into an uncertain future, Irene Butter's memoir will play an important role in keeping memory of the event alive. It also serves as a testament to one person's ability to build a life of meaning and hope in the wake of this horrible event.

JAMIE L. WRAIGHT, PhD
Director, The Voice/Vision Holocaust Survivor Oral History Archive
University of Michigan-Dearborn

Dr. Irene Butter is a remarkable woman who made a conscious decision to be a survivor, not a victim of the Holocaust. Her story has an inestimable impact on students. They witness her dedication to live a meaningful life of activism based on her belief that we can make the world a better place.

SUZANNE HOPKINS
Saline Middle School, retired educator
Saline, Michigan

For many years Irene Hasenberg Butter did not speak of her own experience of the Holocaust but like her brother, Werner, got on with the headlong rush of making a new life in the United States. After the treachery and horror of the Bergen-Belsen Concentration Camp, learning to live as Holocaust survivors was work enough. With this book, Irene has given the world a deeply personal account of her own family's experience that bravely reveals how much all the terrible losses of the Holocaust meant not just in World War II but, sadly, today as well.

JAN JARBOE RUSSELL
Author, *The Train To Crystal City*

Across these eloquent pages, Irene keeps readers by her side as we follow her childhood journey from Berlin to the shadow of German occupation in Amsterdam and into the darkness of the Holocaust. All will be riveted by the voice of Irene, whose love for her parents and brother, Werner, becomes the steady light for her courage. Unlike her friend Anne Frank, whom she sees for the last time in Bergen-Belsen, Reni survives evil and at age fifteen sails into Baltimore's harbor aboard a Liberty ship on Christmas Eve, 1945, with a resilience that still guides her important work with students in the 21st century.

LOUISE BORDEN
Author, *His Name Was Raoul Wallenberg*

Refusing to be an enemy is a choice we must make. Few people understand that stance with as much conviction as Irene Butter, who shares her incredible life story in this powerful and lyrically written memoir. Butter has faced a lifetime of choices, from her childhood during the depths of Holocaust to today. Reading *Shores Beyond Shores* reminds me yet again of Irene's indomitable spirit and her gift of seeking light amidst life's darkest hours.

ROBIN AXELROD, LMSW, JD
Director of Education
Holocaust Memorial Center, Zekelman Family Campus

Distances of time, circumstance, age, and background disappeared every time Irene spoke with groups of three hundred students over eighteen years at our middle school. Irene's thoughtful answers to intimate questions revealed new aspects and insights each year. Eyes of innocence and bravery describing her past then become heartfelt gazes of young people looking deep into themselves and finding compassion, tolerance, and perseverance. Inspiration to always fill the world with love and hope.

JONATHAN BERGER
English Language Arts Teacher
Discovery Middle School
Canton, Michigan

SHORES BEYOND SHORES

SHORES BEYOND SHORES

from Holocaust *to* Hope
My True Story

Irene Butter
with John D. Bidwell *and* Kris Holloway

White River Press
Amherst, Massachusetts

Shores Beyond Shores: From Holocaust to Hope, My True Story

First published 2018

White River Press
P.O. Box 3561
Amherst, MA 01004
whiteriverpress.com

Book and cover design: John D. Bidwell
Cover photo finishing: Jim Gipe/Pivot Media
Photo credits: Irene Butter and John D. Bidwell

ISBN: 978-1-935052-70-8 (paperback)
          978-1-887043-36-6 (ebook)

Library of Congress Cataloging-in-Publication Data

Names: Butter, Irene H. (Irene Hasenberg), 1930- author. | Bidwell, John,
   author. | Holloway, Kris, author.
Title: Shores beyond shores : from Holocaust to hope : my true story / Irene
   Butter, John D. Bidwell, and Kris Holloway.
Description: Amherst, Massachusetts : White River Press, 2018 |
Identifiers: LCCN 2017043082 (print) | LCCN 2017043622 (ebook) | ISBN
   9781887043366 () | ISBN 9781935052708 (pbk. : alk. paper)
Subjects: LCSH: Butter, Irene H. (Irene Hasenberg), 1930- |
   Jews--Germany--Berlin--Biography. | Holocaust, Jewish
   (1939-1945)--Germany--Berlin--Personal narratives. | Jewish children in
   the Holocaust. | Berlin (Germany)--Biography.
Classification: LCC DS134.42 (ebook) | LCC DS134.42 .B88 2018 (print) | DDC
   940.53/18092 [B] --dc23
LC record available at https://lccn.loc.gov/2017043082

In memory of my Pappi, my hero, my idol,
who did everything possible to save his family.
His life was taken when I was a child, only fourteen years old.
With awe I have felt his presence, his protection,
and his loving guidance throughout my life.

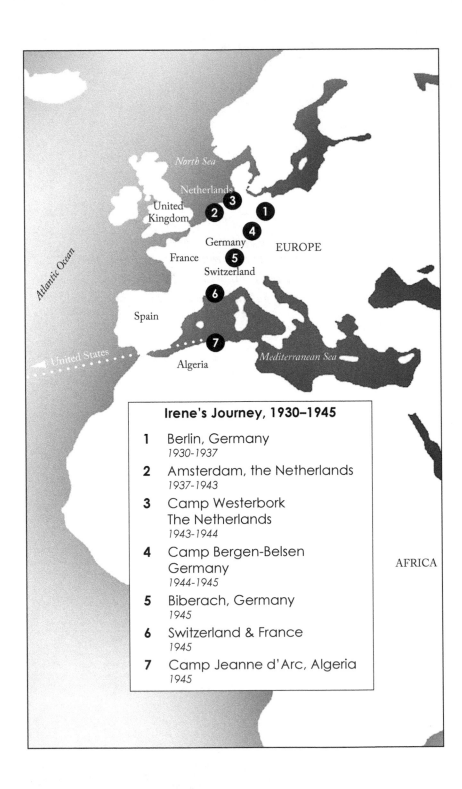

Irene's Journey, 1930–1945

1 Berlin, Germany
   1930-1937

2 Amsterdam, the Netherlands
   1937-1943

3 Camp Westerbork
   The Netherlands
   1943-1944

4 Camp Bergen-Belsen
   Germany
   1944-1945

5 Biberach, Germany
   1945

6 Switzerland & France
   1945

7 Camp Jeanne d'Arc, Algeria
   1945

Contents

Introduction

When I got off the ship that brought me to the United States in 1945, the American relatives who took me in urged me to forget everything that had happened to my family—and to me—in the Holocaust. They told me to never think or speak of it again. I was fifteen years old and they were adults, so I listened to them. For forty years I was quiet. I was not truly free until I started to tell what happened to me as a child. Here is my story.

The Happy Childhood

Berlin, Germany and

Amsterdam, the Netherlands

1936-1940

1

Berlin, Germany

Summary 1936

My birth name is Irene Hasenberg, but you can call me Reni (pronounced "Ray-nee"). Everyone did. I was a lucky child. I grew up in a large, light-filled apartment in Berlin, the sparkling capital of Germany, with my parents, John and Gertrude Hasenberg; my brother Werner, two years older than I, and my grandparents Julius and Pauline Mayer. Our parents and grandparents spoiled Werner and me with attention and toys. My favorite was a red tricycle that I got for my fourth birthday. I pedaled it with speed through the park, and flew across sidewalks, being sure to clean its wheels and shiny handlebars when I got home.

We celebrated Jewish holidays and our birthdays with relatives, always gathering together around the dinner table to eat challah, sing our favorite Hebrew songs, and drink more hot chocolate. Our voices were not very good, but who cared? We were together. We weren't making a record to be played on a phonograph! My experience as a young girl in Berlin was wonderful, despite the fact that Germany was changing.

But what did I know? I was only five.

My grandparents, Opa and Omi, rented a small garden plot not far from our home. One warm morning, Opa announced it was a perfect day for planting seeds, especially for cucumbers and radishes, my two favorite crunchies. We all went. It took a lot of work to dig the ground and "prepare the soil." We carefully put the tiny flat white seeds and the little round brown seeds into the dirt and covered them. Done with my row, I stared at the soil. I stared and waited a long, long time until the top layer dried and lightened in the sun. Nothing happened.

"Reni, are you ready to go?" Pappi asked.

"Let's wait until the crunchies come up."

"That'll take all summer!" Werner said.

"Reni, it takes a long time for the seeds to grow into vegetables," Mutti explained.

"What?"

Tears skidded down my cheeks. Opa knelt next to me, his knees clacking.

"Reni, don't cry. These are special seeds. They grow very fast, for seeds. You need to be patient. Can you be patient?"

"I'm trying."

"That's good practice."

At home, Mutti and Pappi had a surprise: we were going into the city and to the zoo. I forgot about the seeds. But first, Mutti instructed, we had to clean up.

"I'm already clean," said Werner. "I washed when we got back."

It was true. Even his shoes were shiny. I looked at my dress and fingernails. There was dirt everywhere. I brushed off everything with great sweeps of my hands, even remembering to shake my hair.

"I'm all set to go, too!"

"Reni, you are not even close," Mutti said, taking my hand and marching me to the bathroom.

She scrubbed me hard with soap and water, even digging into and around my ears.

"You're breaking me," I protested.

Mutti then wrapped me in a big towel, turned me around, and dried me, like she was fluffing up my whole body. Then it was off to the bedroom to get me dressed in something fancy. Finally, I stepped into the front hall where Pappi and Werner were waiting.

"Oh Reni," Pappi said with surprise, "you are here. I saw a little girl come in earlier, but I didn't recognize her for all the dirt."

"It was *me*!"

We took the big yellow tram to the zoo, the same tram Pappi rode every day to work. Cars and trucks honked here and there, weaving in and out. You never knew where the cars and trucks would go next, but the yellow tram always followed the same track and wires. And it always came and left at the same times, so I knew when Pappi would go to work and when he would come home. The brightly colored tram was easy to spot, so I could look out the apartment window and see it from far away and get ready for Pappi to return, when I would jump into his arms. He told me the other day that he could hardly lift me anymore. I was getting that big.

I looked out on Berlin. It was busy like ants over a picnic basket.

"Mutti," I asked, "what is the black zigzag?"

It was everywhere: on flags as big as buildings, on trucks and cars, and on clothes.

She said it was nothing, so I leaned toward my brother and asked him.

"Really, Reni? It's a swastika," Werner said.

"What's a schweiss…schweiss schick…er?"

"Swastika," he corrected me.

"I'm going to count them all. One, two, three, four, five…"

"Do something else, Reni," Mutti commanded.

"All the banners and flags are for the Olympics in August," Werner said.

"What's that?" I asked.

"Reni, do you know anything?" said Werner.

"I know there are maybe fifty swas…black zigzags," I said, and looked toward Mutti to be sure she wasn't listening. "Maybe more. I've really been counting."

"The Olympics are when sports players from all over the world come here to play," said Werner. "They will compete for medals. I've heard Germany will win a lot, especially in gymnastics and track and field. It's a big deal."

"Yes it is," Pappi added, "and Werner, you and I are going to watch the action."

For once, Werner didn't know what to say, finally eking out "really?'"

Pappi nodded.

"What about me?" I asked. "I want to go."

"You and I will go shopping," Mutti said.

Well, I didn't want to go to the Olympics that badly.

We walked up to the gate for the zoo, and I forgot about the black zigzags.

Inside, Pappi let go of my hand and I ran ahead with Werner, but not too far. Everything was so green: the puffy trees and the bristly grass. Beds of yellow and red flowers hugged tiny fences. The red was as bright as the big flags that floated over the buildings. I wanted to run into all that color, but I had learned to stay on the gray paths. We saw the elephants swing their tails and trunks, and I pointed at the big-mouthed hippos. We fed the goats that circled us and nibbled at our hands. My favorite was the monkey house with the playful, swinging families.

I rested my head against Pappi and his dark suit on the ride home. Then I remembered the magic seeds. *What did they look like as they tossed and turned in their little dirt beds?* I wondered out loud. Werner said I was hopeless, and Mutti pinched his arm. As we walked home from the tram, Mutti suggested we walk past the garden. I saw dots of green and red on the ground: shiny cucumbers and radishes. I ran across the dirt, though I knew I wasn't supposed to, took a cucumber, and bit into it to make sure it was real. It was the juiciest and most delicious cucumber I had ever eaten. Oh, they were special seeds! Opa was right.

"Wait. You need to wash those first, Reni," Mutti called.

I piled as many as I could into my skirt pockets. Mutti and Werner took the rest.

"Opa, Omi, look!" I cried as I entered our kitchen and emptied my pockets on the wooden kitchen table.

"You must have done a very good job planting them, my dear. I have never seen them come up this fast," Opa said.

"Yes, and I've never seen vegetables grow without plants," Werner said. "Like they came straight from the vegetable stand."

"All the more special," I added.

I took another bite of my cucumber. Sure, the seeds were special, but we were also very, very good gardeners.

That night, cozy in my bed, I thought of our cousin Bert's upcoming birthday party, excited that I would be able to wear one of my nice dresses. Maybe my blue-and-white plaid one with yellow buttons, or, if I was really lucky, Mutti would let me wear my white dress with tiny red and blue hearts and the smock, if I promised not to get it dirty and change as soon as I got home. I liked the puffy short sleeves on both, and....

I heard Werner's bed creak. Even without the golden light from my monkey night-light, I knew Werner had gotten out of bed and was standing next to me. I turned my face to the wall.

"Reni," he said, "are you sleeping?"

"Yes, I am sleeping."

"Reni, I want to ask something. Do you think that I'll have a bad dream?"

There was a wobble in his voice. I didn't answer. Lately, Werner had bad dreams more and more—it was a pain. It was like he looked for bad things to dream about. I didn't want to talk with him. I wanted to think about dressing for Bert's birthday. Bert would be six...just like I would be in December.

When I didn't respond he continued.

"It's all the swastikas. They're everywhere now, like the Nazis. And I heard the Nazis are doing bad things. Bad things to Jews. Jews like us."

"Stop it," I interrupted, "You're okay, Werner. No bad dreams tonight."

"Oh...okay," he said. "Thanks. Good night."

With that, he went back to the dark of his bed and crawled under the blankets.

2

Berlin, Germany

Winter 1937

Adolf Hitler had now been the *Führer*, or leader, of our country for four years. He liked people he said who were true Germans. He said they were better than all other people, and if they stayed pure—didn't mix with other peoples—they would take over the world some day. According to Hitler, people who were not pure German were less perfect, and he didn't like them. He said they made a mess of things, like a big smudge on his white tablecloth. This meant lots of people, including Jews like us.

Fear spread like spilled hot chocolate, burning everything it touched. My Opa had worked his whole life building a bank and was now forced to turn it over to someone who was not Jewish. My Pappi also worked in that bank.

One night, as I used the bathroom before bed, I saw Mutti crying. I didn't like to see my parents cry, and I looked away. Pappi came to tuck me in.

"I won't be taking the tram to work anymore, Reni," he said, smoothing my hair. "I will not be going to work…for now."

I was glad to hear that my parents were not upset with something I'd done.

"Does that mean you'll be home when I get home from school?" I asked.

"Yes, I will be home with you, for a little while, but I need to find another job," he said.

"So why is Mutti sad?" Being home more seemed good to me.

"She's sad because finding another job will not be easy. But I am going to try very hard to find one, and I bet I will."

"Okay."

"Go to sleep now, sweetie, everything will look better with the morning sun." He kissed my hair lightly.

Look better? I didn't think things looked bad. Something else must be wrong.

A few nights later, Mutti forgot to read to me. Then, listening from my bed, I heard my parents talking in fast, sharp whispers, keeping me awake. I couldn't hear the words, only the tone. Werner moved in his bed.

"Why are they fighting?" I whispered to him.

"I don't know."

We both crept to the door. I wasn't cold, but I brought my pink blanket. Mutti and Pappi's words flowed down the hall from the living room. I wrapped my blanket around me, and draped it over Werner.

"Even my friends have turned on me," Pappi's voice said. "On us. And these include the men I fought with in the Great War! How in God's name can they not help us? We lived and died in those...those terrible trenches, and fought side-by-side for our...for *this* country, our Fatherland! Together! And now they won't help. It's unbelievable. Even Frank will not get back to me. Frank!" He ended with a snarl that made me shiver.

"John, quiet, we don't want to wake the kids." Mutti said. "I know it isn't fair. It isn't right."

"Don't they know that we've ALWAYS been Jewish? Now. During the Great War. Forever. When did we suddenly become evil?"

I had never heard Pappi yell before.

"John, please. I know, I know." Pause. "What about Charles? Have you spoken to him?"

"It's the same, Trudi," he said in a softer voice. "I stopped by his office, but he wouldn't see me. I know he was there. Everybody is acting strange, even if they aren't Nazis. They are afraid. They are suspicious. It's spreading like a plague."

"There's still Leo."

"Yes, there's always Leo, but he's in the same situation as us. In fact, he mentioned he's thinking of moving the family to Holland."

Leo was my father's best friend in the war. There was a photo in Pappi's study of them standing arm-in-arm, in their smart officer uniforms.

"Maybe we should go, too. There are more anti-Jewish graffiti and posters," Mutti said. "When I go shopping. When I walk to the post office. It's terrifying. The children see them."

"Trudi, there are more terrifying things to be worried about now." He lowered his voice, and I strained to hear it. "Some of the bank tellers heard that they are gathering Jews, whole families, and sending them on trains to labor camps. Rumor is that it's happening in some neighborhoods in Berlin."

I tapped Werner on the shoulder and whispered across the smooth hardwood floor. "What are they talking about? The camps. The posters. And what's graf…?

"Graffiti. It's like drawing bad doodles on buildings."

"Really?"

"And I saw one of the posters. It had a spear killing a snake, and the snake had our Star of David on it."

I didn't know there were Jewish snakes. I didn't like any kind of snake. Yuck.

"My friends at school heard about trains going to the camps, too," Werner said.

Whenever we got on a train, it was for vacation, or to go someplace different and fun.

"Why would people get on a train going to a bad place?" I asked.

"They don't have a choice."

"Who makes them?"

"The people that run our country, Reni. The Nazis."

"The Nazis sound mean."

"They don't like anybody who is not like them."

"Who's that?"

"Anybody not Aryan."

"What's Aryan?"

"Reni! You ask too many questions. Aryans are German. Tall. Blond. Blue-eyed."

"We're German! And I have blue eyes!"

"It doesn't include us."

"But why?"

"Because we're Jewish. Don't you listen to anything?"

It didn't make any sense to me, but *Nazi* sounded like a mean word, a word that could cut you. And getting on a train to a bad place didn't sound like a vacation at all. We listened to our parents' talk float in and out until I was too tired. I left, bringing my blanket with me, and leaving Werner to listen and worry.

3

Berlin, Germany

Spring 1937

A few weeks later, Pappi hugged us good-bye, saying he was going far away to find a new job. He promised to be back soon. I tried to trick myself into believing it was a regular morning, with him dressed in a suit, smiling and walking away, down the sidewalk, going to work. But I knew inside me that it wasn't a normal day. He had a big suitcase, and he wasn't smiling. And then he was gone.

Everyone seemed to change after that: Pappi's leaving cracked open our world and let in the gray; Mutti cried often and hugged me whenever she could. I was thankful that Opa and Omi were there and didn't have to leave to find a job. On my walk to school, Opa started holding my hand. He told me a few of our favorite stories—*Remember last year and the magic cucumbers in the garden?*—but his smile was missing. When he left me off at the steps of my school, I still felt his grip after he let go. My friends at school were quieter. No one seemed to be having parties. My teacher, Mrs. Schmidt, had no energy, like a flower hanging off a broken stem. Even the houses and trees that lined the street next to us grew sadder. Fewer lights were on, drapes were shut, and the new spring leaves on the trees drooped and curled.

"Reni, I had another bad dream," Werner said one night. He sat down on the end of my bed; my head bonked into the headboard, knocking me out of my near sleep. I held my head as if I were in agony and pushed my face deeper into my soft sheets.

"It was horrible, Reni. It was raining really hard. You and I were in the living room. Except it wasn't exactly like our living room, the chairs were yellow and not green and…"

"Werner," I said with a yawn, flopping the blanket down, "get ON with it. You don't have to tell me the colors of the chairs."

"So much rain was thump-thumping on the house. It was pitch black and…and you and I couldn't see anything. Like a big hole was there, or maybe there was never a roof there at all. And all of a sudden I saw that the roof was really burned off and through the big hole, which had layers of rug and wood and metal, I saw firemen outside, and I smelled smoke, but when they started pumping with the hoses, water didn't come out, but snakes. Not water, but *snakes.*"

Yuck.

"You woke me to tell me about snakes?" I asked.

He didn't stop.

"It was snakes thumping on our house. They were flipping and flopping all over our house and then all over us. They got sprayed into the windows and doors and slimed through the floorboards. They were small at first, like in little rolled-up balls, and then they sprang open and lengthened and their heads puffed up to be all big and toothy. You see, Reni?"

He balled his fingers up then sprang them open, showing me the teeth. Now I was really awake. "Those firemen were trying to save us, but they were really just spraying us with biting snakes."

"Stop!"

He waited for me to tell him how stupid the dream was and to go back to bed. That was what we always did. It made him feel better. But I was scared and mad thinking about snakes in the corners of the room.

"Well, Werner, it could happen. If there wasn't enough water in the earth, and they sucked up the snakes that lived down underground instead. It could happen."

"Don't be ridiculous," he said, but drew his legs up onto my bed.

"Snakes will bite anything, you know."

"No," he said, "not true."

I slid my hand under the sheets, grabbing his leg.

"Reni!" He sprang up.

I tried to laugh and pretend it was funny, but it didn't feel funny, so my laugh came out as a dry cough. Werner crept back to his bed without a word. Maybe he'd at least stop bugging me now.

On another day, Mutti picked me up at school, and I could tell she'd been crying again. Her face was growing blotches, her eyes red and looking around fast.

"Reni, was your walk to school with Opa okay?" she asked, pulling me into her side and looking down at me.

"It was okay," I said as we walked out the front doors.

"Oh thank goodness," she said, keeping me close. "No one was mean to you? Or hurt you?"

"Well, kind of."

"What happened? Tell me." She stopped walking and knelt down in front of me. I could smell her perfume, like calm and petals. Her large eyes widened even more on her round face. The short sleeves of her dress hugged her arms, while the hem of her dress puffed and settled onto the ashen sidewalk.

"Karl in my class is having a birthday party, and I'm not invited."

"Oh, oh…," she smiled, her hands resting on my shoulders. "Who is Karl? Is he a friend of yours?"

"Well, he isn't really a good friend. But everyone in the class is invited to his big house this weekend. Everyone, but not me…and not Lisell."

"Oh Reni, you do love parties, but you can't expect to be invited to every one of them."

"Lisell said it was because we are Jews."

Mutti held her breath.

"Karl has a big house and fun parties. Can't I just stop being Jewish for one day to go to the party? Just *one* day?"

"Look at me, Reni," Mutti said, gazing at me hard. "You will always be Jewish. We will always be Jewish, and that's that. You should be proud. You should be…." She was quiet again, and then said, "Karl certainly isn't a very good friend, is he?"

I shook my head. She took a handkerchief out of her shiny yellow pocketbook and dabbed under my eyes.

"He will miss out by not having you there," she said. "They all will. Let's have Lisell over, and we'll have our own party."

I nodded. "Can we have cake?"

"The biggest," Mutti said, standing up.

Then she took my hand and tugged me to the side. A wall of boys was coming our way, all dressed in tan shirts tucked into black shorts. Hitler youth. Black ties hung loosely from their necks, pointing down to big, shiny silver belt buckles. Their sleeves were rolled up like they had work to do, which, according to the loud adult who was with them, was to march in step and sing loudly.

We will continue to march,
When everything shatters;
Because today Germany hears us,
And tomorrow the whole world.

They passed and passed, never looking at us, their eyes stuck on the boys ahead, until they had all thudded by. Mutti looked up the street and behind us before walking.

"Opa will take both Werner and you to and from your schools from now on."

Werner won't be happy about that, I thought. *He wants to be big like these boys who passed. He doesn't want his grandfather walking him.* At home, I went to my room, closed the door, and changed into my play dress. Then I ran to tell Werner.

"You have to walk to school with Opa," I said as I marched in, my chin pointed to the ceiling.

"Did Mutti tell you what happened?" he asked.

"Yup, Opa has to walk you to school just like me," I puffed and crossed my arms.

"Not that."

Then Werner told me that, earlier that afternoon, a gang of boys chased his friends and him in the street. The gang yelled and called them *Judenschwein*. They caught one of his friends and beat him up badly. The friend had to go to the hospital. Werner had crept under some bushes. It was dark, and the moist dirt rubbed into his knees and hands. He tried not breathing, and then breathed as slowly as he could and tried not to think of his snake dreams. Werner had been late getting home and Mutti was upset, but happy when she heard how he had saved himself.

Werner wasn't fast, but he was a good hider.

"Wait until you are big and strong like all the other boys we saw today," I said to make him feel better.

"What boys?"

"Hitler youth."

"Reni, remember? They don't want me."

"Well, anyway, you're brave," I said, "and you were smart to hide."

Werner put on his proud face, and it made me smile.

4

Berlin, Germany

Summer 1937

Pappi called with news. His voice sounded as far away as it was. He had found work at the American Express Company in Amsterdam, in a country called the Netherlands. We would be leaving Berlin and joining him in a few months. Werner and I sat with our mouths open. Nobody else looked surprised.

"Will he come back here to get us?" I asked Mutti.

No. It had been very hard to get out of Germany in the first place. It took lots of work and special papers. The people who gave him the special papers might change their minds if Pappi returned. Then none of us would be allowed to leave. That sounded okay to me. I wasn't sure I wanted to go. All my friends were here. When Mutti passed the phone to me, Pappi said that getting ready to move would be hard work, and Werner and I had to be helpful. Did I understand? I nodded until he repeated his question, and I remembered he couldn't see me. Then I said, "Yes."

After that, Omi asked me to help her get ready for dinner.

"Reni, we won't be able to take everything in this house," Omi said and stopped chopping vegetables to refill my milk glass. We were sitting in the kitchen. She chopped, and I drank. "This house is so big, and the apartment in Amsterdam is smaller."

"Does that mean we have to leave everything?" I asked. "Even my books and my blanket?" My lips trembled.

"No, you can keep those. But you have to leave the big things."

"What about my bed? And my tricycle?" I still loved my tricycle, even if I didn't ride it much anymore.

"You'll have to leave those, I think. You'll get new ones."

I pushed my tears into my belly.

"Okay. As long as I have time to say good-byes."

"You'll have time, sweetie," she said.

"And...and what about the dresses you bought me?" I asked. "The light blue one is new, and it feels springy. Are there parties in Amsterdam?"

"I think you can bring those," she said. "And yes, there are parties."

"I like getting dresses with you," I said, a little more hopeful.

"We are good shoppers, yes?" Omi said, her voice secretive. "We have fun."

"We're the best," I said, my eyes big, and my voice meeting her hushed tone, "I know the best dress stores, and you know how to pay for the dresses."

School started again, and each day when I returned from school with Opa and with Werner, the furniture had been rearranged by what we were taking and what we weren't taking. Our home looked like a different home each time, while Mutti explained how she decided what to keep. The dining room table: *We may not have large parties, so we won't need it.* The hutch where food was stored: *It's big but compact, and it stores so much. We'll take it.* The two bookcases in the sitting room: *They'll fit perfectly in our new apartment.* Mutti let me bring my tricycle into the house, and into Pappi's study so I could ride it in circles, even though I was too big for it.

One morning at breakfast Opa commented on how big I was getting. "Werner, too, of course," he added with a look at my brother, "but Reni has really grown."

I slid forward in my chair and stretched my head to the ceiling to show them my size. Finally, I was really getting bigger.

"I think we should go get a couple of dresses for you," Omi said, "Today."

"Really?" I burst out.

"Yuck," Werner said, "you sprayed food."

Omi continued, "You have grown so fast lately that most of your dresses don't fit anymore. And you will need something nice for when you see your Pappi again. We will be in Amsterdam soon."

I didn't feel I had grown so much that my dresses didn't fit, but I wasn't going to fight shopping, and I wanted to look good for Pappi. I really missed him.

"And a fine young lady deserves a new dress," Mutti added.

"Lady?" Werner asked. "A lady doesn't spit chewed bread."

"Can I get a fancy one?" I asked.

"Yes, any one that you like," said Omi.

"So we can go to Kurfürstendamm, to the fancy stores?"

The Kurfürstendamm was exciting. It was a wide street with cars, trams, lots of people, and the very best shops.

"Yes," said Omi.

"Just be careful," said Mutti, "not every store is friendly."

"We will only go to the friendly ones," Omi promised. I nodded in support.

I jumped out of my chair and gave Omi a big kiss, announcing that I was ready to go. She wiped her cheek with her napkin. She told me to brush my teeth first. It would be the best day. Omi would let me pick out the dresses I loved, even if they were not practical. Mutti would not approve of such fanciness, but Mutti wouldn't be there, would she?

5

Berlin, Germany

December 1937

"Werner, Reni, sit down," Mutti said a few days later after dinner, her voice as hard and cracked as a frozen puddle. "We need to tell you something."

We entered the living room. There, in the middle of the room, on the large rug (*it's always been too dark for us—it will stay*) lit by one standing lamp, were Opa and Omi. Opa's comfy chair, with his back pillow and covered armrests, sat empty (*too old and worn to take*). He had left his chair to sit by Omi; both of them pressed together on one end of the small green sofa (*goes so nice with the painting in the hallway, of course we'll take it*). Werner and I sat next to each other on the other end of the sofa. Mutti balanced on the edge of the rocking chair, facing us. Everyone was quiet, waiting.

"Opa and Omi and I wanted to tell you both how much we love you," Mutti said. "We are almost packed and ready to go to Amsterdam to join Pappi." She paused, slid back, and started rocking.

I looked at Werner.

"But there's been a change in plans," Mutti added. She rocked faster and put her face in her hands.

Werner put his thumb to his teeth, sliding the nail between his front teeth and pulling it out for a look. I slid my hands under my knees to keep still. I grabbed and ungrabbed my legs like I was a cat trying to get comfy.

"As much as Omi and I would like to join you," Opa said, picking up where Mutti left off, "we won't be coming. We didn't get the permits—the right papers—we need. We'll stay here and watch after things. Until you can come home again."

"But why?" asked Werner. "I thought we all had permission."

"Only for the three of us," Mutti said.

"But why?" he asked again. And his question hung there with no one answering it.

6

Amsterdam, the Netherlands

April 1940

What I didn't know as a child was that I was one drop in a flood of Jews leaving Germany. Jews went to Albania, the United States, the Philippines, England, Belgium, China—anywhere they would take us. The United States didn't let many of us in, so we couldn't go there, even though it was Pappi's first choice. Instead, the work Pappi found in the Netherlands meant that at least it was a relatively easy move: "Due west, 650 kilometers," Werner stated. The Nazis only allowed a certain amount of property and money out of Germany, which was the real reason why we had to cut way back.

Imagine having to leave behind all you had earned and saved… for people who hated you. We left our spacious Berlin apartment for a small, two-bedroom one in Amsterdam. A moving truck came, and men loaded all our things at once. My Mutti did a wonderful job of paring down all we owned. Opa and Omi took some furniture, bedding, dishes, and flatware and moved into a nearby apartment. They insisted they only needed a little.

Amsterdam indeed felt like home, with our white dishes with the blue flowered edging, the embroidered linens with Mutti's initials "GMH," some pieces of our heavy living room bookcases, and our large dining room hutch. We hung the oil painting of the meadow with the trembling gold hay and a glazed blue heaven in the front hallway. Just as before, Mozart and Verdi played on the Victrola, our wind-up record player, and filled the apartment with the music we loved.

From 1937 to 1940, life was peaceful and harmonious. We learned to speak Dutch, a language I learned easily and grew to love. Family and friends passed through, some while fleeing from Germany. Opa and Omi were not allowed to move, but they could visit. Mutti's sister and her husband had also moved to Amsterdam, so we felt some embrace of family. Those were joyful days with trips through the country, and bike rides along canals, outlined by the ordered beauty of tulip rows. I found new friends, like Vera and Kitty, who loved biking as much as I did. And our neighborhood had other German emigrants, including a family named Frank. The shadow of Germany was a distant cloud in the vast Dutch sky. But just as a calm and wispy sky can suddenly grow into thunderheads, so did the billowing threat of the Nazis.

My beloved grandparents came for a two-week visit in 1938. My eight-year-old self felt the spike of a more permanent good-bye in their hugs, but I could not have known it was the last time I would ever see them. Hitler was on the move, felling Poland the next year, birthing the Second World War. And then, in the spring and summer of 1940, when I was nine years old, Hitler's armies invaded a string of Western European countries.

One morning, I tightly tucked the sheets and blanket under my mattress so Mutti could fold up my bed into the wall to "save space"—it was a Dutch way of doing things. I brushed my heavy dark hair and ran to say good-bye to my father before he took the tram to work. He usually heard me coming and put some food on his face or pretended to hide, but this morning he just sat there, holding hands with Mutti at the table. I skidded into his arms as he released Mutti's hand to catch me, but he didn't smile like he usually did during our familiar morning ritual. His face was flat and far away.

"Shhh," Mutti warned.

"Shhhh, Reni, it's not the time," Werner said, acting all grown-up.

Pappi just held me close, my fingers settled on his suit coat arm. I pinched at a small thread end, trying to get it between my fingers. I gave up. No one was eating. The toast and jam sat cooling in the middle of the table. I saw the heat leaking away; I preferred warm toast. That's when I heard the radio's voice coming from the large wooden box in the corner. I grabbed two pieces of toast, smeared them with jam, and tried to listen like an adult. I pretended to look thoughtful, cocking my head like Pappi, listening to the very boring voice on the radio. Then I heard the word "Nazi" and froze. It was followed by a voice in German, not Dutch. I was used to German spoken in warm tones at home, but this voice was cold and official-sounding, cutting into our room like a knife.

"What's going on?" I asked. My toast clattered back onto the plate.

"Shhh…." came the answer.

For the next five minutes, we just sat there, and I struggled to understand what had happened. I stayed in Pappi's lap, somehow wanting to be smaller, to be tucked safely into his pocket. Finally, Pappi flicked the radio off and explained.

It looked as if Germany might invade Holland and kill people unless Holland allowed Germany to own the country. If that happened, we might not be safe. Just like before. Living in Berlin seemed like a long time ago to me. Holland felt like home now. I wished Germany would just stay away and let us be.

"How soon will they come?" "What will they do?" "What will they look like?" "Do they look like regular people?" My questions tumbled out like dead leaves in a strong wind.

Werner interrupted me. "Reni, stop! Nothing is happening now. Everything is staying the same. That's what it means." He stood up from the table and put his dishes next to the sink.

Pappi spoke. "We don't know yet what it means. I'm hopeful that Britain and France will fight off the Nazis, and we won't be occupied. But for now, we watch and listen to see what will change."

He got up from the table, hugged us all good-bye, and, from our second story window, I watched him and his hat walk down the sunny sidewalk to the tram. Then I headed off to school, waved good-bye to Mutti with her worried face, and met my best friend, Vera, on the sidewalk outside. We were both in third grade. School was three blocks away. We walked arm in arm for a little bit, skipping over cracks in the sidewalk, our straight brown bobs bouncing. Then she pulled away and reached into her pocket.

"Look what I made for my doll last night," she said. I took the small, perfect miniature dress from her and looked it over. It was bright white like a dove. The blue stitching was even across the bottom skirt with no dangling threads, and both shoulder straps were the same length.

"Oh, it's perfect. I'll make an overcoat to go with it so she can wear it in two seasons," I said.

I handed the small dress back to Vera, and I looked up the sidewalk at the other people. A woman in high heels rushed toward us, her gaze pinned to where she was going. Two men in suits stood on the sidewalk, laughing and talking over their still-folded newspapers. No one had answered any of my questions this morning. Would I recognize a Nazi when I saw one?

"Come on, slowpoke," Vera said. "We'll be late and miss Principal Beuzemaker's 'March of the Students.'"

We walked up the seven steps into our dark-brick school and joined the remaining students in the hallway.

Tap. Tap. Tap.

Principal Beuzemaker stood just inside the hallway. He was bald and forever clad in a light brown suit with a bowtie that struggled against his wide neck. Palm up, fist clenched, he knocked his wedding ring against the stair banister in an even beat that quickened the students' pace into their classrooms.

Tap. Tap. Tap.

Vera and I hung our coats on hooks by the door and sat down at our desks, which were next to each other. We each had a box on our desk that held our ink and pens and a small pile of Shirley Temple cards. These were free in packs of gum that I never chewed. But I loved the cards, as they gave me lots of ideas for doll dresses and hairdos. I thumbed through them now and put the one with Shirley Temple in a green collar and feathered black hat on top. Vera put her favorite card on top, too—the one with the actress's hands in prayer, while she looks sideways at the camera.

Miss Pino, with a tight gray bun and kind face, began to write on the board with clean, looping strokes. I loved learning to write, and I loved Miss Pino. She even invited Vera and me to her house once, and we had tea together.

Part of my love for Miss Pino was also my love for Rudi. She had brought us together: Rudi's desk was on the other side of me. He was absent that day, but when he was here, it was hard to concentrate. He was always one of the first ones to ask questions in class and was always very confident of his answers, but not in a way that was bad. He had wavy hair, like Werner's, but thicker, and he didn't make fun of my Shirley Temple cards like the other boys did. In fact, once he had even picked up my cards when the pile of them had fallen to the floor. A gentleman.

The Start of War

Amsterdam, the Netherlands

1940-1943

7

Amsterdam, the Netherlands

May 1940

K *a-boom*. My bed shuddered in the dark. *Boom. Boom*. More explosions. *BOOM*. A sharp wind blew into the room as glass like hail showered my bed.

"Werner!" I shouted over the noise. "Werner!"

"I'm here! Are you okay?" he said.

"I don't know," I yelled and drew back from the window and billowing curtains. Flames silhouetted buildings and smoke. Werner and I hunkered down behind the end of my bed; Werner put his arms around me.

Pappi and Mutti stormed in.

"Reni! Werner! Where are you?" Mutti yelled. Her breath swooped in and out.

"Here, under the bed," Werner cried.

"Come here, let's go into the kitchen," Pappi said. He held a flashlight in one hand, and guided Mutti with the other.

The horrible noises continued outside as we sat huddled around the kitchen table, which was near the back of the apartment. Beyond the terrifying blasts was the dull drone of planes. Mutti began to cry. And that made me cry. She put me in her lap.

"It's the Germans, Trudi," Pappi said. "It's the invasion; just like they've been predicting."

"The Nazis?" I asked.

"Yes," Pappi said.

The wisps of talk about invasion had felt too unreal to understand. What did I know of war? The meaning slipped through my fingers no matter how serious it sounded, but not the bombs. This was war I could feel in my bones.

Every once in awhile we peeked out the windows. Lights caught billowing clouds as they drifted down from the dark, looking like pulsating jellyfish from the deep-sea waters.

"Parachutes," Werner whispered, as if they might hear us.

German and Dutch planes fought overhead, and Pappi said we could be hurt by either of them. War was messy, and in their fighting with each other, we might get killed if we got noticed. And so it was our job to lie low, keep quiet, and stay together.

Despite the bravery, Holland fell to Germany. Over the coming weeks, we put heavy black curtains in our windows so we'd be less likely to be seen at night by anyone in the sky.

You might think that everything changed in that instant, like going from color to black and white, but the changes were slow to show. The day-to-day became familiar. One morning, when I was on my way to school, I saw my first group of Nazi soldiers. They wore helmets that had the black zigzag and looked like turtle shells, tall black boots, and grayish green uniforms; they smoked and talked together, and when they moved they marched their legs up with purpose as if they were showing off. The first time Vera and I passed them, we quieted down. They didn't even look our way. They didn't ever seem to notice us as we walked to school, and we soon forgot to be quiet.

They didn't seem to notice when Werner went to his junior high school, either. Or when Pappi went to work. Or when Mutti went shopping or kept the apartment clean and prepared wonderful foods for us.

But they were always there.

8

Amsterdam, the Netherlands

December 1939–September 1941

My friends and I went ice-skating on a pond at Vondelpark, the biggest park in Amsterdam. Vera was there, and so was Kitty. Kitty was one of the older girls in the neighborhood like the Franks' daughter, Anne. I looked up to Kitty, glad that she was willing to play with a nine-year-old. The long, twisting pond was filled with other skaters and even some dogs that loped and slid around like comic book characters. We flew like birds along the chestnut tree-lined shore, and then returned home to my house to peel off our soggy layers and put them in a pile near the front door.

Soon their parents joined us for my birthday dinner. Vera started giggling, which meant she knew about some of my gifts ahead of time. The colorful presents—packages wrapped in pink, purple, and blue shiny wrapping and tied tightly with ribbons—sat in a corner of our small living room. Adults sipped their beer in the doorway, as there was not enough room to fit everyone on the two chairs and small sofa. Mutti had told me to unwrap slowly so we could reuse the paper, and so I didn't look too greedy. This was hard. I thanked each friend or family member before moving on to the next gift, though Mutti's eyes hinted that I was not being as gracious as she wanted. As I tore off a corner from a package that was obviously a book, Vera leaned so far forward in her chair she almost fell over. That's when I realized it wasn't a book, but a *Poesie book*.

There were two types of girls in Amsterdam: those who had a Poesie book and those who wanted one. I ran my hands over the rough black leather cover with "POESIE" stamped in gold in the lower right corner.

"Now you have one too," Vera said. She had gotten hers last year.

I opened the book with relish, listening to the binding crack and yield. A blank page stared up at me, a waiting space for me to mark as my own and welcoming the treasures that people would script inside. I couldn't wait to fill it up.

"Oh, thanks, Mutti and Pappi. Thanks. Will you write in it?"

"Yes," said Mutti.

"I promise to write something later," Pappi added. "This is very important. What I write may be around longer than me!"

"But I want it now. Please?"

"Reni," Mutti said, "the point isn't to fill it up right away. People write in it when they are ready."

"That's right." Pappi said with a nod, "Don't you want people to write something thoughtful, and not just because you are impatient?"

I knew what I wanted to say, but I said "yes" instead.

We all sat around the table—my family, and Vera and Kitty with their parents—and ate our fill of pot roast and scalloped potatoes. Then came my favorite, a thick lemon pudding, covered with sugar powdered like newly flurried snow. When we were almost finished with the pudding, Mutti opened a drawer and brought out a white box with blue scrolls on it that read: "Droste." I opened the box and unwrapped the foil to reveal the smooth, silken chocolate. I was allowed to take as big a chunk of chocolate as I wanted, so I cracked off a huge piece and passed it to Werner and the others who did the same. It was delicious. After dinner, I asked for my father's special pen, sat down on the floor, opened my new Poesie book, and wrote in Dutch, in my best writing:

This album belongs to me as long as I hope to live.
Irene is my name given to me by my parents.
Hasenberg also belongs to it from my father's ancestors.

I was about to write that I was from Amsterdam, but I wanted to honor my family, so I went back to my birth and finished with:

Germany is the country where I came into the world.

Later that night, Pappi snuggled me into my bed.

"Did you have a good birthday, Reni?"

"Yes, so good," I said. "I wish I could have them more often!"

He hugged me and swept closed the heavy curtains in around the windows, wrapping me in my cocoon.

"Well, if they happened more often maybe they wouldn't be as special," he said.

"Don't tuck me in too tight," I said. "I still have to read the wishes in my Poesie book."

"Okay," he said. "But don't stay up too late. It's been a long day. Werner will be in soon."

"Is he helping with dishes because I don't have to since it's my birthday?"

"You know the answer to that. Good night, " he said, and kissed the top of my head.

Reading my Poesie book wouldn't take long: I had one entry, from Mutti:

> *Start your day with a happy face and then everything*
> *will work out.*
> *Do what you have to do, and want to do what you do.*

I reread Mutti's second line to make sure I understood. It didn't help.

Mutti and Pappi were right: my Poesie book filled slowly. Very slowly. Pappi didn't write until June the next year, and Werner took until August! Everybody wrote nice things, but I couldn't believe it took them so long to figure out what to say.

Pappi wrote:

> *You sweet little one,*
> *you belong to me,*
> *you belong to me,*
> *you are the most lovable.*

Then Werner:

Dear Irene,
Little person, I wish you in many ways much blessing and
good luck.
Your brother, Werner

I laughed, as I didn't know any other Werners.
And then from Vera:

When later on you are grown up and you re-read
this album
and between the lines you see this verse,
I hope that it brings you joy and that you think of the one
who is writing this now and even if we don't see
each other
you still remain my friend.
Vera.

Well, of course we would see each other. Did she think we wouldn't?
We would be best friends forever.

Someone had written a single line and left it unsigned: *Vergeet mij niet.* Forget me not. How could I forget somebody I didn't even know?

In the winter of 1941, Werner and I returned to Vondelpark, ice skates slung over our shoulders on white laces, and there, on a pole at the entrance, was a freshly painted sign, black letters on white wood: *Voor Joden Verboden.* Forbidden for Jews.

"What?" I asked.

"No!" Werner said. "I don't believe it." He kicked the pole, leaving a muddy print. "What are we going to do? Destroy the park?" He asked the air around the sign. "There's no reason for it."

Then he looked at me, and his face softened. "Come on, let's go home," he added. "It's just one more thing they are taking away from us to make us miserable. Let's not give them the pleasure."

I tried to lift up my chin as I looked through the iron barred gates at all the people within. I saw how the iron fence surrounded the park, protected it, prevented people from going in. Prevented *us* from going in. I saw clearly now, though my eyesight blurred through welling tears.

"I'm not so sure I wanted to skate," I said to him, and to myself. "I think I'd rather play at home."

On our walks to and from school that spring, Vera and I saw more signs—in storefronts, on lampposts, in front of libraries—that forbid Jews from one thing or another. We ignored them as best we could, locking arms tightly as we went.

In Miss Pino's class, Vera and I practiced our handwriting, and Rudi picked my pencils up when I dropped them. Rudi was Jewish, and I wondered if that was why Miss Pino had sat us together. Vera wasn't Jewish, or at least not as Jewish as me, since her family didn't celebrate the holidays we did.

From time to time, classmates would sign my Poesie book when I carried it with me. Lena, one of my classmates, wrote:

> *In the heavens, there are angels.*
> *On earth, there are only naughty people and you are one*
> *of them.*

I laughed.

Miss Pino even signed it, her beautiful handwriting straight across the page as if she could see invisible ruled lines:

> *…to fly high without flickering, that is not what you*
> *should do.*
> *To become smart, no one becomes smart without effort and*
> *without work you don't get anywhere.*

So serious, I thought. Why did teachers have to be so teacherly?

"Rudi, would you sign my Poesie book?" I asked him.

"You know my handwriting is bad. Can I do something else?"

"Um, sure."

"Okay, I'll do it tomorrow. I have to get ready."

The next day he took the Poesie book to his desk and hunkered over it throughout the break, flipping pages and pressing his hand into them.

"Here you go," he said giving it back. "Remember that a picture is a thousand words. So imagine what a few pictures are worth."

On every other page I had stuck stickers in my Poesie book. Pictures of bouquets, boys, girls, planes, a blimp, animals, a horseshoe, an automobile, but the one thing they all had in common was flowers. Every sticker included flowers. Now, scattered throughout the book, were new, non-floral stickers. A pig in a suit with a monocle. The wicked witch from *Snow White*. A boy in lederhosen with a giant cone of candy. A black cat. Rudi's fingers had touched everything.

When I returned home that day, I sat on the small bench by the window that looked out over our street. I watched for Pappi to turn the corner after getting off the tram from work. I wanted to show him the stickers. The sun shone through the slats, the stickers and the writing sparkled, and I felt good. Finally, he was there. Pappi in his hat. I ran downstairs and jumped into his arms as he entered.

"You are getting way too big for this, Reni!" he said, though he caught me with ease and spun me around until one of my shoes flew off and landed in the dining room.

"John, you are going to bring down the house with that ruckus," Mutti said.

"Pappi, I want to show you my book," I said. I waited for him to take off his hat and sit down with me on the sofa.

"What have we here?" he asked.

We read together what people had written.

Werner came from our bedroom and announced the Henki Express was going to new destinations, including the USA! The Henki Express was Werner's pretend travel agency. He studied other countries and when he was interested enough, he arranged pretend trips there. In the kitchen, Werner showed Pappi and me on a map how we would travel by train and then by ship to land in New York.

With summer's start, the sun strengthened, stretching out its warm light farther into the evening. It was June 1941 and Vera, Werner, and I stayed outside as long as possible. Along the nearby canal, we gathered on our bikes to ride along the water's edge. My metal horse and Vera's were fast friends as they flew along at a full gallop. We grasped the looping handlebars and steered the big-for-us wheels ahead. *Go.*

At night, the brick paths along the canals were smooth trails. We barely felt the jiggling space between the bricks as our fat tires traveled over them. The young families were at home, and people roamed leisurely in twos. We sped along, heady with the early night smells of pollen and full leaves. Werner was strongest and could fly up the bridges and back down long before we could. Up and down and around. My ears jumped between the sounds of birds settling in for the night, bugs waking up, water lapping at the canal walls, a far-off barrel organ, and our chains rhythmic straining against gears.

We picked up Rudi from his home. He was almost as fast as Werner and twice as graceful. His long legs and arms moved like a dancer's. We took over a street, and rode side by side, all four of us. Evening lights slowly turned on here and there, reflections shining up from the water in shimmering light.

We came upon a small park in the middle of a square with winding brick paths around small shrubs and statues. Rudi pedaled up, wound between the blackened shrubs, and disappeared. Werner came to a halt at the entrance and held up his hand for Vera and me to stop. We backpedalled on the brakes, both of us sliding into the back of his bike with a crack. Tacked up on a tree was a sign: *Voor Joden Verboden.* Jews Forbidden. In the lower right corner was an official police seal.

"Rudi, come back!" Werner called, fear edging into his voice.

"Rudi!" I screamed.

I looked at the deserted streets and whispered to the night to let him come back before anyone saw. He flew back around the corner just then, almost knocking into us, his eyes wide and filled with light. Werner pointed to the sign. Rudi stopped smiling. All of our bikes, like eager steeds, strained to go on, but we turned back. Our horses had turned into just bicycles.

As summer turned to fall, there were so many "last times."

The last time we went to the cinema, Vera and I saw *Snow White*, and I hid my face behind Mutti's arm at scenes with the awful stepmother. And then I was no longer allowed to go to the cinema, because Jews were not allowed, and Vera had to go without me and tell me about the films. She was a good storyteller, and it was almost as fun as the real thing.

The last time we went to the park on a warm fall day, Vera and I lay in the grass on our towels and talked about how many babies we'd have when we got older. She wanted three girls, and I wanted one boy and one girl.

There was the last time Werner kicked a soccer ball with his friends. And then he was no longer allowed to play on any sports teams.

And finally, the last time I could go to school with my friends.

It was a Saturday when Mutti gave me the news. She sat me down in the living room, a folded letter in her hand, and put her arms around me. On Monday, I was going to a new school. A school just for Jews. No more walking with Vera. No more sitting next to Vera. No more recess, or lunches, or Shirley Temple card swaps. No more Miss Pino. *No!* I stood up, ran down the stairs, and out onto the street. I walked fast to Vera's apartment, the next block over, and knocked on her door. When she answered, the look on her face told me she knew, too. We hugged, and then her mom and dad hugged me, too. We stood there in a small circle, until it got awkward, which it sometimes does with adults, and Vera and I went into her room to play dolls.

"Mom and Dad told me that your school is far away from here," Vera said, putting a blue coat on her doll.

"I don't know where it is," I said. "I don't care. It's just stupid." My hands wouldn't do anything today, not even dress dolls. My fingers just wanted to stay curled and asleep in my pockets.

"We can always see each other after school, you know. I'll keep you up to date on everything that's going on," she said, and put another coat—this one red and white polka dots—on the doll. "And you can tell me about all the new people in your class, and what your teacher is like."

"I don't feel like meeting new people," I said.

Vera put a bigger, yellow coat on the doll.

"Vera, your doll looks like a stuffed animal with all those clothes! Not very fashionable."

We both giggled at the stacked fabric around the doll's middle. We played for the rest of the afternoon. My hands still felt heavy when I thought about leaving for school without Vera at my side.

Two days later, Werner walked me to school before continuing on to his new one. Mutti and Pappi wanted me to have company, at least on this first day. Werner wasn't so thrilled, but he didn't have a choice. He had to go even farther, to a school called the Jewish Lyceum, all the way on Voormalige Stadstimmertuin street. Food trucks rattled by on the road next to us.

"If we were on the Henki Express, we'd get to school faster," he said. "The ole Henki would take us to school and even let us spend weekends in the countryside, or take a boat across to England. We'd see Big Ben and the Tower of London."

"Who's Big Ben?"

"It's not a who. It's a giant clock in a tall tower in London. It chimes like all the churches here in Amsterdam, only much louder. Even the Nazis and their bombs haven't been able to stop the clock. It chimes and chimes."

Time could tick by, despite the Nazis. As if they never happened. Life could go back to what it was.

"I want to see Big Ben with you. Can we go when we're older?"

"Yes. If you have the money to afford my luxury trains and ships," he said. "Anyway, for now, just try to have a good day."

He left, the gait of his walk, quick yet heavy, reminding me of Pappi.

I turned and I faced my new school. It didn't have nice brick steps, or a tap-tapping principal. As I entered the brick building and gave the secretary my name, she pointed the way. I walked down the hall to a classroom. It all felt loose, like a dress sewn too quickly, with stitching showing and uneven. The chairs and desks didn't match, and there were too many crammed into too few rooms. I searched the group for familiar faces. Rudi! There he was. He had saved me a space next to him. It was so crowded that our knees touched together under the table, but we left them there. The teacher, Mr. Pinto, called us to attention. Here we were. Just us Jews.

9

Amsterdam, the Netherlands

1942

S oon being Jewish wasn't enough; we had to show we were Jewish. Starting in April 1942, we had to make sure we wore a yellow six-pointed star, one that looked like the Star of David, on our jackets. Mutti said we even had to buy them, as if we *wanted* them. It seemed to me that the star made me invisible. People looked at the star, and then they didn't look at me. They looked away, or they looked through me. I was eleven and disappearing.

And so were Jewish families all over Amsterdam—literally, disappearing. Knocks on the doors by the Dutch police and Nazis and… *poof*…a family was gone. I had been taught that police were good guys, but I knew that wasn't always true now. There were whispers of places to the east where Jews were gathered and were forced to work on Nazi projects. Shadows where I had only seen sunshine before.

By the summer of 1942, even Werner's hopes of travel were doused by the restrictions. I no longer jumped into Pappi's arms when he got off the tram because he wasn't allowed to take the tram anymore, or a bus, or a taxi. None of us were. Pappi had to walk, so he returned late, sometimes too late for me to see him. Vera and I weren't even allowed to be in each other's homes. Jews and non-Jews could only see each other outside, in the few public spaces that weren't already signed with *Voor Joden Verboden*. Vera, our friend Greetje (who was not Jewish either), and I played outside together whenever we could. Greetje's little sister Gerda had just turned four years old and was so cute. Like Shirley Temple. Her bouncy blond curls stayed perfectly in the hairstyles we tried on her, so unlike my thick dark mass. We played hopscotch. My yellow star didn't seem to bother them.

Mutti instructed Werner to stay with Vera, Greetje, and me now, almost always when we were together. We met up with Rudi and other friends to unharness our metal horses and gallop along the silvery night canals. Until…another day and another rule.

Pappi walked into my bedroom as I was sorting Shirley Temple cards. Shirley was dressed up from her different movies. She looked serious, pouty, and then happy. My favorite was her as Heidi, holding a little goat. I loved that movie as much as I loved the book. Heidi had problems, but she was always happy. Not everything worked out for her, but she ended up with her beloved grandfather in the end because she was *smart*. Pappi pulled back the bottom of the thick black curtain that covered my window. The light poured in. He sat on the edge of my bed. The sun sliced through and long shadows flew across the floor and walls. The colors of the cards laid out across my pink blanket jumped out. I felt the warmth dance along my forearms and travel up my neck.

"Thanks, I forgot to open them," I said.

"I know," he said. "It's easy to forget."

"I wish we could have the curtains open at night. To see the lights and the night sky, and stars."

"Me, too. Me, too," he said with a sigh. "Reni, I have bad news."

"Okay," I said. "What?"

"We cannot own bicycles. We have to put them outside on the street by one o'clock this afternoon."

"Why do they want our bicycles?" I felt tears coming and tried to blink them back.

"I don't know," he said.

"Don't they have their own?"

"They do have their own. I think…I think it's a way to test our strength. And we are strong. But I am so sorry, my little one. I know how much you love to ride."

He hugged me close and left. I let the tears go, sank onto my pillow, eyes closed, face up to the sun. A few minutes later I heard the squeak and roll of Werner coming and sitting on his bed.

"I have to give up mine, too. I think we may be leaving here anyway," Werner said.

"What do you mean?"

"I overheard Mutti and Pappi talking," he said. Then he got up and closed the door and sat down on my bed this time, leaning closer to me.

"I think it has to do with a man Pappi met on the street the other day," he explained, chewing on the skin around his thumb. "The man said he could get us passports from another country so that we can leave Europe and Hitler behind."

"We can't get passports from the Netherlands?"

"No, they will not give them to Jews."

"But we get them from another country? How?"

"I don't know. All we need to know is that they can help us get away from the bad guys."

After lunch, Pappi told us it was time to say good-bye to our bikes. We walked down the stairs and into the front hall where my beloved bicycle, my metal galloper, rested against the wall. And I said good-bye, hugging the handlebars.

"Be glad we don't have a cat or a dog, Reni," said Werner. "Those would be even harder to give up." I had always wanted a puppy, but now I was so glad I didn't have one. I couldn't imagine how hard it would be to give up a pet. I watched Pappi wheel my galloper away, as it disappeared around the corner to join all the other bicycles unlucky enough to be owned by Jewish children.

Summer had always been a time of freedom and space and sun-soaked adventures with friends, away from the structure of school and adult eyes. But not this summer. This summer felt different. In July, we were restricted to our homes from 8:00 p.m. to 6:00 a.m. Werner, Vera, Greetje, Rudi, and I could only gather outside to be together anyway, and now our long summer evenings were cut painfully short, like a fingernail clipped too close. It was hot that summer, and the swimming pools were closed to us. So we hung out by the side of the canals, under the spotted shade of the leafy elms in the early evenings.

On one of those evenings, we walked single file—Werner, then Greetje, then me, then Rudi in the back—along the canals. Yellow star, no star, yellow star, yellow star. The rush and honk of cars on the other side of the trees was on our right, and the cool, slowly rolling water knocking houseboats against the stone on our left. I put my arms out on each side to stay balanced along the cement edge. Then I bent down to grab a stone and, as I got back up, I tripped on the hem of my skirt. I gasped and jutted my left arm out to catch my fall. My arm hit the cement and skidded over the edge just as someone grabbed me around my waist and pulled me back. I sat down hard on my right hip, and turned around. Rudi.

"Oops," I said, a bit embarrassed.

"I know you're bored, but you don't want to go into the canal. You don't know how to swim," he said.

He reached for his gray cap, which had fallen to the bricks in his lunge, and put it back on his head. I glimpsed his short haircut; I knew he didn't like it. That was the reason for the cap. He touched the small visor with one hand and cupped the back with another to straighten it on his head. He'd always taken pride in his hair, we had that in common, but now he had to go to a Jewish barber, who was ancient and had no style or experience except for old, bald heads.

"You okay?" Greetje asked.

"Yeah, fine," I said.

"Klutz," Werner yelled back.

"Don't call me a klutz," I said. "Mr. Henki-Express-who-made-us -walk-too-fast."

We returned home a bit early, early enough to invite Rudi to dinner so he could get home by 8:00 p.m. Greetje wasn't allowed to come in, so she continued on to her house a few houses away. Mutti's face told me she wasn't happy about stretching our food. Not only were there food rations for everyone, but Jews could only shop from 3:00 p.m. to 5:00 p.m. Many times, by that time of day, there was not much left on the shelves. Greetje sometimes shopped for us, bringing us a few delicacies, but mostly we had lots of potatoes, not much meat, old cheese, and days-old bread. This day, Greetje had been able to shop for us, so we had fresh brussels sprouts and carrots, and fresh milk. I knew she was taking a risk as shopping for Jews was not allowed. Mutti did her best to put together meals with what she could find. I savored my memories of the days when Opa and I gardened together. After a day playing, I was starving, but I knew better than to say that and invite the comment, *You don't know what starving is, young lady.*

My birthday, December 1942. In our dining room. The delicate white china dishes with rose print that I usually ate my lemon pudding on were packed away. Some crystal and silver were stored now at our neighbor's apartment upstairs. Max and Stien Bremekamp were not Jewish, but were willing to keep some of our things in hiding. And there was no lemon pudding: no lemons, anyway, and eggs, butter, and milk were scarce. And there were no friends, as we weren't allowed to gather together in large groups anymore. I had my dolls, though and that helped.

Mutti stood up and placed her chair close to the large hutch and climbed up as Pappi held onto the back to steady the creaking legs. She opened the upper glass doors, reached into the back, and pulled down a shining, tinseled package from the top shelf.

Pappi took it from her as she climbed down from the chair and sat at the table. He placed it in front of her, nodded, and she took the large bar that had *Droste* written across top. She began to carefully unwrap each fold. From out of the blue folds emerged a large chocolate bar, wrapped in another layer of gold foil.

Mutti held the bar out to the four of us in her open palms.

"Reni, happy twelfth birthday."

Werner sucked in his breath and looked at the bar. I licked my lips at the thought of the deep brown chocolate just within its thin wrapping, but knew better than to reach for it. Mutti put it back down on the table, and we watched as she carefully folded the foil package back into itself, following all the creases. This time, Pappi got up on her chair as she handed him the chocolate bar and he nestled it back in the cupboard.

"And we look forward to celebrating your thirteenth," Pappi said as he closed the glass doors and kept hope alive for another year.

10

Amsterdam, the Netherlands

March 25, 1943

My classroom was emptying. There were now more desks than students. I looked over the other students and noticed the spaces between. Every week someone was deported, hauled off to work. Rudi was still there, and I sat as close to him as I could, which was more noticeable with fewer students.

"Helen and her brother Joseph are gone," he said and nodded toward the back of the room where they used to sit.

"Yeah," I said, as I looked back at the empty chairs. "It seems to be happening faster."

"Yeah."

I thought about one set of neighbors on our block. One day there. The next day, police pulled out their belongings, everything gone and the apartment closed up, shuttered and dark, an official looking piece of paper nailed to the door, flapping in the breeze.

"Irene," said Mr. Pinto, using my formal name.

"Yes," I said, looking up.

His eyes held concern. He touched my arm. I looked at Rudi.

"The principal would like to see you. Bring your book bag. I'll walk you."

He told the class to read the next chapter and he would be back soon.

Why would the principal call me? I thought. I had never been called to the principal's office before. Had I done something wrong? Had I been late to school? Homework not turned in? I hadn't done anything like that. I gathered my pencil and notebook, my small book bag, and coat, and Rudi mouthed, "You'll be okay."

Then, I stood, facing the principal. I couldn't remember his name; I hardly ever saw him. "Irene, they're waiting for you outside," he said. He didn't look at me, but his hands were on the desk and shaking a little.

What did he mean by *they*?

"Go on now."

I stood frozen until Mr. Pinto walked me out of the office.

"What's happening?" I asked, frightened. "Am I going to a camp?"

"Be courageous, Irene," he said, and hugged me.

My legs shook so hard I could scarcely stand. One of the lines he had written in my Poesie book came to me then... *if sometimes there is a rain shower and everything looks black and gray, be courageous, be a blessing, because things will soon change again...*

I walked out into the bright sun where a rickety food delivery truck sat by the curb. A short Dutch policeman pointed into the back of the truck. His uniform was dark blue with shiny gold buttons and tall, dirty boots.

"Up," he commanded.

I couldn't help it and started to cry. I didn't feel courageous. He motioned again.

"It's too high," I said in a squeaky voice. The back of the high truck bed was like a huge mouth hovering with hunger.

"Reni?" came a voice in the back of the truck.

"Werner?" I cried.

"Do I have to toss you up?" asked the policeman, his hands raised and ready to push.

"Take my hand," Werner said as his face appeared from between the gray canvas flaps.

Seeing my brother melted the icy feeling, and my legs stopped shaking. I grabbed his hand, hung onto the side, and leapt up the side like a cat. We both fell into the back.

"Stay there," said the policeman as he flipped up the tailgate, latched it into place, and we listened to his footsteps make their way to the passenger side. The door opened and slammed.

I hugged Werner tight and let the tears flow.

"Are you hurt?" Werner asked and looked at my face.

"No," I said while wiping my eyes. "But what's happening?"

The truck started with a lurch. Behind Werner were crates of vegetables, boxes of cans, bloated burlap sacks, and a couple of large metal containers that smelled of cooked food. The air was heavy with the smell of rotten cabbage. There was just enough room on the benches for Werner and me on one side.

"I don't know," he yelled above the engine. "But I hope they don't try to jam in anybody but us. I was picked up at school, too. No warning. Just pulled from class. They didn't tell me anything."

I looked up at him, but he looked straight ahead. We both instinctively grabbed the rail as the truck turned.

"Reni. I confess I'm so scared," he said and shuddered.

"Worse than snakes," I said.

"At least we're together," he said, and put his arm across my shoulders.

I had never been so glad to be with him.

We sat wrapped together for a long time. Then I felt something soaking through my dress. I stood up to find that I had been sitting on damp, stinky leaves. Not wanting to get my dress even dirtier, I braced myself against the back frame and tailgate, which had the added advantage of reducing the smell since I could hold open a flap. I made sure my book bag was crammed into a drier corner where it would not slide. I peered outside; Werner peered out, too.

"I know these streets," he said. "I recognize the signs. So far, we are just going through Amsterdam. Heading east."

I relaxed a little at that. We could get back home on our own if we had to. We stopped at an intersection, and then the truck jumped forward, stalled, restarted, and bound ahead through a roundabout. The city's streets stretched out behind us. A woman crossed the road. She turned our way, our eyes locked for a second, and then she shrank into the distance.

"Do you think people are wondering why a well-dressed girl and boy are hanging out in the back of a truck?" I asked.

"Maybe, or maybe not," Werner pondered. "This war has made the very strange seem very normal."

The truck stopped at each intersection. I could taste the urge to jump and run. But it was too far down and too quick a stop to get sure footing. And what would the police officer do if he saw me?

Soon the truck stopped again. We were in front of the old theater, the Hollandsche Schouwburg. I heard the sound of boots: the person who wore them came around the corner.

"Down from there," the same Dutch policeman who'd made me get in now commanded as he unlatched the tailgate.

Werner and I both jumped down with our book bags. I looked around at the crowd of people heading inside.

"In there," the officer said and pointed to the front of the theater.

"Are our parents here?" Werner stuttered but stood straight.

"I...I don't know," he said, sounding like a shy child.

"C'mon Reni," Werner said, reaching back for my hand as he went ahead.

I will not cry, I thought as I again started to feel the fear well up inside. I took a deep breath and smoothed out my dress as I clasped his hand. I hoped Mutti wouldn't be upset that I'd stained my dress.

The theater loomed, its white facade blazing in the sunlight. The last time I'd been there was to see *Snow White* with Vera, Greetje, and Werner. I remembered watching the colors dance across the stage, laughing at the cute dwarves, and hiding our eyes behind our knees when the scary Queen burst into the scene. *Two years ago*, I thought. It seemed like yesterday. Or maybe forever ago.

We walked alone up to the entrance. People were prodded and ushered through the large center doors; Werner chose to enter the unused door farthest to the right where five large guards turned around, looking down on us. All of them had zigzags, all were Nazis.

"Umm," Werner said, "I think we are supposed to be here, but we don't know."

"Well, why are you here?" said the largest one, with a smirk.

"A truck picked us up from school."

"Are you Jews?"

"Ah, yes," Werner replied softly.

"Then you are in the right place. But wrong door," he said, pointing. "Get in line there."

The flow of people slowly pushed us up the steps to the open doors. More Nazi guards stood on each side, and people filed up to talk to them.

"Should we ask where Mutti and Pappi are?" I asked.

"Shhh. No, we could get in trouble," said Werner and squeezed my hand hard.

"Ouch, Werner," I said.

This small injustice was enough to throw tears down my cheeks and drip fear along my back. *What if they aren't here?* I asked myself. *What if they have already been deported? What if...?* I looked at Werner, squeezed his hand back. *What if it was just us now?* It was too much to think about, and I felt faint.

"We will find them," Werner said. He looked straight into my eyes. "We will."

We gave our names, the guards wrote them down, and we entered with eyes down, hearts pounding. My eyes took awhile to adjust to the feeble yellow lights and dark interior. Soon I could see it was no longer a theater. The walls had been stripped of their decorative paper; all that was left were hairy, uncombed shreds. Some of the curled moldings that lined the wall were cracked, which made it look as if they could collapse at any moment. And all the seats were gone. It was a shell, an "exoskeleton" like I was learning in school, with all the guts scooped out. By then I realized that's what the Nazis were good at. Scooping out insides. People were packed inside, standing and walking and talking, and it smelled bad, like there was a toilet backed up somewhere. How could such a fancy place, one that once had carpet that felt like clouds and chandeliers that twinkled like the night sky, become so barren? Was all this ugliness always hiding beneath?

I could make out small groups huddled on the floor. We walked across the rough concrete stubble where the carpeted floor had been, over toward the families, whispering pockets of people. We moved slowly and carefully. We peered into the dark huddles. We would search everywhere, cover every inch until we found them. Every nook and corner. I wanted to be seven feet tall with a big adult voice that boomed above the crowds, "Where are you, Mutti and Pappi? Werner and Reni are here and looking for you!"

We continued. Werner pulled me into the crowds toward where the stage used to be. Scanning through the dim light as if in a dream, my heart beat as fast as a bird's, I was sure.

Then a woman turned around: *Mutti!* I broke from Werner, running to her as she got down on her knees and began to cry.

"Oh Reni, Werner." The words fell from her lips in a cry. Her eyes were red.

"Mutti!" I cried. And then Werner was there, too. And we were all in a tight circle. Home.

"I was so worried," she said at last.

"Where's Pappi?" I asked.

"He went to talk to some people. He'll be back." She looked me up and down. "Are you hurt? Did they hurt you?"

"No, we're fine," Werner said. "But we had no idea what was going on…." He explained how we were picked up at school and how we traveled through the streets in a food truck. The story sounded crazy even though it had just happened. I saw my pink blanket in a pile along with another one of my coats and a pillow and even my favorite doll, Liesje.

"You brought my things!" I said and ran over to them.

"Yes, we didn't have much time. Just a few minutes to grab it all," she said, coming toward me. "I hope I got the right doll for you."

"Yes, you did. Liesje's my favorite," I said clutching my doll. I sat down with Mutti on the floor and snuggled onto her lap. I curled into the warmth and fell fast asleep.

Sometime later, I awoke to a gentle shaking. I was on my side, my head resting on my pillow.

"Wake up, Reni," my father's voice called. "It's supper."

"Pappi," I said and gave him a hug before I fell back into semi-sleep until the sound of so many people talking made me realize I wasn't at home. I sat up straight and saw the wrecked theater with Pappi sitting cross-legged across from me. I crawled over onto his open lap, dragging my pink blanket with me. He held a bowl for me, heaped full of soup. I hadn't eaten all day. I looked into the perfect circle of water and soggy vegetables. I thought of all the food in the back of the truck—here it was. It tasted horrible but my body didn't care. My mother and

Werner were gone, their empty soup bowls on the threadbare carpet in front of me.

"They went to see what neighbors are here," he said.

"Why are we here?" I asked.

"This is a gathering spot," he said. "It's a place where they round us up and then send us to a work camp."

"There are so many people here," I said. "How did they get the work done before?"

"That, Reni," he said, "is an excellent question. And one to which I don't have an excellent answer."

I examined his face, wanting to wipe away the worry lines that grooved his high forehead. They scared me. Pappi always knew what came next.

Then I heard laughter. I looked groggily over at the people next to me: a mom, dad, and four little boys. They seemed to be playing some kind of a game, tossing stones and laying pencils on the floor. Oh, how I wanted to play. No bicycles, no friends over to play, no birthday parties, no skating or movies, no…I felt tears come up my throat and into my eyes as I remembered Pappi's words in my Poesie book.

You sweet little one,
you belong to me,
you belong to me,
you are the most lovable.

We all slept that night, huddled together on the floor with our few blankets and pillows around us. The theater was stuffy, dark, and crowded but I was thankful. I couldn't remember the last time we'd all slept together.

11

Hollandsche Schouwburg Theater

Amsterdam, the Netherlands

March 26–27, 1943

That morning I awoke to groups of people being shuttled out by guards. There was crying and scrambling and everyone was in a rush. Pappi told us to wait, not to go to the toilet yet, and just to be still. So we did. Finally, the space emptied a bit. A few new people arrived with shock on their faces.

"Nice hair, Reni," Werner said.

"Oh, be quiet," I said. There was no mirror, but I was sure my hair was horrible. I looked at his off-centered mop. "You don't look like any movie star."

"Oh?"

With fingers as quick as a cat claws he finessed his hair to perfection. "Now?"

"Hmph. Now you just look like a jerk."

"This is what you're going to fight about? Hair?" Mutti asked. "Here?" Pappi rubbed her shoulders.

I made a face at Werner while trying to tame my hair with spit.

"Where is everyone going?" I asked.

"To a work camp called Westerbork," Pappi said.

Mutti gave him a look that said *be quiet.*

"Come on Mutti," Werner said. "It's not like Reni and I don't know what's going on. Well, at least I know what's going on."

"What we know," Pappi continued, his voice sharp, "is that people leave here on trains that take them to a Dutch work camp, just north of here by a few hours."

Mutti glared at him. He didn't say anything more.

We finally used the bathroom, which was disgusting. Werner said the theater bathrooms were not designed for so many people.

Back on the floor, we sat together in our sleeping spot and ate porridge out of the same dirty dishes we had had the soup in the night before. Also disgusting.

Soon a pale, nervous Dutch policeman came over and spoke with Pappi. They both glanced at me.

"Reni, dear. This nice policeman says that there are children across the street in a daycare that has been set up to take care of the young children, and that they need helpers like you. Are you willing to go?"

I tried to read his face. Was this real? I loved playing with children, at least somewhat well-behaved children, but I didn't want to leave my family. He nodded. Mutti nodded as well.

I stood up and followed the nice policeman along with several other girls my age. I looked back; Pappi waved. *You'll be fine*, his wave said. Outside we went into that same cold sun. Oh, but it felt good.

We walked into a small building across the street that looked like it might have been a library. I spent the day playing with children of all ages. There were about ten of us older girls, a handful of nurses in white smocks and caps, and probably seventy kids. It was certainly more fun than staying in the stinky theater. Even with the changing of diapers, it was a lot less smelly, and even in hard times, I realized, little kids can find a way to play. There weren't any toys, but we made up games and sang songs we learned in school. We all knew "Two Buckets of Water."

To fetch two buckets of water
To pump two buckets of water
The girls in wooden shoes
The boys on their wooden leg
Just ride through my gate.

I loved silly rhymes that meant nothing. I sang and sang and we held hands and danced around in a circle until we collapsed. As the day went on, the babies fussed and cried because they were used to eating whenever they wanted and now they were separated from their moms. Twice that day the moms were allowed to come over from the Schouwburg to feed them, escorted by two Nazi guards. One Nazi guard, a little fat man whose helmet looked like it had been squeezed over his head, told the moms to return to the theater after just a few minutes with their kids. Feeding time was over. One mom didn't want to leave her little boy. He was so tiny and couldn't even lift his head. And he was a little yellow, with a high-pitched cry.

"Please," she said as she covered him with her arms like a cocoon. "He needs me. Can't you see how he needs to stay with me? He is a newborn."

The three or so of us closest to the mom sat stone still, stunned to watch her defy the Nazis. *Let her stay*, I thought, *please*.

The Nazi guard grabbed her now-screaming baby out of her hands. Then the other guard pushed her out the door, and the first guard handed her baby to an older girl next to me and both guards went outside. The girl folded the tiny crying baby into her chest.

The daycare was silent but for the baby screeching for his mother. I was chilled into stillness. *Nazis must not get married and have babies*, I thought. If they did, there's no way they could do this.

At the end of the day, the moms came back to feed their children, and the little yellow baby got to be with his mom again. Then a different Dutch policeman took us helpers back to the theater.

"Did all the moms and dads go to work or something today?" I asked Werner, whom I saw first.

"No, we all just sat around wondering if we would be in the next group to be sent away."

"Why did they have us be with the little kids then?" I asked.

"Ummm, maybe because little kids are like you—noisy and gross?"

"At least it doesn't smell like here."

"Really? A hundred babies, all clean?"

"Yes," I said, "and everyone smells better than you!"

We joined Pappi and Mutti in our small space, said hello to some neighbors, and sipped soup in our disgusting porridge bowls. Then I lay down and looked around at them. Half-lidded, not asleep, but not fully awake either. I knew this state now. The state of existing in-between; it was an almost-dream where what was real could still seem far away, but not so far that one couldn't snap back if needed, if something went wrong. It was exhausted alertness. I closed my eyes.

In the morning, groups of people left and again, new ones came in. And we waited, unmoving. The same nervous Dutch policeman from yesterday came over and spoke to Pappi. Pappi's eyes widened and he nodded and smiled, and said something to the officer who quickly scribbled something on a piece of paper.

"Quickly, gather all your things now," he said. "Let's go, Hasenbergs."

His tone told us not to talk or question. We gathered up our knapsacks and bags. We followed the policeman as he scurried through the crowds, but in the opposite direction from where most were heading. Pappi showed his identification to another policeman at the entrance of the theater space, and he let us through. Into the street. Into freedom. Life swarmed all around us, and we walked as fast as we could around the block and away.

"Oh John," Mutti exclaimed, panting from the pace, "are we free?"

"Yes," he said and stopped to hug her. He looked at Werner and me and hugged us, too.

"It's a miracle," Mutti said with a smile.

"Yes," Pappi confirmed.

"But," she continued, "it will be a little bit of a walk home with all of our things. We stand out."

"Especially walking three kilometers home with our earthly belongings!" Werner said.

Three kilometers, I thought. It seemed farther than that.

"I was able to send word before we left with the officer," Pappi said, "A neighbor will be here to pick us up."

"Oh John, you think of everything."

"I think it is more worrying than thinking."

We waited forever before a car came to pick us up. We all piled inside.

At our apartment on Schelde Straat No. 40, we found a notice tacked to the front door saying that our place was vacant. No one lived here anymore. But we did! Pappi unlocked the door with a spare key he kept in his wallet and threw it open. All of the rest of our belongings were there—even the dirty dishes were in the sink, as if we had never left. I ran to my room and checked my special things: my Poesie book, my other dolls, my cards. Werner confirmed that his maps and his books were still there.

Our neighbors and friends were shocked and happy. No one had ever gone to the Hollandsche Schouwburg and returned. Why we had been released really was a mystery. All week long they filled our apartment with flowers— tulips, daffodils, reds and yellows and pinks. I breathed in the rich perfume, and felt the promise of it all.

12

Amsterdam, the Netherlands

Spring 1943

Vera, Werner, Rudi, and I walked the canals through the mists of spring's coming. On one of our walks, on a rainy Saturday afternoon, Vera told me about a new boy she liked as we strode ahead of Rudi and Werner along the dappled waterway. She didn't have many classes with him, but maybe next year. As I listened to her whispered and exciting news, I looked at the pedestrians. Coats with yellow stars were fewer, and the German soldiers and Dutch police more numerous and always in packs. Germany was draining Amsterdam of Jews. I didn't feel invisible anymore, in fact, I felt sure that my yellow star glowed like a bright beacon in the gray drizzle. Something had changed between Vera and me: unlike me, she didn't live under the threat of disappearing. She could think about next year; I was stuck worrying about today and the next day.

Back at school, Rudi and I sat together as always. I brought my Poesie book in for what classmates remained to sign. Rudi added a few more stickers. Where he got them from, I didn't know. I reread what people wrote, including what Mr. Pinto had written in my first few months at school, especially the part I'd remembered when Werner and I were on the food truck:

> *To write a verse in this book, I do this with pleasure. Let us always remain good friends, even if you live far away from here, and even if sometimes there is a rain shower and everything looks black and gray, be courageous, be a*

*blessing, because things will soon change again. Go through
your life upright and honest, dear child, this is what your
teacher says to you.*

It was as if he knew what was coming, that life would get harder for
all of us. His clothes hung off him now. And he paced back and forth
while he taught, as if he was afraid to sit down.

There was also a new quote in my Poesie book, and it looked like
Rudi's handwriting, though I couldn't be sure:

*As devils pray and angels curse, when cats and mice look
for each other,
when water changes into wine, then shall I forget you.*

He looked down when I read through it, but I thought I sensed
a smile.

Back at home, Greetje's mom brought back small bags of food
from the store almost every day because the shelves were still bare after
3:00 p.m. when Mutti could start her shopping. Many apartments on
our street darkened, their doors tagged with official notices. Mutti
and Pappi said it was time to give away more of our things: it was
better to choose who our beloved things went to than let the Nazis just
take them.

The Bremekamps hid most of our stuff. A photographer named Ri
Ritsema, who lived with them, said she could store things like photographs, and it wouldn't seem suspicious. The photographs on the walls
came down, leaving their shadows where the sun had cast them over
the years. The haystack painting came down, and Mutti's neck and
ears went bare with no jewelry at all. I looked at the emptied wall and
imagined the photos back in place: my grandparents, my parents on a
stroll, Werner and me skating, Werner and me at the beach.

What couldn't I live without? My dolls? Even Liesje, my favorite,
didn't call me to play with her like she used to. When little Gerda came
over with her sister Greetje to drop off the food, she ran right into
my room to see them, lined up on my shelf in their hats and dresses.
I let her pick whatever she wanted. To my surprise, she chose Liesje's

wooden bed, so her own favorite doll could have a bed. *Poor Liesje*, I thought, but I understood. And Gerda was all smiles.

My pink blanket: Mutti said I should keep that.

And then came the late spring morning in 1943, when I showed up in our hollow little classroom, and Rudi wasn't there. He had always arrived before me. I stared at the door to the classroom and willed him to come in. I watched the door all morning. His empty wooden chair stayed naked and alone. By noon he still hadn't shown up. Mr. Pinto came over and patted my back. My tears overflowed, and I asked to go home. He nodded. I ran all the way home, losing my only pencil on the way. I went straight to my room and slammed the door.

"What are you doing home? Are you okay?" Mutti asked, coming in from the kitchen, wiping her hands on a towel.

"I don't want to talk," I said.

She came in anyway.

"What happened?" she asked.

I turned my head toward the wall and started to cry into my blanket.

"Sweetheart," she said and put her hand on my back, like Mr. Pinto had done.

"He's gone," I said. "They took him."

"Rudi?"

I nodded into the pink softness.

"Oh, I am so sorry," she said. And we sat there. I didn't look up, but I thought she might be crying, too.

"We knew this day would…might come," she said.

"Yeah, but it's different *knowing* it might come and then having it *actually happen*," I said. "I didn't even get to say good-bye."

"He knows you care. You showed him that every day. You're a good friend. He knows."

I thought back to the day before. He'd been wearing his brown coat, the yellow star a little ripped off one corner so it flapped down. I remember hoping he wouldn't get in trouble for that. He'd waved as he left with a couple of other boys. We had talked about the weekend coming up, and what we would do if it rained. Hide under the bridges? Duck under the eaves of a store? Construct our own umbrella?

And, now, we wouldn't do any of that.

Rudi's leaving stripped away the color from the tulips and dampened the sunshine trying to warm us after the rains. In the weeks that followed, Werner tried to make me feel better by inviting me to plan Henki Express trips with him. I could choose anywhere I wanted to go. My favorite trip to work on was to Ecuador, the country where our passports were coming from.

Almost every night, my parents talked about the passports. A man Pappi knew was getting them from another man who was Swedish. It seemed a little confusing, but they talked as if the passports were gold. I learned that Ecuador was a small South American country covered with clouds and rain forest. It was ripe with promise because it was anywhere but here.

In May I came home from school and Mutti met me at the door with a big smile on her face. She pointed to the kitchen table. Werner was home too, and he smiled as well. An impish smile. Like he was going to tease me. What was going on? There on the table was a postcard. It was plain tan. One side had two stamps: one green and the other red, with my name and address under them. Rudi's handwriting. *Rudi!* I flipped it over.

He and his family were at Camp Westerbork. They had theater shows at night…some were pretty good…the food was bad…everyone slept in big rooms…life was pretty boring…it would be a lot more fun if I was there….

I re-read it again. And again.

Mutti and Werner hung around, fiddling with things they didn't need to fiddle with.

"Mutti," I asked, "if we get sent away, will we go to Westerbork?"

"Yes," she said. "It seems that's where everyone goes." She paused in her cooking, four small potatoes, peeled and waiting on the counter.

Westerbork and Rudi. I was ready to go.

We heard the Germans would round up Jews tomorrow, then two days after that—no, next week. Rumors changed course like skittish pigeons. We heard that roundups, when they happened, were fast, so we kept knapsacks ready to go. Mutti worried that the passports would arrive too late. What if we were taken away and we didn't have them?

At least we knew what to pack—a change of clothes, things to eat with and eat on, a blanket. Postcards from friends at Westerbork told us what to bring, and the police distributed lists as well. Details were sparse, but we knew one thing: it was not a matter of if they came to get us, but when. After all, every other part of Amsterdam had been "de-juda-ized," Werner said.

"Dejew...dejed...that's not a word," I said as I pulled everything out of my knapsack again. I always seemed to need something I had just packed, like my comb or a clean shirt.

"It is," he said standing over me. "It might not be in the dictionary, but the Nazis use it."

"Who cares about the Nazis?" I blurted.

"Other people say 'dejudaized,' too. Just because you can't say it doesn't mean it doesn't happen."

"Mutti," I yelled, "Werner is making up words!"

I put aside the shirt I needed and restuffed the rest. I would refold it neatly later.

"I don't want to hear it," Mutti called back. "Not that word, and not you two arguing."

13

Amsterdam, the Netherlands

June 20, 1943

The morning air was hot, humid, and heavy. The remains of the night rain trickled down the panes and polished the leaves of the trees outside, which drooped in the breezeless air. The showers had done little to break the humidity. Even with our windows cracked open and the bulky blackout curtains pulled aside, we were already sweating. Wispy white curtains, the few we had left up since the threat of air raids had begun, hung limp. Each of us—Pappi, Mutti, Werner, and me—stirred, getting ready for the day, when I heard charged voices echoing off the cobblestones and brick buildings outdoors. With a brush of the back of my hand, I parted the light curtains of the corner window. Far off, a few cars and meandering bicycles passed through an intersection. It was so quiet and normal, except for a line of Dutch police in dark uniforms spread out across and moving up the wide road like an incoming tide.

From behind, Pappi's voice startled me.

"Reni. Away from the window. It's time to go."

"But we got out of the theater, can't you get us out of this?"

"No, this is a much bigger roundup, Reni. I'm sorry."

He smelled of soap and tea. His hair was combed back, ready for the day. His face was tight and drips of sweat glistened by his ears. I looked at him in the day's new light, but I was suddenly thinking of Rudi, and how the "time to go" would mean that I would see him. My breath quickened.

In my room I rummaged through my knapsack to make sure I had what I wanted. I pulled out everything to make sure my pink blanket and Poesie book would fit in first. After that, I swapped some clothes for others. I shoved it all in and pushed down hard. I'd fold them later. The flap barely covered the top, so I had to yank on the straps to get them to buckle.

"Remember to put on two pairs of underwear," Mutti called.

"Put on, or did you mean pack?" Werner asked.

"Put on, so you have more room to pack," repeated Mutti, "And pack two more pairs."

I unstrapped the knapsack and things tumbled out. How was I going to add any more?

"Reni."

Pappi stood in the doorway, a box in his hands.

"Last chance to leave things with the Bremekamps," he said.

My parents had constantly fussed over what to keep and not keep. If we hid too much, the police and Nazis might be suspicious. We had to be willing to leave some valuables in our home, to protect the Bremekamps and protect the things we really wanted.

"I thought we gave them everything," I said.

"Most of it. Your Mutti and I started a new box yesterday. Anything? Quick, quick, I have to run it to them now."

He already sounded out of breath, just standing there. I felt that I had to give him something, so I pulled the Poesie book from my knapsack and put it on top of our keepsakes. Pappi darted out. I then changed my mind and called after him, but he was gone, our front door clicking behind him. Mutti called him, too, pleading for him not to go. I stood in my room, tasting fear.

A few minutes later there was a knock on our door and a loud voice. I peeked down the hall.

I saw Mutti at the door: "Who, who is it?"

"Me! Trudi, open the door. It locked behind me."

"Oh John, that was too close," she gulped as she let him in. "You shouldn't have done that. It wasn't worth the risk."

"Shhh, don't worry. Our things are safe with Max and Stien…they offered to hide us again."

My parents walked down the hallway, not seeing me.

"I know, I know. It is too late," Pappi continued in a whisper. "The police are too close. We would all get caught. They are already taking a risk holding our things. We can't endanger them."

"Are you sure?" Mutti asked, "Maybe we should hide. This is our last chance."

"I don't think we should, Trudi. I thanked them and left. I told them we would be back later for our things."

Then there was a sharp rap on the door and a sharper voice.

"*Politie.* Open up!"

We froze.

"Coming," Pappi said, his eyes locked with Mutti's.

"Are there Jews here?" the sharp voice demanded.

Pause.

"Yes, we are all Jews," Pappi said. He opened the door and three Dutch police officers swept in.

Even up close, the Dutch police looked the same as they had in the theater with their blue pants and their blue jackets with golden buttons that ran down the front like a trail of geld. They just differed in height.

The sharp-voiced leader said, "You are to come with us. You have ten minutes before we leave."

I backed into my bedroom to get my bag, feeling dizzy and my breath small. Boots hit muffled carpet and snappy floorboards. A head and body in the doorway. The youngest policeman in his pointy cap looked at everything in the room except me. I could smell the leather of his high boots and tonic in his hair. There were stomping footsteps in other rooms. Drawers being hastily opened.

The sharp voice said, "I suggest you don't take valuables."

It was a command not a suggestion.

I realized I hadn't made my bed, so I grabbed the sheets and cover and pulled them up and over my pillow. Diagonal wrinkles spread over the blanket like waves.

I joined Mutti in the living room.

Sharp voice tapped his watch hard enough, it seemed, to shatter the face. It was time to go. He directed Pappi to give him the apartment keys.

Werner looked hot, bundled in too many clothes. We walked downstairs, one officer in front of us and one behind, and the last locking our apartment. The steps down the one flight squeaked under our weight. Outside, we joined a few neighbors who were just as over-dressed. They wore coats and hats and carried duffle bags, suitcases, and bundles fashioned from wool blankets. I overheard an officer refer to us as a "lot," as if we were stuff to be sold.

"What are we doing now?" I asked Mutti.

She shushed me.

"Reni, no talking," Pappi said.

We were lined up and paraded down the street, turning right on the much wider, double boulevard at the end of the block. More people joined us like streams converging toward a river. We became a wide flow, keeping up as best we could with only Pappi marching straight, fast, and orderly, as if he were in a drill from the Great War. I tried to walk in step with him, which I found impossible. People kept shifting their loads hand to hand, and arm to arm. Ropes, strings, and straps bowed shoulders and palms. There was a wooden cart and baby pram. Everybody unbuttoned jackets and shirt collars. Women clutched their purses. I tried to think of Rudi.

As we entered a square, there were fewer Dutch police and more German guards. I realized I couldn't remember how we got here, the route we had walked. The streets, normally filled with people, were empty except for the swelling ranks of us Jews, hemmed in by police and guards. A few faces peered from high, murky windows. A couple of men stood in a doorway, talking. They didn't look our way, as if they didn't notice us. As if rounding up Jews in Amsterdam was normal. They stood safely on the shore as a river of people flooded by.

Finally, we emptied out into a park and were directed to stop. People put their bundles in the grass and let the elderly have the few park benches. Everyone looked confused. Babies cried. In the distance I heard guards yelling. I moved back a few steps until I bumped into Werner.

"Hey, be careful," he said. He spit out something. He had been biting his nails.

"Sorry," I whispered.

A procession of gray trucks pulled alongside the curve of the park. The green canvas flaps were peeled back, and our family and others were ordered to climb up and sit on benches that lined either side. We were packed. I kept squeezing in more and more until I couldn't move. Belongings were piled in the middle. A few people fanned themselves with hats and folded magazines. One man called to have the side flaps opened so the women and children could breathe. The guards ignored him. The man didn't repeat himself, and nobody dared open the flaps on their own.

Fortunately, the ride was short, and we were soon at Muiderpoort Rail Station—the same station our family had always gone to when we went to the seashore where I buried my feet in warm sand and my small pockets pulled heavy with the treasure of white, gold, and blue shells. We dropped out from the back of the truck, shuffling to join hundreds of others who were sitting and milling about outside the station.

Then the sun burned off the last of the clouds, steaming the pavement. We made a pile of our stuff. Werner and I shaped seats from the knapsacks and further unbuttoned our jackets. Pappi and Mutti stayed quiet, so we did the same.

I watched a lone boy standing close to the tracks who looked a little like Rudi, only older. His face was serious, as if he were trying to solve a problem, his coat folded over his arms, his shirt and jacket open, his rucksack between his legs. The knapsack straps strained, despite being buckled to their last holes. Just like mine. I thought about pulling out and refolding my belongings as I'd promised myself. Instead, I placed my chin on my hands and looked around some more. Closer to us, a child held a doll. Some young boys laughed; one of the boys put sticks up his mouth to imitate a walrus. Two passing police smiled at the walrus boy who smiled back before hiding his face. I glanced back to the standing boy. He was like a statue. No matter how often I turned my gaze away, each time I looked again, he was the same. An older man passed by in front of him, pushing a low cart of small, empty barrels, their hoops black and tight.

Then a train engine moved slowly in front of us. It was pulling boxcars. Some of the cars had tops that were flat, others were domed. All had big mushroom-shaped bumpers on the ends.

"That's how they carry cows and horses," Werner said.

"What?" I said. I wasn't paying attention.

"Those rail cars can carry lots of things, but mostly they are for animals like cattle."

I listened for the droning and nickering of farm animals. All I heard were the metal mushrooms knocking into each other and the screeching of wheels on tracks. Either the cars were empty, or the animals had nothing to say.

"Do you see that car with the little tower on one end?" asked Werner. "I suppose you know what that is for?"

He was in a know-it-all mood because he was nervous. At another time, it might have bugged me, but I didn't respond. I was thinking of Rudi and all we would talk about.

"The little tower is to look out for girls who don't know anything about trains," he said.

"I do so."

I rolled my eyes to let him know I wasn't playing along. I looked down at his knapsack, which was the only one not bursting at the seams. I knew, I just knew, that all his clothes were carefully placed inside, just as his folded jacket now sat neatly in his lap.

The cars rolled past until they lurched to a stop with squeals and bumps. German soldiers and Dutch police suddenly seemed purposeful. Some ran up to the cars, sliding open the huge, square doors. Others called everybody to get up, come forward, and line up.

"Pappi?" I asked. "Are we going in those?"

"Let's go, Hasenbergs," he replied without answering my question.

"Aren't they for animals?" I tried.

He nodded, his eyes not meeting mine, and ushered me along with a hand.

At the edge of the car door I smelled barn, and just as I put my hands on the mix of straw and dirt I was pushed up and in by unseen hands. I skidded forward, scraping my finger. We were pressed in further and further, so that we constantly had to reshuffle our things, redefine our family space. We were as cramped as cucumbers in a jar, as if they meant to pickle us. People packed in, making it duskier. Soon, the only light I could see was through a couple of barred windows that were high up, near the ceiling. The heat was thick. Pappi clutched my hand; I squeezed back.

"Push in! Make room! No sitting," came the orders from men I couldn't see.

The cramming stopped.

"Now, put this in the far corner! In the corner! Back there. And put the other in the other corner. Hurry. We are leaving."

Men passed along one of the small barrels I had seen in the cart, over their heads.

"Ugh," Werner said when he was pushed aside as the little barrel wound its way past us.

What is it?" I asked.

"I think that is our toilet."

"What? That? In the open? For all of us?"

"Don't worry," Mutti said. "We'll hold up a blanket to hide you."

With the sound of grinding metal, the square door slid shut. People asked others to move a bit, to give more space. Other voices said there wasn't any space to give. It already smelled of food and bodies. The train jerked forward and back, ahead again, and started rolling. People settled in as best they could, shedding heavier clothes and then lighter ones. Pappi nudged and guided our pile of things next to a wall, sat on top, and motioned for me to sit down. I was happy to join him, despite the heat.

"So Reni, tell me again of your most favorite trips," he said.

CHA-CHINK. Cha-chink. CHA-CHINK. Cha-chink. The train fell into a rhythm.

14

Train Rails North of Amsterdam,

the Netherlands

June 20, 1943

talked about going to the beach in the summer and playing on the canals in winter. Werner joined in, explaining all the trips he planned with his Henki Express: to New York, London, China, and even Africa. I kept steering my questions back to Westerbork and what it would be like.

"Reni, why so many questions about the camp?" Pappi finally asked.

"She wants to see Rudi," Werner answered before I could think of another reason.

"He's just a friend," I said.

Mutti seemed to wake up from a thought.

"Oh, Reni," she said, "We understand. Your Pappi and I are looking forward to seeing people, too, like Aunt Alice and Uncle Paul."

Alice was Mutti's sister, and Paul was her husband. They had recently been sent to Westerbork.

"We have bread and sausage if you two get hungry," added Mutti, checking her bag. "John, make sure the kids don't sit on this."

It had been three months since I'd seen Rudi, and I still ached for him. I missed my grandparents terribly, but my insides pulled for Rudi. I couldn't wait to see his face, hug him, and feel our legs against each other's. The wait would be over. We had heard through friends that his family was healthy, and of course, I had his postcard. Instead of rereading the few lines over and over, we could play and talk. What had I done with his postcard?

Oh no. I'd left it in the drawer by my bed.

I felt bad, but I decided it was fine. I'd take the real Rudi over a piece of mail any day.

Our talk trailed off. Pappi told me to stand, because he needed to stretch his legs, and give more room for Mutti and Werner to sit. I squinted, trying to imagine myself on an adventure, like Heidi from the book and movie when she was on the train against her will. Except that Heidi had been on a nice train and not in a boxcar meant for cows. Except that I had my family, and Heidi had not. I'd rather be with Pappi, Mutti, and Werner than be on a nice train without them. I laughed, remembering the movie scene when Heidi bent over and was butted by the goat, Old Turk.

"What's funny?" Werner asked.

"Everybody knows you can't turn your back on Old Turk," I quoted Peter the goat boy from the movie.

"Well, Old Turk isn't much of a gentleman," Werner replied, quoting Shirley Temple.

Werner smiled and then frowned. "This isn't funny. This is serious, Reni."

I was a lot like Heidi. We were about the same age. We were both close to our grandfathers. Her story took place in Germany and the Netherlands. She helped her grandfather and people around her; I was determined to do that. Of course, Heidi also lived in Switzerland. I wanted to visit there some day.

The hours seemed to turn into bad smells. One man near us had a worsening odor like rotten onions, and the toilet emitted occasional wafts that settled into a stench. Voices complained it was close to over-flowing. That explained why things felt more crowded—everybody was moving away from the offending corner. The real fear, somebody said, was that sloshing could lead to spilling and toppling. I pulled my shirt up to cover my nose. I was covered in sweat and I had to pee, but not bad enough to force my way to the barrel. The push toward evening and into night didn't even cool things down.

CHA-CHINK...Cha-chink......CHA-CHINK.........
Cha-chink.............

The train had slowed off and on throughout the day, but this time it continued. Light flashed through the small barred window. A boy climbed onto a man's shoulders and looked out.

"What do you see?" asked the man.

"It's a town with low buildings," he reported.

"What else?" came a different voice.

"There is a big fence around, with a tower way on the end."

"That must be a guard tower. We must be at Westerbork," said the man, sliding the boy to the floor.

Murmuring swelled and we all started shifting like we were hungry for recess. The train came to a full stop, and the doors banged open. Rays of light charged at the ceiling from outside. People turned away. Flashlight beams streaked across the walls and bleached flinching faces. There were groans of pain and discomfort mixed with sighs as the new night air rushed in. My need to pee was terrible. I thought maybe I could find a place outside on the other side of the car, away from the lights and lanterns.

"*Uitstappen!*"

Men started yelling for us in Dutch to get out. People stretched their necks and backs, and shielded their eyes. An old woman needed help getting to her feet. A little girl cried that her leg was asleep. We tumbled out, dragging our stuff. The handheld lights blinded us, but beyond that was a darkness like I had never seen. I put on my knapsack and realized I was very thirsty. I expected to see guards like the ones who had put us on the train, but these men wore green coveralls with a yellow star on the left front pocket, and they had on black caps. Thin ties were tucked into their shirts between buttons, and thinner belts tightened their slight middles. They reminded me of men who filled cars with gas.

"*Stap uit! Vlug in de rij!*"

"Get out! Get into a line!" they repeated. "Men and boys here; women and girls there!"

Everybody from the train looked a mess. Their nice clothes had become disheveled, and were bunched under their arms. Hair pointed in all directions and all the men seemed to have stubble. People were looking up and down and calling names, coaxing each other to carry and drag bags, suitcases, and blankets. The sick were loaded onto handcarts with large wheels a meter and a half tall.

For the first time I felt scared as we went to separate lines: Werner and Pappi away from Mutti and me. I began to cry. Mutti told me to *hush*, as I closed my fingers around hers. Women—dressed in the same coveralls as the men in charge—counted us. They marched us until we were stopped in front of a low brick building. Yellow light spilled from a single door. Mutti and I waited in line, inching our way closer as women disappeared inside. When I could finally look in, I saw people dressed in light-colored clothing. Then my sight adjusted. And I saw they were…naked.

I had never seen a naked adult. My family walked around the house in at least their underclothes. Pink skin. That meant I would have to get naked, too. *No,* I thought, *no.* Once inside, I leaned against the wall, trying to be ignored. Women were leaning over, pulling down skirts and underwear, pulling sweaters over their heads, and reaching behind, unclasping bras.

I didn't want to cry. I looked up at Mutti. She looked down at me and gave my hand a squeeze.

"Undress, now," one of the women in coveralls said to all of us. She was short, with puffy cheeks, a hooked nose, and hair pulled back in a stylish cut. I froze. What would she look like naked?

"Who are they, the ones giving orders?" Mutti asked a woman, when everyone in coveralls had moved on.

The woman shook her head. She didn't know.

"They are the Jewish Police," said another woman, who smelled of perfume.

"*Jewish* Police?" Mutti repeated.

"They are prisoners, too," the perfumed woman replied.

"They must be better than Nazis," said a third woman, who wore nothing.

I turned away, amazed that she could talk with no clothes on.

"Maybe," said the perfumed woman, "but they don't seem that friendly."

The stubby policewoman came back. Everybody stopped talking, and I pretended to unbutton my dress.

"You're too slow," said the policewoman to me, reaching for my fingers. "Do I need to do that for you?"

Her hand followed mine as I flinched to the side.

"She will undress quickly," Mutti interrupted.

The policewoman took back her hand, using it to push some stray hairs from her face. It was such a sudden, simple gesture that I wanted to think we had something in common. Closing my eyes, I imagined myself back in my bedroom or in our bathroom, alone. I loosened the belt and undid a few top buttons to pull off my dress. I followed with my undershirt and underpants. The air tightened my skin. I couldn't look down at myself, which allowed me to pretend I was wearing something. My lips pulled in and my shoulders hunched as I looked straight ahead and then up to catch Mutti's eye. Her mouth was stiff, but her arched eyes and slight nod looked almost proud. I rocked from foot to foot, fending off the urge to pee on the floor. I was sure the policewoman would not like that.

Old- and middle-aged women, mothers with sagging breasts, and young girls with firm skin. Brown hair, red hair, black, and blonde. The buds of bodies to come and the scars of the old were equally exposed, but almost everybody had their arms wrapped around themselves even in the warmth. I shifted my eyes away to the small, vacant places between bodies, offering the only privacy I could. Others did the same. Their look-away gaze made me feel a little better.

We carried our clothes and shuttled to a smaller examination room. If someone was suspected of having lice, they were shaved. As I got closer to the head of the line, I could see a large nurse running a comb over an old woman's head and peering down onto it as the old woman cowered and shook. Soon it was my turn. Fingers dug through my hair, pushed and pulled on my skin and then around body parts that had only ever been touched by soap. The large nurse moved Mutti and me along, without a shave. I had my clothes back on in no time. Outside again, we marched again. I took my mind off what had just happened by looking around, hoping I might spy Rudi. Or find a bathroom.

"Mutti," I blurted, "I really have to pee."

Nearby women and girls nodded in agreement. Somebody spoke up. Our guide stopped the line by the latrines, and we walked quickly toward the small building. The smell of urine was strong as we approached. There were no stalls; just one long board with many holes. Yuck, but I didn't care. I sat down. My eyes closed. I felt more relieved than I could remember.

Next door was our barracks, a long, low wooden building. Inside was noisy, but all heads turned as our group walked in. Women were already in bed, or standing and talking and getting ready for sleep. The long space was mostly filled with steel-framed, three-tiered bunk beds, with thin mattresses. Windows were high on the short walls; a few were decorated with curtains. It was humid, yet a fine layer of dust seemed to coat everything. The furniture consisted of picnic-style tables and wooden benches. It was obvious that there were not enough seats for all of the barracks' residents at once. Did that mean we wouldn't be able to eat as a family? Suddenly, I was hungry for dinner.

The policewomen were gone, replaced by a woman who told us she was the barracks leader. She directed us to empty beds. Mutti and I found two, one on top of the other. Mutti talked with some of the other women, while I ate some hard bread and rubbery cheese I picked from one of our knapsacks. I found the small washroom off the back of our barracks and washed up. I drank a lot of water, each glass making me want more. Then I crawled to the higher bunk and made up the bed. Mutti settled below. Bits of straw poked from the mattress, like exclamation points. I broke off the worst, tossing the bits on the floor, and pushed in what I could. I doubled up my sheet, but I still felt the little strands poking me. I heard Mutti's sighs and felt her every move.

"Reni, sleep well," she said.

"Mutti, are Werner and Pappi okay?" I asked, my eyes watering.

"Yes. We will see them tomorrow. The other women said the men and boys are fine."

"Okay. I'm still hungry. And it's dinnertime, and we are sleeping." I yawned.

"It's been a long day," she said. I felt her stir. "We have some more food, but we should wait and see if we need it for later. Go to sleep; it will all seem better in the morning."

"Okay, Mutti. I love you."

"I love you, too."

I silently cried into my blanket, not wanting Mutti to think I wasn't strong. I had never gone to bed this hungry before. I didn't want to have to go to the bathroom again, not with other people. I was sure Mutti was as tired as me, and I wanted her to believe that I believed her. If Mutti felt the bed shake from my crying, she didn't say anything. Then I thought of Rudi and let go a long sigh. Maybe he was with Pappi and Werner and the other men and boys.

Prisoner

Camp Westerbork, the Netherlands *and*

Camp Bergen-Belsen, Germany

1943-1945

15

Camp Westerbork, the Netherlands

Summer 1943

The next morning. Werner jolted me awake. I leapt from my upper
bunk and hugged him, kissing his head over and over.
"Blech," he said. "You're like a puppy."
"You're here!" I said.

And there was Pappi talking with Mutti. I ran to him and held
on; he hugged me back so tight I almost couldn't breathe. Pappi and
Werner had slept in the same barracks as we had, just at the other end
in the men's section. We sat at the picnic table with some warm coffee
and bread. Mutti was right: this wasn't so bad.

With nothing else to do, it was time to explore. I found myself
looking at every boy with dark hair, which was just about every boy. I
also kept my eyes open for Rudi's parents. Pappi and Mutti met people
they knew, made boring small talk, and we followed pointing fingers
until we found my aunt and uncle, Tante Alice and Oom Paul. It was
the widest smile I'd seen on Mutti's face in a long time. The day's young
sun brought out the gold in her brown hair. She was beautiful.

"You don't look so bad," Mutti told Tante Alice after the sisters
pulled apart and looked at each other close up.

"Well, it isn't awful here. We have food and there are shows with
skits, singers, and dancers. Some big theater names, actually: Max
Ehrlich, Johnny and Jones, Jetty Cantor, Kurt Gerron...."

"Max Ehrlich and Kurt Gerron as neighbors?" Pappi interrupted.
"Who would have guessed. We've come up in the world!"

"Oh yes. Under any other circumstances you couldn't buy your way into such company," added Oom Paul.

"So, you are used to it? Living here?" Mutti asked, ignoring the men.

"In some ways," said Tante Alice. "Honestly, though, there might be a lot of people here but there is a…distance. We're physically close, not emotionally."

"You never know who might be gone the next week," said Oom Paul. "Why get close?"

"Gone?" asked Mutti.

"The weekly train that leaves for other camps," Tante said. "It arrives each Saturday and leaves on Tuesdays. The Germans order the Jewish Council here to make a list of who will go. The Germans give the quotas."

"What's a quota?" I asked

"A number," said Werner, from the side of this mouth.

"Then they get on the train," Tante continued. "The train pulls away, and nobody hears back from any of them. Not a one. From here, at least, we can send postcards, like we did to you. And we can get mail. But nobody seems to send or get anything from the other camps."

"Well, we have heard…" Oom Paul interrupted.

Tante gave her husband a warning look.

Oom continued. "We have heard that notes have been found in the boxcars when they come back from the other camps like Sobibor and Auschwitz. We haven't seen the notes, but there is talk. The Jewish Police find them, sometimes carefully hidden. The notes say the other camps are…" He looked at Werner and me. "…Really not good."

"The train leaves tomorrow," said Tante. "So names will be called tonight."

The adults all looked at one another.

I pictured the men in their coveralls, ties, and caps sweeping out the cattle cars as if they were cleaning up from any other daily chore, just getting things back in order like I should have done with my bed yesterday morning. *Snow White*'s "Whistle While you Work" played in my mind, and I pictured one of the men bending down and squinting at a crack between two boards, not far up from the stained floor, where he spies a fold of white. His fingers clamp on a paper corner and pull it out.

Little discoveries could feel like treasures, rare and light, but these sounded heavier.

"Hm," Mutti said, "we got your postcards. Didn't you get ours?"

"Yes, yes. And we so appreciate all the food you sent to us," Tante continued. "We still have some of it left."

I had gotten Rudi's postcard, but I hadn't sent him food. I wished I had thought of that.

"There are rumors about what happens," Oom Paul continued, "but they are only rumors. We just hope the people who leave are okay, but who really knows?"

Yes, who really knows, I said to myself. I decided to ignore what Oom Paul said about bad rumors. What did that mean anyhow? Westerbork was small and cramped, but we were still together as a family. We'd found our tante and oom, so we would find Rudi.

That afternoon a man in coveralls assigned work to everybody but me because I was too young. Jobs started at thirteen, and I was only twelve. Pappi was to report to the Metaal Werkplaats, or metal workshop. Mutti was assigned to the kitchen, and Werner was to be a messenger. He was so happy at having such an important job, and thrilled when he learned he would have a bicycle. The bike was black, its paint pitted and scratched, with a brown leather seat. A rack sat over the back tire, with wire cages on either side to carry things.

"It's nice," I admitted.

"I know," he said, running his hand over its smoothness. "I haven't ridden a bike for…"

"…since they took ours away. Over a year ago." I remembered. "Can I try it?"

"No, this is an official bike, Reni," he said, too seriously.

Mutti told me I still had to work: it was my job to keep our things clean. This wouldn't take much, as we only had a few pots and not many clothes. It left plenty of time to search the camp for Rudi.

Westerbork was square-shaped, and big enough that I couldn't see from one end to the other. It was cut in two by a railroad track, and had a trench around the outside that made the barbed wire fence just beyond look even taller than it really was. It took about fifteen minutes to walk from side to side, if I didn't stop. I strolled about, poking my head into barracks and workshops. One tall chimney piped skyward against the low horizon, seeming like a cloud maker. Wind sailed across the plain, blowing dirt everywhere. And there were little biting bugs. Amsterdam didn't have many bugs, and I quickly realized that I didn't like them. There were so many people: thousands, it seemed to me. I scanned all the faces, recognizing a few. I would make small talk and politely answer questions about my family. Just before we ran out of things to say, I asked them about Rudi's family. Nobody knew.

I was surprised there were not more Nazi soldiers. A few were around the gates and in the towers. It was the Jewish Police who really seemed to watch over the camp. Most seemed eager to be bossy, so I didn't walk near them. I could walk everywhere within the camp except the quarantine hospital and the punishment barracks, which were inside the camp but cut off by barbed wire. There was a field where men and bigger boys played football. I thought for sure Rudi would be there, but he wasn't. Evening came and went, and then it was time for bed. My second night in Westerbork, and I still hadn't found him.

I was sound asleep when the lights came on. The barracks leader, a woman about Mutti's age, began to yell. Two police stood beside her. I bolted up and looked down at Mutti and the other women around me.

"Get up. Get up. Out of your beds. If I read your name, you are to report to the train early tomorrow morning. You will be going to work camps in the east."

Mutti looked up at me. Her eyes were huge. I jumped down and sat next to her.

"They are calling the people who will leave," she said and smoothed my hair with a shaky hand. "If we hear our name, we must go find Werner and Pappi."

I sat next to Mutti as we listened to names. *"Berkowitz…Borman…"*

"Alphabetical. They are calling names in alphabetical order," I said.

"Yes," Mutti said.

And so we waited.

"Haas, Hanef, Hirsz…"

No Hasenberg. The alphabet passed us by. Mutti kissed my head. Others readied themselves to go. The barracks was alive in the middle of the night. Some people were crying. Pappi and Werner came in and sat down on our bunk.

"This isn't paradise, but be thankful for every week we get to stay here," Pappi said.

"Pappi," I asked, "how many people go on each train?"

"I don't know, Reni," he said, and shook his head.

"I do," said Werner.

Of course he did.

"It depends on the orders from Berlin. Mostly, it is eight hundred to over a thousand."

I rolled my eyes.

"Pappi," I tried again, "why does the train leave every week?"

"Reni, I just don't know. But it seems that it leaves a lot since there are new people arriving every day and Westerbork can't hold us all."

"And the other camps don't always have the room, either," Werner added.

I was going to tell him to shut up, but I didn't need to. Pappi gave him a stern look.

A few days later we received a food package from friends in Amsterdam. We got canned goods, chocolate, fruit, and something resembling a meat salad that had spoiled. The smell was terrible and the only reason we opened it was that Mutti said she wanted to send an accurate thank you.

"Werner, Reni," Mutti commanded through a pinched nose, "come closer."

"Do I have to?" I asked.

"I need to get going. I have to deliver messages," Werner tried.

"This will not take long," she insisted. "Just tell me what is in here."

"Beef?" Werner guessed from a safe distance.

"You have to actually smell it. Come here," Mutti said. "I can see some vegetables...."

"I can smell it from here, Mutti," Werner said. "Honestly."

I took the smallest whiff possible. "Pork?" I coughed out.

Mutti gave up, penning that we were very happy to get their "excellent dish."

Werner promised to get me an "excellent dish" for my next birthday, but only if I was nice enough to him.

16

Camp Westerbork, the Netherlands

Summer 1943

On another night, after our first week, our family talked about their work as we ate some soup and the last of the sausage and bread that we had brought. Pappi's hands were cut and he had a burn on his thumb.

"I have to get used to this new work," he explained while softly rubbing red scratches.

"And keep your hands clean," Mutti added. "You don't want an infection."

Mutti said her work was boring. She had to sort dry beans, the good from the bad.

"And not many of them are that good," she said.

"So you are really throwing out the worst of the worst," Pappi said, laughing. "That's good!"

"No, it's bad, because we are told not to waste too much, and the best of the worst is never enough. If only I had a magic wand to turn bad beans into good."

"And a wand that turns beans into ones that don't make you fart," suggested Werner.

"That would be magic!" I added.

"And turns sisters who fart into ones who don't."

"I don't fart!" I yelled.

"Reni!" Mutti snapped.

"Okay, maybe a little…," I confessed.

"That's not what I meant!" said Mutti. "No such talk and keep your voice down."

Werner was smiling.

"And that goes for you too, young man," she said.

"That's not why I was smiling." he said. "I get to hear everything with my job."

"What do you mean?" Mutti asked.

"Who's in charge. Who's working where. Talk." He looked a little smug.

"Can you find out about friends from home, like, say, Rudi and his family?" I asked.

"Don't you mean just Rudi?"

"No! I mean anybody. Everybody."

"I'm sure I can."

"Be a little careful," advised Pappi.

Over the next few days we found more friends. It was nice to see them and eat together. It was just a matter of moments before I found Rudi, or he found me. I was sure of it.

Then the train arrived. It was Saturday afternoon when I felt, more than heard, the rumbling, especially as the huge black tube of the engine ground past, dragging a long link of faded black or brown cattle cars, slithering through the entire length of the camp. The Jewish police threw open the heavy doors and jumped up and inside with buckets and brooms, looking around to make sure nothing was left.

Whistle while you work

And cheerfully together we can tidy up the place

The boxcars sat there, doors open, looking empty and hungry. No matter where I was in the camp that weekend, there was the train. When I went to the bathroom. When I walked to dinner. When I hung out the clothes to dry. When we visited others in nearby barracks. I noticed numbers were written in chalk—*74 Pers*—on the sides of the cars. Werner said this was the number of people each car held from the last trip. Smears of past numbers were there too, as faded, smudged, and unreadable as the people they represented. Carefully counted, quickly erased. On to the next.

That evening at dinner Werner was less talkative about what he was hearing. His excitement about his work had faded, his lips were tightened, and he bit his nails.

"What is it?" I asked as we sat outside on the steps of our barracks.

"Nothing," he repeated. "Leave me alone. Don't hassle me about your Rudi."

"He's not 'my Rudi.'"

Werner didn't make a comeback, nor did he tease me or get frustrated as much as I bugged him.

"Reni," he said picking at his cuticles. "You know this is a transit camp, right? A camp that sends people to other places?"

"Yeah. Tell me something new."

"You know I've been looking high and low for Rudi, like you have. His family was here, but they boarded the train a few weeks before we arrived. He's gone. I found out yesterday...."

"Why didn't you tell me?"

He paused, then said, "Because I heard other things, too. And I wanted to check on them. Rudi left for that camp Auschwitz. Auschwitz is worse than here. A lot worse."

"How can Auschwitz be worse than this? We've been taken from our home. Who knows who has all our stuff we left behind. We're bored and doing stupid work. The food we brought is gone, and the camp only has gross soup and stale bread. And we have to use a big open bathroom with no door!" I felt panic rising in my throat.

"Reni, you don't understand...."

"I understand. I understand that you didn't tell me about Rudi right when you knew!"

"They don't just bore you or even starve you at Auschwitz. They kill you. I had to hear it a lot before I believed it. They kill people at camps like Auschwitz. They kill Jews like us...and like Rudi." His voice rose and he choked on the last words.

"You don't know that for sure," I cried.

"I know they left. I know they left on that train. And I know they kill people where the train goes."

"You don't know what happened to Rudi!" I covered my face in my hands.

He put his hand on my back. There was a rushing sound in my ears. I thought of telling Werner again that he didn't know anything, but instead I got up and stormed off in the direction of the evening sun.

I marched the camp, making sure to go through all the barracks again. None of it made sense. Sure, the Nazis were mean, but why would they use all this effort to kill us? We didn't do anything to them. The Germans had a war to win. Why bother with us? The next day I ran through my chores before going through Westerbork again. I fought the fear that came when I saw the smudged numbers on the train cars. Is that what was left of Rudi? For the first time I missed dinner; my appetite was in a hole.

The next day, outside our barracks, Mutti and Tante Alice were crying as they stood with my Pappi and Oom Paul. Mutti said the name of a camp "Theresienstadt" and the name of my Omi and Opa.

"Have we heard from Omi and Opa?" I asked, hoping to hear something good.

Before Mutti could say anything, her red eyes told me what I feared. *Omi and Opa are dead. Maybe like Rudi.*

"No Reni, we have not heard from them," Tante Alice said. "We are just very worried about them. They are old and the camp they were sent to months ago is much harder to be in than we first thought."

"So, no postcards come from Theres…"

"No, none yet," Pappi said,

Mutti dabbed at her eyes. "We just don't want them to be sick."

Omi and Opa are dead, I thought, but I pushed that away, squaring my shoulders.

"Omi and Opa are strong, even if they are old," I said.

Everyone nodded. I realized that uncertainty had been my hope. But like a fire slowly dying during the night, that hope was being smothered under a cinder pile of stories. We didn't know much, but maybe we knew enough. Killing camps existed. I turned from my family and retreated to my bunk and buried my loss in my blanket. I would never see my grandparents again, and I might never see Rudi.

I was silent for days, entombed with my thoughts.

I paced the camp and noticed a few birds perched on the top of the barbed wire post or on the peaks of the barracks. In a place that had quickly become routine, the birds didn't fit in. I watched them because I could never guess how long they would stay, or what direction they would fly. They flittered up and over the fences. And out. Watching them, I felt something drill down through me into the earth, tapping into a well of sorrow that I never knew was there. Who knew such sadness existed just below my feet?

Within a few weeks, my sorrow shifted to numb tedium. The weather cooled and the camp's few trees began to drop their leaves. For the first time in my life, the season did not mean school, new clothes, new teachers and friends, paper, pens, and books. I missed it. I talked and played with girls my age, making up games with rocks and pieces of paper. I met a girl a few years younger than me named Rachael, and we became friends. Werner, Pappi, and Mutti weren't much fun. They were too tired. Pappi had to do a lot of heavy lifting and work with hot torches. This manual labor was harder than his work at the bank and American Express. He seemed to be always in a state of healing from scrapes, cuts, and small burns. In addition to sorting beans, Mutti was working in a sewing circle, mending clothes.

One morning, Werner was overly fussing with his unfailing hair in the washroom, something he didn't need to do. No matter how he pushed and pulled, it flopped into perfection.

"What's wrong now?" I asked.

"Um, nothing," he said while running his teeth under his index finger nail.

"Don't do that. There's dirt under your nails. You'll get sick, just like Mutti says."

Werner gave a quick look of disgust. "It's my work. I'm delivering more food now…like taking it from the kitchen to Jewish leaders. Things like that…."

"All that fresh food?" I said. "What's the problem?"

"I've started tasting it." he said in a small voice, and paused. "What if I get caught?"

"I don't know. Stop taking it."

"I'm not taking. I'm only tasting. And I only taste when there is a lot of something, like one sweet roll if there are twenty. No crumbs left behind."

"So, why are you telling me?"

"I don't know."

"I know. Because you feel bad." I said, "Well, you should. If you get caught we will all be in trouble."

Werner looked like he had just been hit. The camp police were becoming stricter.

"Forget it, Reni. I'm sorry I said anything."

I wasn't going to let him off. I'd lost Rudi, and I realized I was still angry. Werner was feeling guilty only because he was getting tastes of fancy food. I knew he wouldn't stop. He might feel bad, but at least he got what he wanted. I would never get Rudi.

Another Monday evening: tension had been building in the camp all day as night approached. People walked through the camp, past the black, slumbering train. When the beast woke up, it would be hungry. It was like living with a lion. Satiated, it rested, and we could afford to let down our guard. Awake, panting and ravenous, we knew some of the herd would be stalked and caught. The stress followed the rhythm of the week, wearing on us over time.

There were more angry words and curt replies. Smiles were rare. After dinner, sitting on the front steps, I overheard Pappi telling Mutti how lucky we were. It was hard to think of anything here as lucky, I thought.

"Our names were on the list this week," he said. "To be called tonight."

"Which list? The train list?"

"Yes."

"Oh my god. What happened?"

Leo Buschoff, Pappi's buddy from the war, had seen our family on a list to go to Auschwitz. Leo had influence. I thought about Pappi's old war photos, standing or posing with fellow soldiers. I liked Pappi's war pictures. He looked happy with his friends. He looked strong.

"Anyhow," Pappi continued, "he took our names off the list. I think we are safe for awhile."

Pappi was right—we were lucky. It almost seemed like a miracle. A war pal Pappi knew from twenty-five years ago just happened to see our names on a list, and happened to erase them.

Another Monday night came and the barracks door shot open, and the two Jewish police came in. My heart started banging as the door closed behind them. Barracks' leaders read the names of those who would leave tomorrow: A's, B's, C's, down to the G's and finally the H's. I put my hands over my ears. I went rigid, then felt Mutti's touch. Safe again for now.

"Mutti," I said. My lips were dry.

"Yes, Reni." She moved beside me. "You've been so quiet. And I know that you and Werner have been fighting."

"I'm sorry," I said.

"It's okay. Rudi being gone is hard."

"That's not it. I'm sorry about Omi and Opa. I'm sorry they…your parents are gone."

Mutti's eyes dampened. We were in that deep sorrowful well, but together.

"Thank you, Reni."

For days, I continued to only poke and sip at my food and drink. Then I began to bubble to the surface. When my appetite returned, it roared in. Now that the food we had brought was gone, there was only one meal a day. And though it was nothing like Mutti's cooking, I found it delicious. I savored my portion of the carrot and potato stew or the sweet and sour bread soup. I actually hoped Mutti could remember how to cook these meals when we got out of the camp.

17

Camp Westerbork, the Netherlands

Fall 1943

had trouble getting used to all the people, all the time. There was never privacy. I was used to having my own room, and our own apartment. I was used to family always being around, but if I wanted, I could go to my bed, or even a quiet corner where I could make a nest of blankets. Just me, by myself. In Amsterdam, I would look out the window at the rain, blue sky, or snow. At Westerbork, all I saw when I raised my head were the tortured twists of seven-feet-tall barbed wire fences and, beyond that, the armed soldiers high in the watchtowers watching everything that happened.

Mutti let out a breath that she must have been holding; it smelled of the onions from dinner. Behind us, I heard a woman crying. I turned to see Rachael's mother. Rachael's family had arrived only three weeks ago, and now I had to say good-bye. This was not the first time. It seemed that I lost friends as quickly as they got here. At this point, after three months, we had become one of the old families. Rachael, her family, and the others started packing; their friends and their friends' families helped.

"Let's go, Hasenbergs," Pappi said.

We toured the camp, stopping in on family and friends, to see who had been listed. Almost every time, we knew somebody, or at least Pappi and Mutti knew them.

We spied Tante Alice and Oom Paul just after going into their barracks. They looked normal to me, but Mutti picked up on something. She sucked in her lips and lightly said, "Oh, my God."

Mutti and Tante hugged for a long time.

"Sobibor," Tante said when they pulled apart.

Mutti's hand went to her mouth and then cupped the side of her face.

"I promise to send a postcard if I can," Tante said with a forced smile.

"You better," Pappi said. "You don't want us to worry."

"A beer when this thing is over," Oom Paul said.

"As many as you want," said Pappi. "I'll pay."

"That goes without saying. You're the banker."

Tante got around to hugging Werner and me, telling us to be good.

"We will see you in the morning," Mutti said as she hugged her sister again.

"Yes, the morning," was all Pappi said to Oom Paul who didn't reply, only nodded.

We headed back to our barracks, crisscrossing others' paths. We walked silently, close to one another. It was a chilly November evening. Searchlight beams moved over and between the buildings, carving the night from guard towers sitting on spindly stilts.

Mutti and Pappi encouraged us to sleep. Sleep was always hard on Monday nights—too much commotion. Adults talked, deciding what to bring and what to give away. That Monday night was impossible. Sleeping must have seemed like the wrong thing to do if your family was about to go away, maybe forever.

The next morning we gathered for good-byes. Tante Alice and Oom Paul held hands like young crushes. My brief friend, Rachael, was in her best dress like she was off to her first day at school. They were ordered outside and we were ordered to stay put until the train left. We sat until the train's whistle shrilled far off and away. Mutti collapsed against Pappi.

That night was cabaret night. Our Camp Commandant, a man with the last name of Gemmeker, loved the theater, so he allowed famous Jews to make music and perform for us. As prisoners, we didn't see Commandant Gemmeker much, except at the cabaret. I sat between Pappi and Mutti, with Werner just beyond Mutti on the right. It was humid, and I could smell the work on my parents: oil and sweat. Pappi's fingernails were black on the ends, chipped, and his fingers stained and nicked. Mutti's head rested on Pappi's shoulder. Two men at pianos in front of the stage bobbed their heads and marched their hands back and forth across the keys. Men with violins jabbed the air with their bows. A series of small skits and coordinated dances swept the small stage in front of a dark red drape. In the end the performers joined hands, bowed, and waved to all of us as the curtain swept away the last of the show.

That night I dreamed of guards' harsh voices chanting "Hasenberg" until it became a scream and I awoke damp and sweaty.

Mutti cried for days.

A few weeks later my Pappi received a package. Other than the food, we had received no mail at the camp.

"It was forwarded from our Amsterdam address," Mutti said as she turned the small brown package over in her pale hands. "Who would send us something with no return address?"

"I don't recognize the handwriting," Pappi added.

"I've never seen forwarded mail," said Werner. "Even with all my deliveries."

I felt more excited than I could remember. The fall morning was bright and dry; sweet-smelling leaves blew around the camp, having escaped the far-off trees to visit us.

"Should I open it, or wait for a birthday?" teased Pappi.

"Open it, just open it!" I practically shouted.

Pappi's thick, rough fingers tore away the crisp paper to expose four small white booklets. The words *República del Ecuador Pasaporte* were above an official looking seal that showed a bird with spread wings sitting on an oval, surrounded by flags.

"What are they?" I asked.

"*Pasaports*," Werner said. "That looks like Spanish. They must be the passports."

"I can't believe it," mumbled Pappi as he flipped through them, looking at every page. Most were blank, yet he stared at them in wonder.

The three of us asked to see them. Pappi gave us each one. The inside page had uneven typed words that I couldn't read—they were definitely in Spanish, Werner chimed—and there were official red stamps and signatures in black. A school photo of me was stapled in. I looked at my smile, remembering when the photo was taken. We had filed onto the stage one at a time, sat, were directed to look happy at the camera, and then we filed out.

"They're real." Mutti said. "The contact in Sweden came through."

"Yes Trudi," Pappi said. "I don't know how or why these things made it here, but they did. This is…remarkable."

"They are really from Ecuador," I said.

"Ecuador's in South America," Werner stated.

"I *know*, Werner. Are we going really going there?"

"No," Pappi said. "At least I don't think so. These just mean we now have the status of *Austausch Juden*, 'exchange Jews.' We can be traded for German nationals made prisoners by the Allies. That's the value of our Ecuadorian passports. We are worth something to the Nazis."

"So this is good?" I just wanted to know.

"Yes, very good." He turned to Mutti. "These should protect us from being sent to Auschwitz. We have a chance now."

"We really might get out of here," she said.

It couldn't happen soon enough. Winter pushed away fall. Thin barracks' walls that gave some summer comfort now let in cold drafts. I buried deeper into my pink blanket and moved closer to Mutti. Food and supplies were harder to get. There was less soup to eat and less soap for cleaning. One thing was plentiful: bugs. The bathrooms were full of flies that seemed to want nothing more than to be in your mouth, and little white worms wiggled on the ground. I learned to not look into the latrine holes where the surface moved from so many of them. The worst were the head lice. I started itching and scratching my head, even in my sleep. I tried washing my hair, but the cold water and lack of soap couldn't get rid of them.

18

Camp Westerbork, the Netherlands

Winter 1943

started to not feel well. I was tired, achy, and had a slight fever. "Just a cold, Reni," Mutti said as she tucked me in. "Stay in and rest more."

After a week I felt worse. My pee was dark, even though I drank more water.

"Her skin looks yellowish," Pappi commented.

Mutti took me to the small hospital. We sat, my head in Mutti's lap, the solid bench hurting my bottom. I heard moans around us. We were led into a small, silvery room that smelled like chemicals. A white-clad nurse and doctor looked me over top to bottom. It was too warm in there.

"She has to be quarantined," the doctor with the tiny round glasses said. "She has jaundice."

Mutti asked what that meant exactly.

The doctor said that quarantine meant I would need to stay there, by myself.

"Alone?" I asked Mutti.

"Yes. We can't see you until you are better."

"How long?"

Mutti looked into the small round glasses on the doctor's face.

"A couple of weeks, maybe longer," he said.

The hospital barracks was similar to our sleeping barracks except that the beds were single, not bunk. There seemed to be only two types of people. The first were sick, quiet, and resting or sleeping. The others acted weird. Some stared, barely blinking. Some rocked back and forth, or yelled. I was so tired, but not tired enough to know that I didn't like this place. Mutti talked with a nurse, and then walked to a window near my new bed.

"Reni," she said when she came back, "you see that window? Just beyond the window is the fence. We can come to the fence, and you can look out the window so we can see each other. We will come every morning and evening. See? We will not be far away."

She smiled. I knew it was forced since I had not seen her smile for a long time, and I had never known her to smile about sickness. I returned her smile with a small one to make her feel good and so I would look brave. Mutti gave me a long kiss on my forehead and tucked in the sheets that didn't need tucking. She reminded me she loved me, and I told her the same.

I fell asleep, and dreamt of worms in bathrooms. The bugs opened their mouths to talk, getting louder and louder until I awoke to screaming. The noise was from the other end of the building, near the door. A bushy-haired man was crying out the name of someone named Sarah over and over. Two big men in white pushed him down and tied him to his bed. The bushy-haired man howled, straining his head up off the pillow. A calm doctor leaned over him and stood back up with a syringe. In a few minutes, it was quiet again. I closed my eyes.

I awoke to shaking. A nurse told me to get up: my family was outside and wanted to see me. Did I need help walking to the window?

"Can I have some water?"

She brought me a glass, which I drank so quickly I coughed. She wiped my face, reminding me to go to the window. The air around the glass was cool. Standing beyond the outside fence was my family. Werner was kicking at something. Mutti and Pappi were looking my way, and tapped Werner's shoulder when they saw me. I couldn't hear what they were saying.

"Can I open the window?" I asked.

No.

I shook my head at my parents with my hand to my ear to show that I couldn't understand. Mutti moved her mouth slower: "How are you?" I smiled and nodded my head a little. In reality, I didn't feel any better, and I was scared. We smiled back and forth until Pappi mouthed that they had to go to work, and they would be back. I was sorry to see them go, but happy to get back into bed.

That night was filled with more moans and screaming. A voice yelled in the dark to "shut up." I hid under my sheets, telling myself that even though they were threadbare, they could protect me. I missed my blanket so much.

The next day I learned from other patients and patches of conversation that all kinds of people ended up here: the sickest of the sick, even from other camps. There were people who had tried to commit suicide, their wrists swaddled like diapers, or their stomachs pumped. Others were so broken that they just stared or yelled.

Being sick was good for one thing; I slept through a lot of noise. As I got better, it was harder to sleep to escape the craziness. I looked forward to eating, when I could drown out the scary noises with the heavy taste of thick soups, bread, and actual sweets, which the nurses said were good for making the yellow in my skin and eyes go away. I ate very slowly.

Pappi, Mutti, and Werner came almost every day to the fence. We couldn't do much except look at each other, and mouth out "Miss you" and "Love you." Looking at them like that, I realized they looked different. I played a trick on my mind, pretending to be looking at them for the first time, as if I didn't know them. They looked older. I probably did, too, so I decided to think about other things: Mutti's gentle touches on my cheek, Pappi's tight, bright smile, and Werner's funny comments. The details helped to keep the shouts and moans at bay. I couldn't wait to see—no, *touch!*—my family again. I rubbed the window so I could see them a little better, and I watched them leave until they were fully out of sight.

Never in my life was I as happy as when they let me out. I had to keep myself from running ahead of the nurse who was leading me to the gate. I fell into Mutti's arms, promising to never let her go. Then I hugged Pappi until he chuckled, and I even squeezed Werner until he coughed. I vowed to stay healthy and do whatever I needed to stay with my family: I didn't ever want to hear, smell, or see that hospital again.

For an afternoon, Westerbork seemed like freedom. Even the long, black, heavy train sitting on its wiry rails didn't bother me. That night, we ate as a family. After dinner, Mutti and Pappi had to share some bad news about a distant relative who had died recently here at Westerbork.

It was Omi Silten, the grandmother of Gabi, who was some sort of cousin to us, but I didn't know exactly how. Gabi, Omi Silten, and her family had arrived here at the same time as us. Her family had come to some birthday parties and holidays in Amsterdam, but Gabi was younger than me so we didn't play together much unless there wasn't anybody else.

"Wait, Omi Silten wrote in my Poesie book," I said.

I remembered Omi Silten's note not because she was close to me, but because I had liked her words. They had reminded me of my heroine, Heidi. She'd written about the importance of being helpful and strong, because that would help lighten the load of others. Those words became more important the longer we were in Westerbork. I had a job beyond keeping things clean: to be helpful and strong.

"I'm sorry," I said. "Gabi and her parents must be sad."

Later that evening Werner finished the story.

"Gabi's dad is a pharmacist here at Westerbork," he said. "When Gabi's grandmother found out that she was going to Auschwitz last week, she begged her son for drugs to help her die."

Werner's face twitched, and he bit his nails. "Reni, he helped his own mother die rather than see her forced to get on the train."

19

Train Rails East of Camp Westerbork,

the Netherlands

February 1944

I felt almost giddy. We were out of Westerbork, bound for the camp called Bergen-Belsen. The shock of having our names called to leave was lessened by the fact we were not surprised, and also because our train was so nice. Pappi's contacts and our passports had kept us in Westerbork longer than most people, almost nine months. What was amazing, though, was the train that pulled in to take us away. It had boxcars, but that wasn't all—it had passenger cars with seats, big windows, and heat. And that's what our family got to ride in. For the first hour after departing Westerbork we stared through the hard windows at vast fields of snow that looked porcelain blue under the half-moon. The stars sprinkled the heavens like spilled sugar. My spirit plowed the deep moonlit drifts, sailing through the softness. It was all so beautifully different.

Hearsay wafted between the cars, kept afloat by a lack of details. The rumors trailed behind the German guards who patrolled the aisles. Some prisoners believed we were bound for someplace bad, referring back to the notes found in the cattle cars. Most felt it would be better. Pappi said to focus on what we really knew, and what we really knew looked promising. We were on a nice train and not in cattle cars like the ones that had taken us to Westerbork. We were sitting in compartments with leather benches. The train was heated. There was a toilet with a door that closed at the end of the car. These were sure signs—at least likely signs—that things were improving.

"Really, would the Nazis bother putting us on a train like this if they only meant to take us to a worse place?" asked Mutti.

"Doubtful," said Pappi.

I shrank into weariness, comforted by the adults' chatter. I looked out at the occasional passing light or village, though mostly I watched Pappi and Mutti talk with their friends Mr. and Mrs. Loewenberg. Pappi and the Loewenbergs sat across from Mutti, Werner, and me. The three of them looked cramped, but they insisted that Werner and I had space to curl up and sleep if we wanted. Talk revolved around Bergen-Belsen. What was the camp going to be like?

"I bet when we get there, we'll even eat on tablecloths," Mr. Loewenberg said. "And oh, how we will eat: tender meats; soup so thick it will not fall off your spoon even if you turn it upside down; the chewiest, crustiest, steamiest breads; chilled butter and fresh jam and desserts piled on silver platters."

"And oh, how we will pass gas from eating such rich delicacies!" Pappi said. "Gas galore from such gluttony, and yet we will never be happier."

"My, such a poet," Mutti said in a high voice, fanning her face.

Was that Mutti playing around? Werner and I exchanged the same look of amazement. Mrs. Loewenberg turned her face towards the window and blew cigarette smoke before breaking into a grin.

"What about punishments?" Werner asked.

"Yes," Mr. Loewenberg said with an overly serious face, "you are right Werner. The Nazis do like to punish, but...but you will only be beaten if you don't mind your manners, or don't eat all your chocolate tart! The commandant will march up smartly to our table, click his heels and say, 'That spoon is supposed to be on the left!' 'That linen is wrinkled!' 'You did not finish your plate!' 'No second helping for you, young man!'"

Mutti gave a sharp salute. I laughed along with everybody else. I would be happy if only a little of this was true.

"I've heard," Pappi said, "that Hitler is a busboy at Bergen-Belsen... but only on weekends."

"Hitler is a rather busy man," said Mr. Loewenberg. "Invading and killing takes a lot of time and can be so exhausting. Nobody really understands the stress that comes with being the Führer. He needs a place to get away to and relax. He has been known to even kick off his boots at Spa Bergen-Belsen. When he's not bussing tables, of course."

Mrs. Loewenberg gave her husband a focused smile, eyeing him from down the bridge of her nose, before tapping her cigarette ashes on the floor. A few flakes found her skirt, which Mr. Loewenberg brushed away.

"Sorry darling," he said, and looking back up at us, he added, "Kids, I may be exaggerating, just a little."

Mrs. Loewenberg pulled deeply from her cigarette. She looked fancy and content when she smoked. "Since you seem to know sooo much, darling, will Bergen-Belsen have enough cigarettes?" she asked.

"Oh yes, they grow on the trees, but in the off-off chance they don't, you know I'll find them for you."

"I know," she said, making big kissy lips at him.

Werner leaned over toward me and whispered, "Old Hitler might be a busboy, but 'everybody knows you can't turn your back on Old Hitler.'"

I giggled, thinking back to Shirley Temple's *Heidi* movie and the mean goat Old Turk. Werner made big eyes at me, waiting for me to deliver the next line in the movie.

"Well, Old Hitler isn't much of a...."

Werner widened his eyes, making me laugh harder.

"Well," I started again and finally finished in a rush, "Well, 'Old Hitler isn't much of a gentleman.'"

We doubled over. The adults joined in.

"I don't even know why I'm laughing," said Mutti.

"Because they are," said Mr. Loewenberg with a finger in our direction. "That seems like a good enough reason."

Our fits sputtered and calmed.

The window glass radiated cold. Deeper Germany was in front of us, the Netherlands behind. Though Mutti reminded me that this land used to be my home, it was hard to imagine that now. Mostly, I remembered my grandparents, and the powdery warm smell of my grandmother, and my Opa making breakfast, bending over the garden plants, and joking.

Had it really been eight months since we were last on a train and I'd thought about *Heidi*? I was Heidi again, on another adventure, in a story where things always worked out for the best. I dreamed of Switzerland's tall mountains and Heidi's loving grandfather. Like my heroine and her grandfather, my Opa and I were sledding together, coasting downhill and being pulled by horses through villages that looked like they had been dipped in icing. At least leaving the Netherlands and entering Germany took us a shade closer to the Alps.

Except that not everything worked out all the time. Heidi had her grandfather in the end. I wouldn't have my grandfather again, but I had something Heidi didn't: my immediate family. Things working out didn't always mean everything worked out, but the important things did.

At some point, I drifted off.

20

Camp Bergen-Belsen, Germany

February 1944

was in the cavernous, lavender-colored, smelly stomach of a whale, eating colossal beets that reeked of wet earth. They were as big as my head and bright purple, lined up on long tables. A floating hand gave me a fork, and a vague voice said to eat as much as I wanted, and as soon as the prongs pierced the tough, rippled skin of the beet, it turned into one of my favorite foods like anise cupcakes or chocolate. But as I brought the food to my lips, expecting a rush of flavor, it turned back into beet, as rancid as the great belly that trapped us. I gagged, except that I was so hungry I bit down, my teeth touched tines, and I scraped the mush down my throat. The floor moved with a low rumbling, lurching back and forth. My ears filled with growling. But it was the whale. My stomach felt sick. Hissing and squeals. Sharp screeches. Words. Barks.

Where was I? I thought, eyes wide, light-flooded.

The barking got louder and louder until I covered my ears. Our compartment door was thrown open and a young German guard stood there, shaking, saying nothing. I searched his face for what he wanted. He had thick blond hair under a moss green cap pulled so low that the back tapped the collar of his sweeping overcoat. His boots reflected the lights, as shiny and new as if the cobbler had just delivered them. His lips were red, red enough to be rouged. I thought he started to smile, so I relaxed a little. And then there was a whistle and he began to yell.

"Get out! *Raus!* Get out now!" he yelled through his loud red lips.

He swore, using words that I knew were bad, even if I didn't under-stand them. The German he spoke sounded as hard, high, and brittle as an icicle, not like the lower, softer German of my parents.

"*Raus! Raus!* This train is too good for your kind!"

He jabbed the air with a baton so smooth it caught the light. Pappi stood, putting himself between the boy soldier and the rest of us, nodding at Werner and my mom, using his gestures to say, "We hear you. We are moving." Passengers and German soldiers shuffled past in the passageway, pushing the young guard into our compartment. He stumbled into Mr. Loewenberg who caught him by the shoulders to stop his fall. The boy soldier regained his balance, shoved away Mr. Loewenberg, and recoiled back into the doorway. His whole face was now red. His eyes seemed to see something invisible to us. He raised the baton higher and stood trembling.

"Let's go, Hasenberg family. Let's go," Pappi commanded.

He and Werner pulled our few belongings off the rack above the seats. I folded my pink blanket, and tucked it tightly under my arm. The boy soldier backed into the aisle, stick still raised, as we slipped into the stream of people. The thin hallway smelled of grease, and soot, and too many people. As we stepped down to the platform, German soldiers were everywhere, and large tan and black Shepherd dogs with long snouts snarled from the ends of leashes pulled as tight as piano wire. I tripped on something, falling to my knees on the frozen, pock-marked ground. An immense bristling dog jumped at me and would have bitten me if not restrained. I screamed.

"Reni, look at me," Mutti said. "Look at me. Dogs that bark don't bite."

I looked at her, then back at the lunging beasts, then back at her.

"Did you hear me? Dogs that bark don't bite! Look away."

My eyes jumped upward to the sky. Dawn clawed at the tree line.

This is all wrong, I thought as I got up. I had not really expected Bergen-Belsen to be like Westerbork, but this felt like a trick. Nearby, a man tried addressing a guard.

"Excuse me sir, but there must be a mistake," he blurted. "We... we are to be exchanged...we are to be sent to a different...not this...."

The guard looked like he was chewing something, then his mouth curled just as he hit the man across the face. "Shut up! Move!"

I turned away. The glowing fields washed into the distance, broken by clusters of wiry trees. Orders to move. We walked. Orders to run. We did. The road paralleled the rail line before breaking off to the left. We were a crowded current; a human river whose banks were steeped with toothed and rifled predators. I bumped into Werner and then Mutti as I tried to hide in the middle. Pappi breathed heavily. Werner, Mutti, and I fell behind with him, the guards screamed, and our fear forced us forward again. My blanket fell. Without thinking I turned to pick it up, almost getting run over by a panting couple. Werner grabbed my arm, his eyes pleading for me to not get sucked into the undertow.

After about twenty minutes we slowed. People doubled over, but those who stopped were ordered to *move*. Our collective breath fogged around our faces, floating and disappearing into the cold, now blinding morning sun. Squinting, I could just make out the grid of a high fence.

"Women to the left and men to the right!"

Mutti and I were shoved to one side and Werner and Pappi to the other. I began to cry. My mother held me close as I struggled to get loose and reach my father.

"Pappi! Werner!" I called, even when I couldn't see them. I looked for their familiar legs, a big pair and a smaller pair. A Shepard growled, its fangs frothy, and a dark crust had formed along his muzzle.

"Pappi, we are over here!" I screamed. "Here!"

Other prisoners screamed. The guards yelled louder.

"Reni, stop!" Mutti said with yank on my arm.

"But what about Omi and Opa?" Daring to speak my grandparents' names. "They were taken from us, and now they're gone for good!"

Was this what Opa and Omi last experienced? Were they separated before they were killed? When did their hands last touch, their eyes last meet?

"Stop it! That wasn't here. Opa and Omi didn't come here!"

She's right, I repeated to myself, but the lines on Mutti's face showed fear. Now she studied the growing distance between us and the men and boys.

We were shuttled through a large, double gate next to an ugly shack. Inside, a guard glanced at his watch with a yawn. Gnarled barbed wire wrapped around and stretched between poles. Large rolls of the wire curled through the snow to keep people from even getting too close to the fences. Shards of shattered skin-thin ice fringed the edges of twisted potholes. Mutti and I walked briskly, our group led by a tall woman guard. My head didn't even come as high as her shoulders. She was huge, and I would have confused her for a man—she was so square and her jaw set so tightly—if not for the stiff skirt. She looked straight ahead as she kept a fast pace along the main road that ran down the middle of the camp like a spine.

Bergen-Belsen spread before us, as structured and orderly as school graph paper. It was bigger than Westerbork, with low row buildings and roads that angled off into paths. It seemed we walked forever in one direction. I turned around to see from where we had come. Dark forms shuffled. So many people everywhere, all moving as slowly as caterpillars nibbling the edge of a leaf. An old woman passed. She carried a glass jar of brown liquid, clasping it as if it were a baby. Was she wearing clothes, or was she just draped with cloth? Three girls stared. Their hair was pulled back, tight and dirty under handkerchiefs. They didn't look at my face, but at my dress and our belongings. I clutched my rolled up blanket more closely and moved beside Mutti, grasping her sleeve.

"Reni, what?"

"How long will we have to stay here?"

"I don't know," Mutti said. "Your father is doing everything he can to help."

"What's that mean?"

"Stop asking questions. Don't cause any trouble."

"But I'm NOT. I'm just asking one question: How long will we be here? And where's Pappi and…"

"Shhh!"

I got the answer I didn't want. It looked like nobody left here. They just stayed, getting dirtier and thinner. The female guard stopped in front of a building and read off a series of names: "…*Haas, Hasenberg, Holtzman, Kolb…*" Our barracks.

A woman shoved past us and darted inside. Then another came from the other side and pushed us in the other direction. Mutti caught the energy, pulling me in. We skirted to the left and then to the right. It was dark and dank, with rows of bunks. The smell of sweat and sleep was so thick I could feel it on my tongue.

"The choice spots are in the middle, away from the cold walls," Mutti whispered heavily to me.

She threw her jacket and other clothing onto two lower bunks just before another woman claimed one of them from the other side. The woman glared. Her high cheekbones widened her already square face. Mutti spread her blanket out and fell onto one of the bunks to claim our property in the flesh. She told me to do the same.

"I only see two of you," the woman said, moving toward Mutti.

"These are for my husband and son," Mutti said.

"This barracks is for women only," said the woman.

"Not true," Mutti replied, advancing on her.

"Mutti, I think it's true," I said, butting into the conversation. "Look, there are only women and girls here."

Mutti kept her eyes on the square-faced woman.

"What's going on here?" an approaching woman asked. She was older, with a tight, long face, hooked nose, small dark eyes, her dark hair piled high.

"Who are you?" asked the square-faced woman.

"I'm Mrs. Mandel. I'm the leader of this barracks. I'm in charge. Again: What's going on?"

"She is claiming too many beds," said the challenger.

"They are for my husband and son," Mutti explained.

"No men, no boys sleep here," Mrs. Mandel said. "Anything else?"

Mrs. Mandel glared at Mutti and the square-faced woman.

"No," said Mutti, "… nothing."

"Nothing," agreed the challenger, and sat down on the bed.

"We will be reviewing the barracks' rules to make sure 'nothing' happens all the time," said Mrs. Mandel, who then swept her head toward the sound of another quarrel and stomped off.

The squared-faced woman smirked, and Mutti grabbed her coat off the bunk.

Mrs. Mandel kept her promise soon after, reviewing rules upon nitty-gritty rules to us new arrivals. We had to keep the barracks clean, make our beds, and we had to report quickly to the *Appell*, or roll call.

A voice asked about the men and boys.

"They are in other barracks," said Mrs. Mandel.

Another voice asked if we could see them.

"You will see them tomorrow."

What about tonight?

Mrs. Mandel glowered.

"Listen closely," she said, "This is not Westerbork. You don't ask questions. I'm in charge. I will tell you what you need to know, when you need to know it. You will leave these barracks when I say so, unless you need the toilet. You will not go anywhere until after *Appell*. You will see your boys and men. Tomorrow."

She continued to stare. Nobody said a word. She walked away.

I realized why Mrs. Mandel seemed familiar. She reminded me of *Fräulein* Rottenmeier, the strict and nasty housemaid from *Heidi*.

The other women—the ones who were here when we arrived—came over to look for familiar faces, and to tell us what they felt we needed to know. Every day started with *Appell*, where everyone had to line up in rows outside to be counted by the Germans and *Kapos*.

"What's a *Kapo*?" asked Mutti.

"Prisoners who are forced to work for the Nazi Germans," said a woman. "They supervise the forced labor here. They can be terrible. Terrible."

"Some *Kapos* are decent, considering their work," added another. "The Germans choose them. To refuse is to be punished. Some figure out how to serve the Nazis while helping us. Others are less…subtle. They become more like the Nazis."

I didn't understand all her words, but I understood enough. Be careful: the *Kapos* can be bad. Even if they were prisoners like we were.

"Mandel?" asked Mutti.

"She is a favorite of the camp commandant, and she plays favorites herself, though not in the same way. Avoid her bad side."

"Avoid any side of her," said another.

"The *Appells* are serious?" asked Mutti.

"Very. It is not just individuals who are punished for mistakes. We can all be punished. Hundreds of us, if they choose, even for one person's mistake."

Women went on to further describe the *Appell*. The *Kapos* and officers didn't call names, and we were not assigned a number. The Nazis just counted us over and over, as if we were coins to be deposited. The tiniest problem—a whisper, a wrong glance—meant we would stand longer. Problems larger than tiny ones could mean a beating.

Later that night we climbed into bed. Around us, the women talked about recipes and food, and what they would eat when the war was over. I thought of our family meals together, and I asked Mutti if we would bunk again with Pappi and Werner.

"Reni, at least we are in the same camp as your father and brother," said Mutti. "We will see them very soon. Trust me."

"I do," I said.

It was Mrs. Mandel I wasn't sure about.

21

Camp Bergen-Belsen, Germany

Winter 1944

Just like on the train, I felt like I had no sooner fallen asleep than I awoke to shouts of *"Raus, Raus. Schnell!"* "Out, Out. Quickly!" I sat, spinning my head from side-to-side at the thought of rabid dogs lunging toward me.

"You are to report to *Appell* in a half hour," Mrs. Mandel barked. "It is five-thirty-one a.m. You now have twenty-nine minutes."

A voice from two bunks away asked about breakfast.

"Westerbork pampered you. There's no breakfast here. That is why I let you sleep in. Move."

I was so nervous putting on all my clothes and getting a drink of water that I suddenly realized something just as Mrs. Mandel announced we had eight minutes.

"I have to pee," I said to Mutti.

She pulled in her lips. Her eyes widened.

"Please. I have to go badly," I almost whined.

"Be quick. Very quick."

I waded through the swelling sea of dressing women and girls. Some were all ready, and lingered by the door.

The brunt of the outside cold knocked the grogginess out of me. I walked at a quick pace, keeping my eyes on the ground after almost falling on the dark patches of ice. The women had told us that each of the barracks had a couple of single toilet stalls, but they were broken and filthy, used only by the sickest and most desperate who couldn't make it outside. The working latrines were separate buildings. There was a line to get in, and I took my place at the end, burying my hands deep into my jacket. I fidgeted with the growing hole in my right pocket as I looked ahead to see if the line was shortening, and I glanced back at the barracks where there was shouting.

A woman leaving the latrine hissed: "Don't be late! We will all be punished."

I thought about running back, but I didn't want to pee myself. That would make me really cold.

"Move. Move. Move," I prayed.

As quickly as people burst from the latrine—smoothing down their skirts and buttoning their jackets—others rushed to take their place. Finally, I was in. The stench almost made me gag. I held my nose. How could this be so much worse than Westerbork? There was a long bench with two rows of holes running down the middle, set at a crisscross so that if you leaned back you wouldn't bump the person behind you. I scanned the seats in the gloom to see which one was cleanest, wanting to stay away from anything damp or lumpy. Then in one graceful act, I pulled down my leggings, lifted my skirt, and sat. I gathered what privacy I could, moving my skirt to keep covered and warm. I looked ahead and down so as not to catch the eye of my neighbor. There was very little sound; only occasional moans. I had to go so badly, I hardly cared.

I breathed through my mouth. Werner told me that smells were actually little bits of actual stinky things in the air. I didn't like the idea of breathing in tiny pieces of poop, especially through my mouth, but it was better than the smell coming into my nose.

I closed my eyes and listened to the guard yelling orders, somewhere out beyond. I tried pushing out the pee. Nothing. I counted and relaxed, producing a small leak. More yelling and my pee dammed up. I did math exercises in my head to get started again. Three-plus-three-equals-six, plus-three-equals-nine, plus-three-equals-twelve…a dribble turned into a stream…plus-three-equals-eighteen, plus-three-equals-twenty-one, and so on, up to thirty.

Nobody was left in the latrine but me. When was I last alone? I peered into the murky corners where the floor met the wall, the walls hit the roof, and where the roof peaked. I wanted the aloneness to last. All the lightless corners seemed to tug at me, offering something, anything other than what we were facing.

Yells. I needed to get out. There was no paper. No sink. No water to wash my hands. Disgusting. I pulled down my skirt and ran outside, joining the tail end of the last stragglers who included my very worried Mutti.

"Thank goodness, thank goodness, Reni. Don't ever do that again," she said, shaking and visibly upset.

We hurried together to the gathering *Appellplatz*; as we entered the square framed by the barracks, I gasped. There were hundreds of people. All bundled up, scurrying, and being pushed and prodded into straight rows.

"Oh, oh," Mutti whispered. "Look for your father and Werner. They must be here, too. There are so many. So they must be here."

Guards and *Kapos* writhed between us, forging us into columns five deep. Mutti and I were toward the back. I scanned my eyes left and right, but I was too short to see much. A guard moved toward us, and I dropped my glance. It was so cold. To keep warm, I pulled my fingers into the palms of my gloves and balled them together, feeling the jagged fingernails that needed filing. I moved my toes up and down, up and down. A guard counted as he paraded between us; after he passed once, he passed through again, counting again. And again.

"Dirty Jew," a guard yelled at someone.

"Stand straight, dog. You stupid Jew, is standing still too hard for you?" yelled another.

Who are the stupid ones? I thought. *You have to keep counting because you can't get it right the first time.* I pushed down my words, afraid that my face would betray me, or my thoughts would burst from my mouth like a pheasant flushed into the blue. Rather than think about what not to do, I focused on the coat of the person in front of me. I counted the rows of bleached stitching, lost count, and started again. A fragile snowflake landed on the black wool. I expected it to melt or blow away, but it stayed. I kept counting rows, and checking back, and always the flake remained, looking like a lovely, lonely, shimmering star.

We stayed there for hours, standing and doing nothing. New guards replaced the old. I pretended the man in front of me was Opa leading me to our garden, around Berlin and Amsterdam, and even to the Alps like Heidi's grandfather. *That's so far! How will we get there?* I asked. *Why, the Henki Express of course,* Opa replied, surprised that I hadn't thought of it. I followed my Opa's coat on all sorts of adventures: to plant seeds, milk the goats, hike hills, and slide down trails on sleds with great rounded rails like the horns on mountain sheep. The *Appell* ended. I thanked Opa and told him I was looking forward to our next trip.

Everybody ran to the latrines and the barracks where they clustered around the stove and buried themselves under blankets to warm up. Once the worst of our shivering had subsided, Mutti and I prepared to search for Pappi and Werner, but they found us first. I recognized Pappi's familiar frame, and ran to him as he rounded the corner to our bunks.

"Oh, sweet Reni," he said and cupped my face in his hands. "You have no idea how good it is to see you."

"Oh, yes, I do."

He hugged me and hugged Mutti.

"Hello, little sister," Werner said and even gave my arm a little squeeze. I squeezed back hard, grabbing him across the chest, and gave him a big kiss. Pappi said that there was little chance of living together, but we were allowed to see each other.

We also agreed on an *Appell* meeting place so we could stand together. Pappi said some roll calls would be relatively short, others long. Sometimes, there would be several in a day. The *Appells* were going to be hard, but they were routine, and at least we would be together as a family.

"Nothing is certain at Bergen-Belsen, except the *Appells*," Werner said, having already pieced together a truth from what he had heard.

But the more the four of us shared what we had each learned and observed in the past day, the more we realized that the lack of food, hard labor for Mutti and Pappi, and the cold were also certain. There was little heat in the barracks. Some had small woodstoves, but they mostly rested like useless relics because there was so little firewood, and two hundred barracks' mates wouldn't all fit around it anyhow.

Werner had talked to other boys his age—he was now fifteen—and had learned a lot in a short time. Bergen-Belsen was about one-and-a-half kilometers long, west to east, and half as wide, forming an equilateral rectangle. We were in the Star Camp—a camp within the camp—named for the fact that we didn't have to wear the grey and white striped prisoner's uniforms, just the Star of David sewn to our clothes. There were several thousand of us, mostly rounded up from the Netherlands. The Star Camp was in the middle of Bergen-Belsen, almost entirely surrounded by other smaller camps. The camps were all sectioned by barbed wire. So everywhere we looked we just saw more camp, except for a small section looking east over fields, a road, and a line of deep green trees beyond. It was the one scene free of camp buildings and prisoners.

To our west was the Small Camp, about the same size as the Star Camp, and to the east were a few camps for Hungarian Jews, prisoners of war, and others. The west fence ran along the edge of the road that formed the spine of Bergen-Belsen. The road was lined on both sides with a ditch and on one side with a row of poles, each with a high-placed light like the head of a shower. At the east end, we were told, was a small crematorium where the dead were turned into ash, one body at a time. All the low buildings, some with chimneys pushing smoke skyward, reminded me of a large farm. High barbed-wire fencing fanned out from wooden watchtowers that looked like four-legged monsters ready to chase down prey.

The camp officials gave jobs to prisoners who had passed their fourteenth birthday, so that included Werner, but not me. My parents were assigned—Pappi called it "recruited"—to work outside the camp. They left after morning *Appell*, Pappi to dig trenches and Mutti to work in a drafty factory. Werner was assigned to take apart old shoes so the parts could be re-used.

No matter how hard they worked or how exhausted they were, Pappi kept a clean face. He still had his shaving kit: a wooden box with a notch for the razor, and a package of blades that he swapped out and sharpened. When the shaving cream ran out, he frothed up soap. When there wasn't soap he rubbed his face briskly. Then he pulled the blade slowly over his face in short strokes, using his free hand to rub and feel for stubble since we didn't have a mirror. Mutti reminded him how much she preferred a smooth face, and how handsome he looked. After running her fingers over his cheek, she combed the hair back from his high forehead and pushed down a few strands near his temples.

"What are these grey things?" she asked. "Are you aging?"

"Hmmm, signs of wisdom no doubt."

"What does your wisdom tell you?"

"That we'll all get out of here."

"Good, because I don't ever want to see another pair of old underwear again."

My Mutti's work was to cut up and repair used soldiers' underwear, separating the parts that could be saved and piecing them together again. She risked punishment if the guards felt the tiniest scrap was being wasted. Pappi's work sounded harder, as he worked in all weather, scooping, carving, and pushing the earth to make long troughs along roads, fields, and fences.

But I thought her work was grosser.

"Mutti is like the Dr. Frankenstein of undergarments," Werner suggested.

"They're alive!" I added, thinking back to kids joking about the monster movie.

My brother chuckled.

"Reni, that was good!"

I beamed.

22

Camp Bergen-Belsen, Germany

Late Winter 1944

"What's it like outside the camp?" I asked Mutti one evening. I was tired of being cooped up in the Star Camp without them all day.

"Just a big, cold building with women working," Mutti said. "You are not missing anything."

"Do you see other people? Other places?" I pressed.

"Reni, stop," Mutti said, "There is nothing to see."

I asked Pappi the same question when he returned near dinnertime.

"It's a lot of work," he said.

"Do you get to eat off silver platters at lunch?" I tried, thinking back to the playful conversation on the train a few weeks back.

"Do we what?" he responded, and then relaxed into the thinnest of smiles. "Oh, not yet. I promise to let you know when we do."

"And is Mr. Loewenberg finding cigarettes for Mrs. Loewenberg?" Werner asked.

Come to think of it, I had seen very little smoking at Bergen-Belsen.

"A few, I'm sure," Pappi said. "It's not easy. I think he is trading food for them."

"Bread for tobacco? You can't live on cigarettes. Though, God knows, she tries," Mutti said, then added, "Mrs. Loewenberg never looks very happy."

"Who does look happy here?" asked Werner.

"Vogeltje does," I said.

That was an easy answer.

"Vogeltje's crazy," he said.

"No she's not," I pushed back.

My brother rolled his eyes. "She's strange!"

"She's out of the ordinary," Pappi said, "I will grant you that, but Vogeltje isn't crazy, she is rare…like a gem."

"Like a gem?" repeated Mutti, her brown eyes widening.

"But not as rare as you, Trudi," he said quickly.

Mutti snorted.

Vogeltje, or "Little Bird" in Dutch, was a sweet, caring woman in our barracks. She was small, not even a head taller than me, who wore her hair pulled tightly behind her ears and loosely around her shoulders. Vogeltje didn't have a family in the camp and she didn't talk much, but she could be caught smiling and singing to herself or to the littlest children. That's how she got her name, for singing all the time.

"She's so graceful," I said, thinking back on how she seemed to glide across the barracks' uneven floors.

"I find her rather plain," Mutti said.

Vogeltje was nondescript. She could be like any of us, any age, with any features. To be honest, I probably would never have noticed her before coming to Bergen-Belsen. She would have blended away if not for the smiling, laughing, and singing. For that, she was rare. I didn't think Vogeltje was crazy, but even if she were, I didn't want to be normal if normal was being unhappy, or even mean, all the time. There seemed to be enough of that here.

"Anyhow, kids," said Pappi, clearing his voice, "I'm just thankful I don't have to buy your mother's love with cigarettes."

"No. You just need to get us out of here," Mutti said.

Weeks went by with a sameness that was life-sucking. My parents worked without breaks and without food, or heat, or time to visit with each other. When they returned late in the day, they were more and more exhausted, often resting in bed until dinner. They ate their soup with trembling hands, a sign of starvation, Werner said. Within the month, they became thinner and my hands began to tremble too.

I was assigned to the role of cleaning the barracks and our clothes, which meant that Mrs. Mandel and I crossed paths too often. Over two hundred people slept in our barracks. All I had to clean with was a bucket, a rag, and a short broom that constantly lost strands of straw. No mop, no soap. I pushed around the dirt, dust, and mud, trying to make sure nothing littered the rutted and stained floor. I bristled whenever Mrs. Mandel was within view, because she always found something wrong.

"You are a spoiled girl," she took to saying. "You call this clean?" She jabbed a speck of dirt with her shoe toe, grinding it to dust.

I swept her mess onto a piece of torn cardboard stamped "Red Cross." Standing up, I came face-to-face with her leaning over me, a rigid piece of straw sticking straight up from her cracked fingers.

"And this!" she said from behind the strand. "Cleaning up doesn't mean leaving pieces of your broom behind! You are a spoiled, spoiled girl. You and your family."

She let the straw tumble to the ground. I trembled. A single dark eyebrow hair over her left eye pointed up to the lines that crossed her forehead. As I bent over to pick up the straw, I thought she would kick me and grind me to dust. Instead, she stomped off.

Pappi, Mutti, Werner, and I each had two sets of clothing. Weekly, I washed whichever wasn't being worn. I had to be very careful not to wash too hard and wear through the material. Pappi had a pair of blue pants and a pair of gray pants. Mutti had a grey wool skirt and a crimson dress. Werner had brown trousers, and blue shorts that fell below his knees needing long socks in the cold. I had two dresses: a brown one and a red one. I was glad I hadn't brought my white or yellow ones. At least dark colors didn't show the dirt. Because we had had these clothes since leaving Amsterdam, all the colors had fallen away.

The washroom was at the end of the barracks; its concrete floor—with a hole for drainage—was permanently wet. Over the hole were wood slats that looked like the deck of a boat and apparently were a constant source of temptation to those who wanted to throw them into the stove for an hour of warmth. Taps spewed only frigid tan water into long concrete basins. I tried my best to get out the dirt and grime, but I could only do so much, especially with no soap or hot water. I kept pulling my hands from the water, trying to warm them in my sleeves, pockets, and against my skirt. They would turn bluish and were slow to move.

I'm so sick of wearing the same things, I said to myself, intertwining my fingers and stretching them until the joints cracked. *I hereby promise that when we finally get out of the camps, I will never wear dark, dull colors again.*

One day as I was cleaning, Werner returned early from his work. He used a stubby knife to cut the stitching and pry apart shoes and separate the parts into different piles.

"Reni," he said, "You have never seen so many shoes in one place. The pile of shoes, it must be four or five meters tall, and that doesn't include the smaller piles. They look like a small mountain range."

"Where're they from?" I asked.

"All over. The military mostly. Others from prisoners, I guess."

Where had those shoes been worn? What battles fought? What parties danced? What cafés had they sat in before ending up here? What countries did they walk?

"Do they smell?"

"Yeah, like leather."

"Not like feet?"

"Well, not like *your* feet, at least. Compared to you, they smell like flowers," he said. "Mostly, they're clean. Some have dirt and somebody else's had dried dog poop…"

"Eww, poop?"

"Yeah, you just scrape it off. But you know what I really hate? I hate that I'm a shoe slave. I have to help the Nazis get better shoes while mine are getting worse."

"Can't you sneak ones?"

"Are you kidding? The *Kapo* knows my crummy shoes. He knows they're too small, because he makes fun of me. He would beat me if he saw me in anything else."

I looked at Werner's socks bulging from the open toes of his shoes. He had recently cut them to make room for his growing feet. Pappi said he was amazed that Werner could keep growing with so little food. "You are strong," he'd said to Werner. "Both of you," he'd added after looking at me.

"Don't believe that old saying," said Werner, rubbing his toes now. "It isn't the cobbler's kids who have the worst shoes."

One of my other jobs was caring for smaller children while their parents were working. I had always thought little kids were fun, but also thought they could be a bother: all the excitement and running around and getting into stuff. Here, they were different. There wasn't any excitement or running around, and there wasn't anything to get into. They were like small ghosts, shadows of the playful energy they must have been before the war. All they seemed to think about—well, all *any* of us could think about—was food.

One boy, Joseph, would wait too long to go to the bathroom, panic, then pee himself. His pants were almost always damp.

"Joseph, did you pee?" I said as he approached in tears.

He nodded, looking down.

"It's okay," I said. "It's okay. Here we go. Just stop crying and we will take care of it. Come here."

He came over and settled next to me. I didn't care about the pee anymore. He leaned into me. The pee got cold. Then I heard the heavier steps of an adult. *Oh no*, I thought.

"What's that on the floor?" demanded Mrs. Mandel. "Is that urine?"

"The…the boy is sick and he…"

"What are you doing!" her voice came out like a storm wave. "Was I not clear? There are to be no accidents on the floor, and God forbid if there are, you are to clean them up immediately! Why are you coddling him? Clean it up immediately!"

Her instructions were clear, but I was too shocked to move. Joseph buried himself deeper into my side. Everything was quiet except a ringing in my ears.

"Immediately means now, *du kleine dreck!*"

I dumped Joseph in my haste. He started crying while I ran to get the bucket and rag.

Mrs. Mandel yelled at me the whole time I scrubbed. The rag caught on a jag in the floorboard and ripped. Mrs. Mandel repeated that I was spoiled.

"We aren't spoiled," I said under my breath.

"What did you say?"

"Nothing."

"Look at me. *Look at me!* Oh, I know your family. You are all together, and you are all spoiled. *Clean up!*" The last words sprayed from her mouth. Her hands clenched and unclenched.

Even after my shaking died off, I was jumpy the rest of the day, and only settled after Mutti got back. I told her about my day with Mrs. Mandel.

"Keep clear of that woman," Mutti said.

"Are we spoiled?" I asked.

"What?" Mutti snorted.

"Are we?"

"Oh Reni, honestly, you…we are not spoiled," she said, meeting my gaze. "Well, maybe we spoiled you and Werner a bit before all this. But here and now…really? Yes, some have it tougher than others, but none of us is spoiled."

"Okay."

"Did Mrs. Mandel say that to you?"

"Yes," I whispered.

"Let your Pappi and me know if you have trouble again. Understand?"

But it wasn't easy. I kept my distance without trying to look like I was. I was more attentive to the children and got better at reading the signs when they needed to pee, poop, or throw up. Wising up, I kept a bucket of water and rag close by. I did a better job of not leaving anything on the floor as I swept, and Mrs. Mandel found other people to harass. But it didn't change her idea of our family.

23

Camp Bergen-Belsen, Germany

Early Spring 1944

At Bergen-Belsen, our typical daily menu started with a small piece of bread and flavorless "coffee" brewed from acorns. It finished with another small piece of bread and a small ladle of soup in the evening. A few shreds of potato, beet, or onions in the soup were a treat. Otherwise, the soup was just water and turnips. Now and then there was a little extra flavor like some pickled beets or a smear of jam. Then there were the days when there was no food, because the Nazis claimed that the kitchen workers weren't working hard enough. And sometimes all we had were just the bitter, hard turnips, my least favorite food in the world. At first, I gave my portion away to anyone who wanted it. Then, I gave my portion to my family. Finally, I ate them, remembering Mutti saying, "You really will eat anything if you are hungry enough," and finding these words to be true.

Not having enough to eat was hard, but Mrs. Mandel made it harder. She was in charge of serving meals, a task she took seriously because food was power. Mrs. Mandel showed preference by the ladle. She gave her friends more soup and dove deeper into the kettle to scoop out the vegetables that settled and swirled around the bottom. The food line nudged ahead. I held up the larger of the two brown cooking pots we had brought from home. Mrs. Mandel didn't look at me, but she knew who was in front of her. The ladle in her hand bathed just beneath the surface, pulling a watery portion from the top. It reminded me of the wash water after I had cleaned our clothes. I moved up to get some dry bread. Mrs. Mandel made small talk with the woman behind me in line, and I watched the ladle sink deep enough into the kettle to wet Mrs. Mandel's fingertips. I thought of saying something to Pappi and Mutti. It was unfair, but I decided it was better to work harder. The price our family was paying was my fault, and it was my job to turn that around.

Every night before bed the women chattered about food and complained about all sorts of people and things, especially standing at *Appell*, but I came to want the *Appells*. *Appell* time was guaranteed family time. We couldn't talk, though we weren't talking as much, anyhow. Mutti was in bed earlier. Pappi didn't say much, except to ask how I was doing and if I was healthy (I was, compared to most). Just being near each other was a gift.

New friendships, like with Hanneli Goslar, made up for not seeing as much of my family. I looked up to Hanneli since she was two years older than me. She was quiet, but she seemed to know so much. Her long face always looked calm and neutral. An important man in the German government until Hitler came to power, her father was forced to quit since he was Jewish. Like our family, Hanneli's had moved from Berlin to the same neighborhood in Amsterdam, thinking they had distanced themselves from the Reich. Before being sent to camps, her mom and the mom's newborn had died in childbirth, so it was just Hanneli, her father, and her little sister Gigi, who was four years old. Normally smiley, one day I noticed that Gigi was sleeping in Hanneli's lap; her head was wrapped in a stained bandage.

"How is she?" I asked.

Gigi had had a boil on her head that had grown as big as her fist over the past week. Yesterday, Hanneli and I had decided to take the little girl to the infirmary. It was not an easy decision since so many people who went to the infirmary seemed to die. A doctor there lanced the boil. There wasn't anything for the pain. It was terrible listening to Gigi cry and whimper.

"She's okay," said Hanneli. "I hope they got out all the infection. I keep checking and washing it. But she hates it."

Gigi didn't move; she was sleeping soundly. A couple of little ones wormed their way into my lap. I welcomed the warmth. I licked my thumb and wiped the goo from a boy's eye and some dirt from a girl's cheek. A nearby boy named Henry put a filthy thumb in his own mouth. Hanneli told him to pull it out.

"I'm hungry," Henry said.

"That's no excuse for eating dirt," I said.

"Or your hand," Hanneli added.

"Come here," I said.

He crawled over, and I wiped his thumb on my jacket. I cleaned the dirt from under the tiny nail as best I could.

"Okay, now you can suck on it, but no eating it!"

With a serious look, he nodded.

Hanneli smiled.

"Hanneli? Reni?" one girl asked. "My stomach hurts. I have to go to the potty."

"I took the last two kids," said Hanneli.

I got up, moving the two in my lap to the floor.

"What's your name?" I asked. The girl had arrived within the last few days.

"Lila," she said and repeated that she didn't feel well.

The latrines were mostly empty. I lifted Lila and sat her on the edge of the hole, balancing her with one hand so she wouldn't fall in. Lila was not so small that she would tumble all the way through, but she could get stuck. With my other hand, I held up her skirt. She shivered, and I heard the splash of diarrhea. After a short time, I asked if she thought she was done.

"Think so," she said.

I helped her down, carefully pulling up her underwear so as not to get any mess on my hands. There wasn't any way to wipe her.

"I feel like throwing up," Lila said.

I turned her around and she rested her hands where she had just been sitting. I held back her matted hair, and her sickness fell into the blackness. Her belly groaned. When she was finished, I carried Lila back to the barracks. I fumbled with the door latch with my one free hand, and I almost walked into Mrs. Mandel who was coming out. She glared at me holding the child.

"I assume you made it to the latrine this time," she said.

I stopped my tongue.

"There is sweeping that needs to be done in a corner near your bunk. You missed it," she added and pushed past us.

I got so mad that I wanted to scream. All day, I was taking care of sick kids, and trying to make neat a floor that refused to be clean. My voice itched to follow my heart, to tell her she was unfair, that she was doing the same as the Nazis—deciding who was "in" and who was "out," and showing kindness to friends only. But she was bigger than me, just like the Nazis were bigger than all of us. She was in charge. She controlled the barracks. She controlled the food. So I willed my mouth shut. I didn't want to make it any worse for my family.

"She's so mean!" I blurted after sweeping.

"She's Jewish, too," Hanneli said.

"I know. So what?"

"It's not easy for her," Hanneli said.

"Whose side are you on?"

Hanneli ignored my question.

"She fled to Holland. And she was sent to Westerbork. And she is here. Like us."

"And yet, she is not acting like she's one of us at all," I challenged.

"True," Hanneli said with a nod, "but she doesn't have any family here, like we do. She's alone."

"Where's her family? Did she used to have one?" I wasn't sure I wanted the answer.

"She has two daughters. One was sent abroad and escaped. Rumor has it the other is in hiding."

"Good for her. For them," I said, not really feeling good for Mrs. Mandel, though I did feel a little good for the girls.

"Her husband died here. So did her brother."

I didn't know what to say. Then I did. "That's not an excuse."

"No, it's not an excuse," Hanneli said. "I just mean that the biggest difference between her and you is that you have your family here. You are together, and you are all alive."

I thought of Hanneli. She had lost her mother and her baby sister. So many others had lost loved ones. I had lost my grandparents and Rudi and probably my aunt and my uncle. I couldn't imagine not having my parents and Werner. Mrs. Mandel had control, but she didn't have family.

"But she calls us spoiled," I sputtered.

"She's jealous."

Now I was really at a loss for words. I went back to picking small things off the kids' clothes and putting them in my pocket to throw outdoors later. All my brave, clever responses, all the things I wanted to yell at Mrs. Mandel, dimmed.

24

Camp Bergen-Belsen, Germany

Spring 1944

I felt unruffled for about a week before Mrs. Mandel started wearing on my nerves again, but then it didn't make a difference. With the arrival of more prisoners, the barracks were reshuffled. I was so happy to leave our old barracks and leave Mrs. Mandel, but I was even more surprised when Mutti and I walked into our new home.

"Trudi! Reni!" It was Pappi's voice.

"You came to help settle us?" Mutti asked, almost tripping over the small lip of the doorway.

"No! We are living here, too. We'll be together!" Werner blurted.

We all hugged as if we had not seen one another in years. Our family was given two neighboring bunks, one for Mutti and me, and the other for Werner and Pappi. Nobody was happy about sharing bunks, but it would be warmer, and I could keep an eye on Mutti, who seemed weaker every day.

With the new barracks came new children to look after in addition to familiar faces. Gigi and Lila got better, but sickness rolled from one child to another. There was diarrhea from cholera and dysentery, fever and pain from typhus, coughing from tuberculosis, and paralysis from polio.

The one infection that had gotten worse since Westerbork was lice. Not just lice on our heads, but all over our bodies. We hated them. The sesame-sized bugs crawled through our shirts and underwear, along our scalps, and between the creases of our bodies. Our skin was their city, our blood their food, and our clothing their maternities. We were covered in little red bumps and rashes that turned our skin dark and thick over time. We were told not to scratch, because it spreads infection, but I couldn't help myself. Mutti and I bumped each other awake with our scratching, tearing away scabs that took weeks to heal, only to be replaced by more. The red bites never went away—they only seemed to move around. The children who inched into my lap couldn't settle down and nap. I would gently rake my fingers across their scalps to offer some relief, careful not to draw blood that might cause infections like what Gigi had. Thorough delousing was impossible. We were overrun.

The days began to stretch, lightening the horizon and softening the soil. Only a few snow mounds remained where the sun couldn't reach. Theft crept into Bergen-Belsen and flourished, feasting on the lack of everything. Food and clothing, even the smallest scrap and swatch, disappeared. Starvation made us sick and slow, but for some stoked a desire to survive so strong that they stole others' means of surviving. It was every soul for its own. Jewish camp leaders had to deal with more arguments and accusations. Their goal was to make sure matters didn't get out of hand. Their one task was to avoid the attention of the Nazis. As best as possible, *don't draw attention.*

It was evening, after work and after dinner. Mutti was lying down. Pappi was in the washroom. My stomach rumbled. All I could have was more water, so I took some, but not enough so I would have to get up in the night. Werner's face had grown leaner, his eyes older, but his hair was still perfectly coifed.

"We're all like those thieves," Werner said. It was one of Werner's "observations" as Pappi called them.

"Why?" I took the bait.

"A thief's goal is not to be noticed. Not draw attention. We do the same. We lay low around the Germans. Then we lay low around the *Kapos.* Now we try to hide from each other. We try to hide from the thieves, and the thieves try to hide what they do. All hiding."

"And?" I asked.

"That's it. We're all the same."

"No we aren't. We hide to protect what little we have. Thieves hide to take what little others have." That came out better than I thought it would.

Werner looked surprised. "It's the same: survival."

"Well, maybe all survival isn't the same."

The edge of the cool metal cup rested on my bottom lip as I took a quivering sip.

He looked out from under his bangs.

"Maybe you're right, Reni," Werner pondered. "Maybe survival isn't worth it at all costs. Maybe it matters how you survive."

After washing the clothes the next day and hanging them on the outdoor wire lines, I sat down in the dirt next to Hanneli and some other girls, leaning against the barracks. I turned up to face the sun, looking at the pulsing red life behind my closed eyelids. I was careful not to lean back too much or my hair would snag in the rough grain of the wood. I didn't dare close my eyes for more than a few seconds. In particular, we kept a lookout out for two boys who lurked around corners of buildings, dashed out to grab what they could, and ran off before anyone could catch them.

I thought I knew one of them, a boy only eleven or so, whose mother wore a dress washed to rags. I turned away when I saw her, embarrassed by the glimpses of her body, parts that were red and chapped from the sun, lice, and exposure. Could I blame her for sending out her son to steal, or her son's willingness? Still, I couldn't let them take our clothes, so I stayed alert. And I daydreamed of eating, of riding my bicycle along the canals of Amsterdam, of listening to my parents' laughter float down the hall from our dining room, but mostly of lying in my old bed with my belly full of dinner.

"Over there," Hanneli said.

A few of us stood up, taking a few steps toward the clotheslines like dogs moving to the edge of the yard as a stranger approached. The boy pretended to kick something and then waved. We didn't wave back.

"I heard that girl Henny De-something is having an affair with a Nazi officer," said an older, red-haired girl who was with us.

I wasn't sure exactly what an "affair" meant, only that it was some kind of secret since the word was always uttered in a hushed voice.

Riga, Latvia (Sept 6, 1918): Irene's father John Hasenberg (right) with friend and fellow World War I German officer Leo Buschhoff. While they were all in Westerbork during World War II, Leo got Irene's family off the list to Auschwitz concentration camp.

Berlin, Germany (December 15, 1927): Gertrude and John Hasenberg's wedding day.

Irene's Mutti, Gertrude Hasenberg

Irene's Pappi, John Hasenberg

Berlin, Germany (1934): Irene and brother Werner

Berlin, Germany (1928): Irene's brother Werner with their grandfather, Julius Mayer, or Opa, as he was called by the grandchildren.

Berlin, Germany (1935): Irene and Pappi

Berlin, Germany (1931): Irene with her maternal grandmother, Pauline Mayer, or Omi, as she was affectionately called.

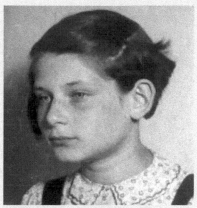

Amsterdam, the Netherlands (1943): Irene's identity card photo. German identity card photos required that the left ear be visible as an added identity detail.

Amsterdam, the Netherlands (1940): Irene's Poesie book entry from Pappi: "You sweet little one, you belong to me, you belong to me, you are the most lovable."

Amsterdam, the Netherlands (1943): Irene, Mutti, and Werner before being rounded up by the police and deported to Camp Westerbork.

The Netherlands (1943): Student artwork of the train from Amsterdam to Camp Westerbork.

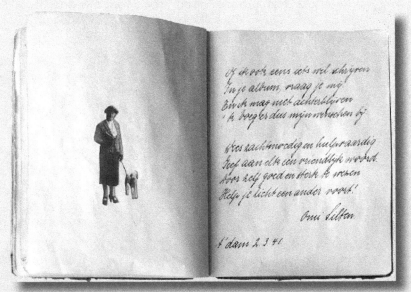

Amsterdam, the Netherlands (1941): Omi Silten's entry in Irene's Poesie book, talking about the importance of being helpful and strong, because that would help lighten the load of others. Those words became more important the longer Irene was in the camps.

Camp Bergen-Belsen (1944-45): Student artwork and poem, "What is hope? Hope is the lone flower fluttering in the breeze above the hell and hot water, between hate and love, heaven and hell. Would you pick me, or wait until I bloom?"

Biberach, Germany (January, 1945): Student artwork of the train station and Pappi.

Camp Jeanne d'Arc (Algeria, 1945): Irene gains enough weight that she feels she needs to go on a diet.

The Netherlands (1946): Lex Roseboom, Irene's boyfriend in Algeria.

Camp Jeanne d'Arc (Algeria, 1945): Vitek, the traumatized Polish boy.

Camp Jeanne d'Arc (Algeria, 1945): Irene (front row, far right) with friend Mieke, to her right.

New York, NY (1949): Irene
graduates from Walton
High School.

New York, NY (1946): Irene's
brother, Werner

Amsterdam, the Netherlands
(1957): Irene as a newlywed
with her husband,
Charlie Butter.

New York, NY (circa 1950s):
Irene's Mutti

Ann Arbor, MI (1990): Irene with Wallenberg Medal recipient Elie Wiesel, Nobel Laureate, author, and Holocaust survivor.

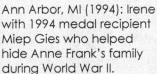

Bergen-Belsen, Germany (1991): Irene and her brother, Werner

Ann Arbor, MI (1994): Irene with 1994 medal recipient Miep Gies who helped hide Anne Frank's family during World War II.

Ann Arbor, MI (1994): Irene with the Dalai Lama, the 1994 Wallenberg Medal recipient.

Ann Arbor, MI (2013): Irene's opening remarks at Wallenberg Centennial Celebration.

Laupheim, Germany (2014): Irene at her Pappi's grave.

Irene's husband, Charlie Butter

Irene's daughter, Ella Butter

Irene's son, Noah Butter

German seashore (circa 1920): Pappi

"What do they do?" I asked. "There's nothing to do here."

"I bet they eat together in his barracks," said a new girl with big ears. "Meats and breads and lots of desserts."

"Really?" said the redhead with a weary look. "Are you serious? We're talking about sex. Oh, I bet she gets food, but do you think she gets her food for free?"

I blushed. The boys disappeared around a building, and we sat back down.

"I bet she doesn't have a choice," Hanneli said.

"Sex? She has to touch him?" asked the acne girl with a surprised face. "Like hold his hand and kiss him?"

The rest of us turned our heads toward the red-haired girl, the obvious expert.

"Don't you know what sex is?"

Big-eared girl's nod was as slight as a breeze. I had some ideas about sex. The details were fuzzy, and I wasn't brave enough to open my mouth, and not around the red-haired girl.

Hanneli jumped in. "Sex can be kissing. It can be a lot more of other touching. The male guards in particular like other kinds of touching. They will pay for it with favors."

Kissing sounded…possible, with the right person. Never with a Nazi. And I would never want them to touch me in any other way, no matter what that "other" was. But what if I had to?

"Aren't the guards ever nice just to be nice?" the acne girl asked.

"Never," shot back the red-haired girl.

"Sometimes," I found myself saying, and added, "There was that *Kapo* who was nice to the nurse."

"Yes," said Hanneli, "he got her supplies she needed to help others, but I heard he was punished for it. For being nice."

"And what about the German officer who took the cook to the hospital? You know, the cook who cut her finger?" the acne girl asked. "I heard he helped her because she looked like his sister."

"Hmmph," snorted the red-haired girl, "Nobody is really nice here. The Nazis are the worst, but we do the same. Look at the boys trying to steal our clothes. The women giving their bodies to guards for a piece of bread…."

"Forced to," added Hanneli.

"Whatever. Any of us would give up anything, even being good, in order to live."

I thought back to my talk with Werner. I knew what she was saying, but I just couldn't believe it was like that for everybody, but maybe the good people don't make the best survivors. Was it a choice? I prayed it wasn't. I wanted to be both: good and a survivor.

As much as I appreciated sharing space in the barracks with Werner and Pappi, being back as a family wasn't all I had expected. Werner was surly that I didn't have to work at a "real" job as he put it.

One morning, at the end of *Appell*, I had crawled back into my bed. Something shook me: I blinked to see my brother beside my bed.

"Oh, sorry, I didn't mean to bump you," he said, "princess."

My eyes fluttered, and I dozed, only to wake up again, curled in a ball with my hands tucked under my chin. My blanket was on the floor.

"Sorry. I must have knocked off your pretty pink blanket."

I reached down, pulling my cover over me again. Werner glanced at me as he got ready for work, but my eyes stayed open so he left me alone. He had succeeded in waking me. Werner was right, I had wanted to retreat to bed, but not because I was tired. Watching my family leave every morning without me was painful. I worried that something would happen to them. Every morning good-bye was possibly the last.

"Have fun sleeping," Werner said as he left.

After a half hour, I got up. I needed to be ready for the younger children.

"Werner is being a jerk," I said to Hanneli when I first saw her.

"Still?" she asked. "You're smart. Can't you come up with a way to get back at him?"

"I used to tease him about his nightmares when we were younger. Before going to bed, he'd ask me if I thought he would have them that night. I would say yes, and he would. That doesn't work here."

"No. Not here. There are too many real nightmares," Hanneli said.

I looked up at some of the little ones who were huddled under my blanket. They didn't cry or say anything unless they had to go to the bathroom. I kept a close eye so they wouldn't get sick in my bed.

"Back home, I could put something itchy, like sand, in his bed, but now we have lice. I could wake him early, but the guards do that. I could put something funny in his food, but we all have upset stomachs."

"The Nazis really kill fun, don't they?" Hanneli agreed. "They take things way too far."

25

Camp Bergen-Belsen

Late Spring 1944

At first, hunger was a pesky neighbor, sometimes noisy at night, interrupting sleep. Then it was a nagging visitor who came rapping on the door more and more. Finally, it had the keys. Hunger marched in and settled down. As the spring months dragged on and the cold raced across the camp, through every crevasse, under every blanket, hunger went from a distant stranger to an annoying acquaintance to a constant companion. There was no place to escape, no room to retire to. It became an ever-present, day-after-day rumbling.

As mothers, fathers, and relatives started returning from work in the late afternoons, I left my job watching kids to get our daily rations. I waited in the long line with other kids and some adults. With food becoming increasingly scarce, adults started pushing the kids out of the way to get ahead. I watched carefully. We were free of Mrs. Mandel, but it always paid to be attentive when it came to food. If needed, I asked servers for more vegetables. And I measured the hunk of bread. Again, I protested, but only if needed. I wasn't loud, but I was quick. Then I returned to our bunks and waited.

I sat on my bunk, arms around our pail, pulling what warmth I could and inhaling the smell. Hunger sat beside me, whispering in my ear to eat it all. It would be easy. There wasn't much, and for the first time in almost a year, I would be able to go to sleep with a full stomach. I slid my finger around the inside edge of the pail, feeling the moisture build to drops. When nobody was looking I put a shaking finger to my tongue. My senses bounced between the all-absorbing taste and listening for my family's approaching footfalls: Mutti's delicate gait and Pappi's longer shuffle. The barracks darkened with the evening. The food cooled. Every few minutes I collected drops of soup telling myself it would have evaporated anyhow.

I couldn't wait any more. With careful measure, I took my portion of food and devoured it. Instead of feeling better I found myself ravenous. I dipped my spoon with my shaking hand into the pail a few more times and picked off and ate the uneven bread ends. As the food hit my lips, my body wanted to slurp down every last drop and chew down every crumb. Maybe this is how vampires feel about blood, I thought. I kept thinking I heard my family, only to realize I was wrong. Then there was no mistake. I was terrified that they would say something about the portions or read my guilt. But also relieved that I was free of further temptation.

They said nothing. Pappi sat, took off his worn out shoes, lay down, and closed his eyes. I looked over at Mutti who stayed upright, but leaned her head against the frame of the bunk.

"Okay, Reni. Do you have something hearty for us?" Pappi asked after a few minutes. In the past he might have added that he "was starving."

"Of course, " I said, and took the brown pot out from under my blanket.

"Have you seen Werner?" Mutti asked.

I shook my head. She took a deep breath, looking around. Pappi moved to her side, resting his hand on her bony leg. They both looked at me and nodded. They refused to eat until I did.

"I already had mine," I said.

"Do you need more?" Pappi asked.

"No, I'm fine."

"Take more, Reni," Mutti said, "I'm not hungry."

"I'm fine. My belly doesn't feel well today, " I lied, and then, seeing their concern, added, "but it's not bad. My belly, I mean."

And so they passed the brown pot and the bread, saving more than Werner's share for him.

"Has anybody heard or talked about an exchange?" I asked, eager to think about something else.

"Nothing," Pappi said, starting to gather the dishes.

"No, Pappi," I said, "leave them. I'll clean them in the morning."

Mutti took off her shoes, removed her cap, and laid her short, matted hair on the pillow. She moved to one side and patted the space next to her. I settled in, feeling terrible. Before surrendering to sleep, I gazed up at the swirling shapes made by the woodgrain of the bed slats above me. The knots stared at me as my eyes fluttered and closed.

I was standing on a mountain of Dutch yellow coins in a world of gold that was all mine. The glint was blinding. I blinked and squinted, turned and twisted to make sure no threats approached. This was *my* gold. I slipped and slid down, falling faster and faster. Stopping was impossible. I grabbed at the coins, but the handfuls just passed between my fingers. I woke to something being pulled from my hands. I clenched them tightly and called out: "No!"

"Reni, it's okay. It's just me," Werner whispered.

He had his hand on mine. I sat up. It was darker; my eyes adjusted. Mutti and Pappi were asleep. I looked at Werner and saw that his left hand was bandaged.

"What happened?" I asked. "Where have you been?"

"I cut myself, and I'm late because of collective punishment. A guy, Bernie, was really sick and spent too long at the toilet. The guards beat him in there, on the toilet. And then they came and beat us, and made us work two hours longer," he said, and caught his breath. "One of the guards kicked me, and my knife slipped. I cut my hand."

"Badly?" I asked.

"Not really," Werner said. "They forced us to look at Bernie, his body. He was a good guy, Reni. He didn't do anything wrong, except be sick. God, we are all guilty of that here."

Werner stopped for a moment. I thought he was done talking. I handed him the soup pot and its remains. He took it, but rather than slurping it down, he took a sip and frowned.

"I heard a story today," he continued. "Everybody was talking about it. It happened at an *Appell* in another section of camp. This one guy was about to be beaten when he told the guard 'Kill me if you must, but don't lay your hands on me. Don't beat me. Don't hit me.'"

I wasn't sure I wanted to hear the story, but Werner needed to tell it.

"The guard let him go. He just let the guy go. Talk about courage. No compassion for a sick guy, but they let another one go for standing up for himself when they normally would have beat him. None of it makes sense."

We kept trying to make sense of everything, as if an understanding would make the things better. There didn't seem to be any understanding and certainly no promises, so I clung to the simple notion that good people were capable of surviving.

"You are lucky, Reni. You don't have to leave camp and go to work. And see things like that."

He slowly ate his cold dinner. Then he turned away and curled into himself next to Pappi. He didn't understand what it felt like to be left, not knowing if they would come back. Every day waiting to see if I still had a family. I promised to stop sneaking food, but I had learned that such a promise after a meal is worthless. I needed to keep it while staring into the soup steam.

26

Camp Bergen-Belsen, Germany

Summer/Fall 1944

I t was teetering on summer. Little by little, day stole from the night. Longer and warmer days made for easier travel, so the number of arrivals began to increase. They came from other camps and from countries like Italy, Spain, and of course, the Netherlands. All this movement was promising, some adults said while in the food line. It was a sign that we would soon be exchanged.

Wasn't that the reason we were in Bergen-Belsen in the first place? Yes, and we were in the special Star Camp section. Even if we were not traded, others said, the war would end soon. Germany would lose. If we just hung on a little longer, something would improve.

Except that rumors and opinions cut both ways. Others chimed in saying that hope was crazy. The Nazis could not be trusted, no matter what they said. One way or the other, they would do whatever they could to make things more difficult.

"What do you think?" I asked Werner one morning when our parents had gone to the latrines. "Will we really get out of here? Pappi and Mutti haven't said much."

I pulled myself up until I sat cross-legged against a corner of the bunk, folding my pink blanket and putting it at the end of the bedding. I leaned forward and tilled my soiled hair with rough fingers, pushing wayward strands behind my ears. Meanwhile, Werner's hair performed its magic. In the time it took to lower from the upper bunk his hair had just fallen into place, a part as straight as an open book.

"They're careful, Reni."

"But this could be it. We could get out."

"Could be," he said. "Or it could be something different. Remember, nobody has actually ever left here alive. They just keep arriving."

I pressed Pappi about it later that day after he returned from work. I waited until Mutti had walked off to get some water. He balanced on the edge of the bunk for a second, before deciding to sit back on the mattress, the bedside board jutting up his knees a bit. This never looked comfortable, and it could put your legs to sleep if you stayed like that too long. Instead of giving me a straight answer, he asked if I had heard the saying that truth was born from consistent rumors. My head glided back and forth. That meant, he said, that the more you heard something, especially from different sources and over time, the better the chances it was true. If there was only one source, it was usually wrong. He told me to ignore talk that flits about like a field of grasshoppers.

"Like the fact we are exchange Jews?" I asked. "And we are privileged...I mean compared to others?"

"Well, yes, the exchange piece has been consistent, yes?" Pappi quizzed me.

"Yes," I said.

"But when we are to be exchanged and with whom...that keeps jumping about. So what does that mean?"

"That there will probably be an exchange, but we don't know the details."

"Right."

Pappi's proverb ruled out most of what was rumored, so I tried to ignore those whispers. Then one took hold. With each repetition, its roots crept deeper, and it flowered. A small group of mostly Dutch Jews from Bergen-Belsen would be sent to Palestine, to be traded for German missionaries living in the city of Jerusalem. We didn't know any of the people involved, yet it was a story worth following. Somebody getting out of here meant that any of us could get out of here.

Several times the chosen group of about two hundred prisoners were ordered to be ready for departure the next day—the news flew through the camp—only to find out that the deal had been cancelled. I began to learn that frustration was, well, frustrating, but it was also a gift, a morsel of hope. Frustration required energy that the people who had truly given up didn't possess. It meant they still cared. And so did I.

The days continued pulling and stretching. More prisoners rolled in by truck and train. Nobody left. Soon there wasn't a single word about the Palestinian trade, much less our own exchange. Our Ecuadorian passports, supposedly our lifesavers, seemed worthless.

"They leave tomorrow. I just heard," Pappi said before even greeting us, as he arrived back to the barracks from work one evening. He had a slight smile and sat down next to Mutti and me on the bed. "Trudi, are you awake?"

"I'm awake, Pappi," I said, got up, slid onto Pappi and Werner's bed to shake Werner who I knew wasn't asleep.

"Reni, stop!" Werner said. "Pappi, do you mean the people going to Palestine?"

"Really? They are being allowed to go?" asked Mutti, turning her head toward him and sitting up on one elbow. "How? When?"

Pappi repeated the news. *At this moment*, I thought eagerly, *two hundred prisoners are gathering their belongings.*

"Pappi, do you believe what you heard?" I tested him. "Is it consistent?"

He nodded yes. He had heard it from different people.

When I thought of the Holy Lands, all I could think of were school history books of a land cleaned bright by the sunlight bathing everything in gold, and bushels of olives, bread, and meats. All the food you could want. Paradise: warmth, food, cleanliness. It felt like something hanging almost within our grasp.

"Still, it is always possible that this is a German trick, but I don't think so since the Germans are talking it up," Pappi said. "Even the Nazis need to look like they have a heart from time to time."

Mutti raised her eyebrows.

We all smiled a little. This was the first sign that an exchange was not just a false promise. But how long would it take for the next "exchange" to be organized, and I thought in wordless fear: *would we live long enough to be part of it?*

More and more, the flat, distant hum of planes washed over Bergen-Belsen. Pappi explained that the Allies—the good guys fighting against Hitler—were up there. The skies seemed to support it. High between the clouds, flocks of bomber planes migrated east to bomb German cities and then west, back home, to rest and clean wounds. We stood for the *Appell* one late morning, herded for another forgettable reason.

"Maybe," Werner said, "shouting for us to line up and keep quiet makes the Nazis feel like they're in control, especially since they don't seem to be in control of the skies."

The hours rolled by, but at least it wasn't cold or raining. A few of us tilted our heads at the sound of a single plane passing overhead. I squinted into the blue. What did those men see as they looked down? Did they know we were a camp of prisoners, or did we just look like another farm, factory, or town? If they bothered to give a glance did they see people, or just buildings and roads? If they saw us, did they wonder why hundreds of people would bother standing around in the shape of a square? My heart beat faster. An air attack earlier in the spring had sent bombs and bullets into a section of the camp, killing some prisoners. That low-flying plane had come and gone before the guards had been able to react. It was scary to me that the good guys might bomb us again. Maybe they thought only about killing the Nazis and not about saving us.

"Pappi," I said quietly, "tell me again why we don't have to worry about the planes up there."

"Because the Germans didn't react when they bombed us earlier," explained Pappi, "The Germans didn't fire back, which means the camp isn't a threat. The Allies poked the camp with a stick, and we didn't bite, so they won't do it again."

I needed to hear that. His words put me more at ease, at least during the day. Sometimes the air-raid alarms, or *Fliegeralarm*, went off several times a day, their wavy drones like the heavy breathing of sleeping giants, breaking conversations in mid-sentence and work in mid-chore. At those times, we were ordered to our barracks, as if thin roofs, walls, and blankets offered protection. At nights, the buildings were blacked out. Even the lighting of a match was strictly forbidden, lest a single flame catch a pilot's eye.

"Werner, what do we do if the Allies bomb us by mistake?" I figured he'd have a good answer, since he thought and worried about it so much.

"I don't know. Nothing, I guess. What can we do? We can't tell where a bomb is going to fall. We might try to escape, only to run into one."

I hadn't thought about that. "Aren't you worried?" I asked, surprised by his calm.

"Not about that. What can we do? Besides, the Allies have so many planes up there, it must mean they are winning."

In the inky darkness, late in the night, I listened. When we'd first arrived here five months earlier, I felt that we had been devoured and were in the swollen belly of some hungry beast. Now, hearing our rustling bunk neighbors and hundreds of dozing strangers, it felt like we were in the billowing lungs. We were breath itself. We were important—if only to this monster's survival. Without us, the camp would have no purpose. It would wither and die. With us "exchange Jews," the Germans could hope to get back some "real" Germans to help win the war. In our own sick way, we really were needed. Somehow, that made me feel better.

Summer grew weary. Daylight burned to embers earlier and earlier. The night circled closer, like a pack of wolves. October began. Coolness and rain followed. Between the streaked gray weather, we stole glances at the ceaseless bombers. Smoke rose to the south—Pappi said it was likely from the city of Hanover. Some German newspapers made their way into the camp. They were read and destroyed, their stories shared by mouth since outside news was *verboten*, forbidden. News reports said that German soldiers were dying heroically in battle. There was no mention of victories, only courage. Pappi said that was another sign the Germans were losing.

It was also telling that our guards started changing, with the young men replaced by older men and young women. The new guards may not have been as young or as big as before, but they were more nervous and unpredictable. The war was not going their way, so they took out their frustrations on us. We stood longer. They yelled and threatened more.

One morning at *Appell*, after standing over two hours, a small, older lady in front of me sat down in the mud and hugged herself to her knees, rubbing one leg and shivering.

"Get up," Pappi whispered to her, adding what we all already knew. "You aren't allowed to sit."

"Tired," was her reply. "Legs are cramped."

I couldn't see her face, only that her head bobbed a little. Pappi repeated his words.

Get up, I thought, *get up*. The orderly row ahead of me was now broken as if a tooth had been knocked out. I glanced left and right and saw the closest guard look over, like a spider that senses the first vibration of a fly caught on a sticky strand.

Get up, oh please, I thought. The woman tried to rise only when she heard the guard's voice.

"*Was ist das hier in einer Judenschule?*" What is going on here in the "Jewish school?" Anything the Germans didn't like could be blamed on a Jewish education.

The old woman planted her right arm in the mud and pushed her body up, her wrinkled and gnarled hand sinking into the muck reminding me of tree roots along a riverbank. She fell back. Pappi leaned forward a bit as if to help, then straightened as the guard emerged from our right. I glanced at the guard's face expecting anger, but his droopy, puffy eyes and full bottom lip that turned up at the corners made him appear disinterested. I knew better: don't judge a bully by his expression.

"*Aufstehen, dreck,*" he said, in a voice as bland as an adult ordering coffee. Get up, filth.

As the old woman moved, the puffy guard wheeled around as briskly as a paw's strike. I was confused at first. I thought that the old woman had slipped, like an ice skater's awkward breakneck sprawl. Then I saw the whip dangling from the guard's tight, white fist. As the woman sat spread-legged, blood ran from under her gray hair, down the back of her neck, and disappeared into her coat. Her hair darkened and thickened. With the second whipping, she cried out to stop. Her arms raised, the sleeves falling, revealing skeletal, blotched, and scabbed arms.

The guard's eyes looked bored, though he flushed a deeper pink as he hit and hit, his trunk of an arm pumping in blunt strokes up and down, up and down. The whip ends wrapped over the old woman's shoulders, and curled around her neck. Falling to her side, I saw thin red trails over her cheek and chin. I snapped my eyes shut. I now knew the difference between the sound of leather hitting wool and ripping skin. She hissed and screamed like a cornered cat, spitting and weeping. Then silence, except for what I took for a mad dog's panting. My heart banged to escape. I opened my eyes to blurry slits, just enough to see the black pile. The old woman was buried under her coat and skirt, but for one root-like hand still looking to pry apart the earth. I saw mud-splattered boots turn from view, and then I heard steps marching off.

I stayed stock still, trying to slow my breath, forcing myself not to cry, and then willing the tears to dry on my face. I didn't dare even a quick move of my hand to wipe my cheeks. *Don't draw attention,* I repeated to myself, *disappear.* I was afraid to even look at my family. If they could do that to a weak, old woman, they could certainly beat us, too. My toes cramped, curled under as far as they could, as if every part of me was trying to hide into itself.

Even with my eyes closed, I couldn't escape. Like a movie newsreel, the scene of the old woman's beating kept spinning through my mind. I heard new guards taking over, teasing the other guards to rest after such an exhausting shift.

The old woman was carried off in a wheel cart, and we never saw her again.

27

Camp Bergen-Belsen, Germany

Fall 1944

f Hitler was losing, why was Bergen-Belsen still growing? The guards moved Pappi, along with other men from the Star Camp, from road and trench work to building more barracks. I asked him if he liked not having to walk so far on the first morning of their new assignment.

"Work is work, for the Nazis, Reni," he said.

"Is it easier, at least?"

"All work is hard here, don't you agree? You are right, though. I don't have as far to walk at the end of the day to see you."

Beyond him, a man I knew as Mr. Cohen proclaimed in a loud voice intended for more than his wife sitting next to him: "It's another sign they are losing."

"*Ja*," agreed a man in the next bunk, running his hands through his beard, "they are getting desperate. It is unfortunate, but the fact they are losing control of themselves in here only means they are losing control out there, too."

"Oh, good," retorted Mrs. Cohen. "The more they lose, the higher the stakes for us. What good is their loss if we are all dead?"

I looked at Pappi for confirmation.

He studied me as he buttoned his shirt. "You okay, Reni?"

"Yes," I lied.

He let the lie go this time. Who was I to complain? Hanneli and Werner were right: suffering was relative. Our family was sick, but standing. I was hungry, but I had all my teeth. I could eat. We had not been beaten. We had not been carried from the *Appell* in a cart. I reached for the hem of Pappi's sleeve.

"Your button is loose," I said, rolling up his cuff with the button safely tucked away. "I'll try to fix it later."

He put his other hand on my shoulder. "I'll be just beyond the fence, in those trees. I will look for you, and I will wave." Pappi stared into my eyes. "And be very careful. The only thing worse than a smiling guard is a scared one."

It was an old lesson worth repeating. We were like mice that had seen our companions caught by the cat. We twitched at the slightest sound and movement, and we knew the safety of shadows, whether to scurry or stay stock-still.

"I know you know, Reni," he went on, "but please, you and Werner, avoid drawing attention and do what you are told. Please, for Mutti and me."

He and the men marched off through the gates.

"Hanneli," I asked later that morning, "can you watch the little ones? I want to see if I can see Pappi working."

Hanneli glanced at the eight children lying or sitting on the barracks' wood floor, and then back at me. The children moved little, except to ask for food we didn't have. One picked at a knot on a floorboard.

"I think I can manage."

In general, Bergen-Belsen was barren, alternating between hard-packed earth and mud depending on the weather, but there had not been time to clear the trees in the newest section with the newest barracks. Instead of being built in tidy rows like the rest of the camp, the new section had roads that curved through trees and barracks at odd angles to each other. It looked haphazard.

I walked to the barbed-wire fence. A guard tower stood to my left, jutting three stories into the sky. It was made up of four solid wood walls, widening at the top with a slight peaked roof to protect the men inside. One guard was looking toward the new construction. The other must have been sitting since I only saw the rounded top of a helmet.

My eyes followed the guard's. In the distance, beyond the double fences, past the camp's center highway rarely touched by prisoners' feet, beyond the second set of fencing, I heard hammers and workmen yelling. Yelling workman all sounded the same, whether in Berlin, in Amsterdam, in Westerbork, or here. The sounds of sawing carried on the breeze, along with a whiff of smoke, which could have been coming from the crematorium.

I glanced up at the tower to make sure nobody was looking my way, then back through openings in the wires into the old trees and new structures, the fresh barracks' beams looking like bleached bones against the dense green trees. Shadows swallowed shadows. I followed figures closely, but could not discern one from the other. They all looked dark and hunched and drab even when they caught the sun, and not one waved at me. I walked back.

A week later, Hanneli said, "Those new women here look terrible."

We were watching the little ones from the barracks' stoop at midday. It was brisk, but the sun was shining. We kept one eye inside and another outside as the kids were spread out, mostly sitting and staring; a few were playing in the dirt. I had thin, little Henry in my lap. All he did was sleep now. His face was dirty, except under his nose where the snot ran. Pulling down my cuff with my fingers, I used a piece of my sleeve to wipe him clean. Then, I adjusted my weight to get more comfortable. I was beginning to feel bones that I didn't know existed—knees, ribs, and hips. My clothes didn't pad enough.

"Yes, the women are so sick," I agreed. "I heard they all have diseases."

"It seems like we're all sick," Hanneli said.

A couple of boys tossed small stones on the floor of the barracks, and I took note to remember to clean up when they were done.

"I guess there is healthy sick and sick-sick," I said.

A small girl, Sara, came up to us. Her hands were balled in her eyes; I wondered how she could see to walk. Muddy fists and cheeks were streaked and wet. I shifted Henry again, who didn't wake up, and made room in my lap. Sara leaned into me, smeared her face in my dress, and quieted. I wanted to say she stopped crying from comfort, but she probably just ran out of energy.

"You know what it means, right?" Hanneli said. "It means less food, less space, and more problems. You'll see."

The outburst was un-Hanneli-like. Gigi came over and leaned into her sister.

"Bah," Hanneli continued. "I'm hungry. Sorry. I am blaming these women when it's not their fault."

Still, there was truth in what she said. The ill newcomers came so quickly that there wasn't time to build them all new barracks, so they got huge tents. Instead of the straight, evenly spaced barbed-wire fence posts, tree trunks, stripped of their bark and branches, had been hastily thrust into the ground. Between them barbed wire was stretched and nailed, patterned in irregular rectangles. Very un-German.

A short section of the new women's camp neighbored our Star Camp. The women cooked over fires under tarps that had been rigged up over branches. Smoke hung like a fog. A few shirts and skirts were draped here and there to dry on the fence, their owners guarding them with darkened, hollow eyes. Even on the warmer days they dressed in overcoats to keep their thin frames warm. Hanneli and I watched the tent city grow. I hated the thought, but it made me more thankful. The new arrivals were in rags. Every time I thought we had it bad, I glanced over my shoulder at them. We were cold, but they were no doubt colder. We suffered—they more. I never thought such a big space could feel so crowded. I remembered my first impression of Bergen-Belsen: that we were like tiny marbles being tossed onto a vast dizzying plain. Now, ten months later, there was no space between us.

My family was shuffled to another barracks, this one with less space than the one before. The huts were noisier with more people, a growing number of sick ones, and more time spent indoors because of the cold. It was a constant chorus of coughing, sneezing, and sighs. There were so many children, but I couldn't remember the last time I'd heard a child laugh.

Keeping clean was a continuous challenge nearing the impossible. Toilet paper didn't exist, and even coarse scraps of paper and soap continued to be rare. I cleaned our clothes in cold water with no soap. I washed myself in splashes of cold water. I fought my thick, dark hair and its itchy, lice-infested scalp with frigid water. We used sticks, frayed at the ends, as toothbrushes. The smell of close bodies and mouths barely scraped clean was normal.

Watching the children with Hanneli became easier as they mostly just slept now, which was good considering our own low energy.

"I would do anything for a warm bath," I said. "To get clean and warm."

"Food first, then a good cleaning," Hanneli said, "in a large tub where I could sit for hours. Washing and washing all of, all of this, away."

"And getting fed while in the tub," I continued. "As long as we had enough bubbles to cover us."

"I wouldn't care. Just feed me."

"Really?" I asked. "No bubbles? You would let people see you?"

"Well, maybe a couple of bubbles in just the right places."

A smile escaped me.

"I want to be served pancakes and breads," I dreamed, "and butter and jams. And tea. And no turnips under any circumstances."

"Not even a turnip pancake?" Hanneli asked.

"No, not even the tiniest bit, even hidden in ice cream."

Hunger was the ache in every moment. Sleep was our lone escape. I awoke from the same dream, born of constant craving. I was the pet dog of a wealthy family. The family enjoyed huge dinners heaped on silver platters. There was lamb or beef, different types of vegetables, fruit and bread, and pies and ice cream galore. I sat patiently under the table, alert and waiting. At the end of the meal, they scraped the leftovers onto a plate and lowered it down. I wagged my tail and gulped down everything at once, slobbering everywhere.

Darkness became cover for what became known as bread thieves, whose numbers were growing. The clothing thieves you could watch out for, but the bread thieves struck at night. Back in Amsterdam and Berlin we had more than we knew, cradled in comfort and with enough food to fill the bellies of all our visiting family, or anybody who visited. We would have been so mad had a thief broken into our home and stolen our silver, but all we really would have lost was an heirloom—a family memory—and a pinch of pride. Now, the stakes were higher and for so much less.

I heard about a parent who stole from kids to feed her own children. Pappi had said that stealing from the deprived to feed the deprived was immoral. And Mutti had instructed us with an added shake of her head that we were never, ever, to steal from someone like that.

Still a silent question haunted me: Did I want Pappi, Mutti, or Werner to die in the name of doing the right thing? Mutti was getting weaker. She drifted from work to bed to work like a ghost. She seemed to be working less and sleeping more. She spent more time going to the latrine. She wasn't alone. Often, the sick couldn't make it to the latrines so they used the backed up toilet at the end of the building, or went in bowls by their beds. The rising stench was like disease's advance horse, as if we could smell the coming typhus, dysentery, cholera, tuberculosis, and polio.

I shuddered and told myself she was strong and would recover. I had put a piece of bread under my pillow to save for our breakfast before bedding down, and I reached for it with my fingertips just to make sure it was really there. I tapped the bread one more time, pulled my pink blanket more tightly around me, wished away the bread thieves, and closed my eyes until morning.

A week later, I was en route to hang wet laundry on the fence when I spotted a long pile of clothes in a shallow ditch. They looked old and dirty and it seemed unlikely to be of any use, but it was worth a look. It wasn't stealing if they were abandoned, I figured, and I seemed to be lucky enough to be the first one there. I stopped. Something didn't make sense: the shoes, the gray smooth skin hugging a skull and hands. I stared into something timeless and empty. Did I know this person? The face didn't look like a man or a woman, an adult or a child. How could a face be so faceless? The body was still. Not even the thinnest clothing moved.

I ran as fast as I could back to the barracks, clutching the damp clothes, and forgetting about drying them. I had to get as far away as possible. My mind went back to the old woman at the *Appell*. Even if the old woman had died, and in my heart I felt she had, I had never… really…been certain. Never like this. This time was for sure. The taut face, eyes, hands, and feet would be in my dreams. I just knew it. I shook under my blanket in my bunk until my breathing slowed. *Help*, I thought. Pappi. Mutti. Werner. My whole family was at work. There was no one. I lay still, willing my mind to think of other things: Switzerland and Opa, running on the beach with Werner, playing with Vera, Heidi getting knocked over by a goat.

My promise to myself was to not tell Mutti or Pappi what I'd seen. They had enough to worry about, and I had to start acting like a big girl. I heard other people talk about the dead body—it turned out to be a man—and they didn't seem upset. But I couldn't help myself when Mutti asked if I was okay. Mutti listened to me when she got back. She only said she was sorry. I was glad we were sleeping together.

Over the next weeks, as winter drew closer, there were more dead. Through the spring and summer, I had known that a few people had died each day; few enough that I'd only heard about it. But those numbers marched steadily upward through the fall. Outside, bodies were in ditches, by buildings, and sometimes hanging on the fence. Inside, families tucked their dead in their bedding until they were piled in carts to be wheeled to the crematorium. I had not seen the crematorium, but had heard it described: a wooden shack, like a garage, with a metal chimney jutting heavenward like an accusing finger. It burned all the time, but the lone oven could no longer keep up. Ashes and bodies were buried in a nearby pit. Not a graveyard, but an expanding hole.

"They are talking about having to dig more pits," Werner said.

I had never thought about what happens to your body when you die. I had assumptions. One was that you were put in your own grave. Another was that you got a gravestone with your name and a little information. Friends and family could come by and pay respects and be sad and remember good times. I became hardened to the point that a dead person was as normal as a fallen leaf, but I was bothered by the lack of respect. There didn't seem to be any of that when so many bodies were dumped into one unmarked hole.

Death itself became a living thing. Before Bergen-Belsen, death was only an idea, like Switzerland or Africa, something you would think or talk about, but was unknown. Then death started soaring closer, like a rare bird you might glimpse from time to time, and finally it just came and went as it pleased, like dozens of pigeons you paid no heed.

Death was daily, and like all daily things, it was tied to little things. It could be as simple as just not being able to get up. The only difference between the living and the dead was a movement, even the tiniest. Death was just a posture you couldn't change. Twitch a finger, or sit up in a handcart and—*poof*—it was gone.

I became used to the lifeless piles, though I refused to scavenge their clothes. I simply let the dead—nameless and quiet—become part of the landscape.

28

Camp Bergen-Belsen, Germany

November–December 1944

One cold November night a storm blew in. The heavy rain was deafening on the metal roof. Wind screeched through the tiniest cracks and rattled the windows in their frames. Pappi had developed a bad cough. His sudden loud rattles jolted me from dozing off again. I snuggled closer to Mutti for comfort, her slow breathing calming the tempest.

The next morning the earth was drenched. Flurries raced here and there as if uncertain what direction to take. I looked over at the women's camp. The storm had collapsed tents. People picked through the debris, gathering what they could from puddles, piles of garbage, and slimy, smelly mud. I felt compassion for these pitiful women, and I felt grateful. I had my family. I had Hanneli. We had a solid roof. I could get up and out of the soaking ground. We weren't on that side of the fence.

Pappi awoke the next night hacking and sweating, peeling back the blankets. As much as I was concerned by his constant cough, I came to fear not hearing it. If I awoke in the night and it was too quiet, I'd train my ear in his direction, not breathing until he cleared his throat, or I was convinced I heard his breathing.

"I'm worried about Pappi," I said to Werner.

"I know. We're not used to seeing him so weak."

"Maybe he should go to the infirmary," I said.

"Are you crazy?" Werner asked. "Do you want to kill him?"

Then he couldn't get out of bed. Werner and I talked with Mutti, who wasn't sure what to do, so we decided to ask a friend of my parents, Mr. Wolf. Mr. Wolf was a teacher, at least he had been before, and was most notable for being a dwarf, except that he never seemed short. Werner told him we thought that Pappi probably had pneumonia, and we were considering the infirmary.

Mr. Wolf's gaze passed over Pappi before looking up at us. "Mr. Loewenberg died there," he said. "In the infirmary."

We knew this already. It had happened a few weeks before. Supposedly, he had joked up until his end. I wondered where Mrs. Loewenberg was now scrounging up smokes.

"I know. I'm sorry," said Werner. "What does that mean for Pappi?"

"The infirmary is not good, but we must take your father there."

We told Mutti.

Werner bit his nails.

"He will be okay in the infirmary," Mutti said from bed. "Remember what Pappi says: We are valuable because we are tradable. He will get extra care."

Pappi didn't get extra care. No medicine. No additional food. At least he wasn't working.

"And I have my own bed," he said between coughs. "See, I can spread out my arms and not bump anybody."

"You are spoiled," I said.

I stayed by his side, giving him all the bits of bread, soup, and water that we could get and he could manage. Mutti was too tired to visit, and Werner couldn't get time away from tearing apart shoes. I didn't like the looks of the infirmary. Instead of being open like the barracks, a narrow hall stretched down the middle with vertical paneling that made it look like it went on longer than it did. Doors opened to patients' rooms. All the beds were full with the sick curled under gray blankets. Some people were even on the floor and in the hall. Everyone's lips seemed thin and dry. If they weren't whimpering, crying, or coughing, they stared. Everything was the color of least resistance. Blues, greens, golds, and reds all became gray. I vowed to keep my pink blanket bright.

After three days of almost constant sleep, Pappi crawled back to health. Seeing him drag his body back to work was painful; the toll was more and more visible. His hack had greatly diminished, yet he had become thinner, and smaller, and grayer. Just as he was rallying, Mutti's health slipped, but since she didn't have any specific symptoms, she had to stay in the barracks. Besides, after seeing the infirmary and knowing it was only getting more crowded, I agreed with Werner that it was best to keep Mutti away from there.

"I can't help with the children," I told Hanneli. "Mutti isn't able to get out of bed. I need to stay with her."

"No problem, Reni," she said, looking around at the few children left. Most were too sick or weak to need care as they just stayed in bed. I hoped they were still alive. Little Joseph hadn't been around for weeks now. "What's wrong with her?"

"What isn't wrong with her? Well, I mean she isn't coughing."

"That's good," Hanneli said.

I was at Mutti's side through her pain, fevers, chills, and delirium. She never complained, though she did apologize a lot.

Adulthood felt like it was falling in around me in ways that I had never expected. I always thought of getting older as having fun in new ways, like flirting with boys and trading in my heavy hair and girl's outfits for a proper coiffure and eye-catching dresses. I looked down at myself. I probably looked older, but not how I wanted.

December came and with it, my birthday. I turned fourteen without anyone noticing. Groups huddled in the candlelit corners of the barracks in the evenings, quietly celebrating Chanukah. They had a spit of oil and threads of cotton and prayer. Werner came back and shared the Rabbi's words from that evening.

"Despair is the opposite of being a Jew," he reported.

"That sounds like Heidi," I said.

"But Heidi's Christian."

"Well, I guess she'd make a good Jew."

Days after the lights of Chanukah dimmed, the Germans could be heard singing Christmas carols, their voices carrying on the freezing breeze, and a week later we were in 1945.

29

Camp Bergen-Belsen, Germany

January 19, 1945

"Anne is here, Anne Frank!" Hanneli said a couple of weeks later as she ran up to me outside the barracks. "I saw her last night."

Of course, we both knew Anne and her family from our Amsterdam neighborhood, but Hanneli was closer to her in age, and they had been friends.

"She's here?" I asked.

"Not in the Star Camp, in the tent camp. I was homesick and heard there were some more Dutch, so I snuck by the fence to ask who was there."

"You shouldn't have done that. The guards…"

"Yes, well, anyhow, I started talking with a women who turned out to be Mrs. Van Pels. Do you remember her?"

I did, a little.

"She said Anne is here, and asked if I wanted to talk with her."

"Really?"

"Yes, a few minutes later I heard Anne's voice as if it were yesterday. We just looked at each other through the fence, and we both started to cry," Hanneli said, her voice shaky. "Oh Reni, she looks so sick and skinny." She took a breath and continued. "I can't believe she is here. I thought, I don't know, I thought her family had escaped to Switzerland. She hid with her family and a few others including the Van Pels. They were in an attic for two years and never left once. Then somebody told the Germans about them. Her family was split up and sent to different camps, including Auschwitz."

Auschwitz. That camp had a bad reputation, even here.

"Anne and her sister came here in November. They were in the tents during that big storm."

"That's terrible," I said. "They've been here almost two months!"

"Yes, all that time and so close, and we didn't know."

"At least they're alive."

"I know, but Reni, Anne is as thin as a twig, or paper, and so pale. She's afraid that her mother and father are dead. Her sister Margot is so sick that she couldn't get up to greet me, and might be dying. Probably typhus. Anne's clothes are rags. And, of course, the lice...."

Typhus had become the talk of the camp. It was spreading, mostly because of the lice. At first typhus looked like the flu, but then it caused a rash over most of the body, a high fever, and then the mind failed until the person died. I thought of a spider wrapping prey with her long, black legs, then the dry carcass dangling by a thread, whipped and loosened by wind until it fluttered to the ground. Soundless and insignificant. So easily brushed aside with countless other weightless carcasses.

"Can we help?" I asked.

Dirt smudged Hanneli's cheek. She smeared it with her hand as she wiped her eye.

"Yes. Anne and I agreed to meet tonight. I really want to bring her food."

"Can we get her any? Does your family have anything left from the Red Cross rations?"

We heard that Red Cross packages arrived all the time, but the Germans kept most to themselves except last month, just before Christmas, when they gave us two cardboard boxes with red crosses in the upper right corner. Each box was the size for new shoes: it contained powdered milk, sugar cubes, jam, and some canned goods. Considering the state of Werner's feet, he was sorry they weren't shoes.

"We don't have anything left," said Hanneli. "We finished ours last week. Even if we had something left, I'm not sure my father would let us give it away."

"Yeah," I said. "We ate it all, too, especially trying to feed more to Mutti. I'm not sure we could get any food from anybody at this point."

"But we could get clothes," said Hanneli.

We gathered some clothes and a bit of bread, and bundled them in a ball as if we were readying to run away from home. Darkness and cold fell, and the fear of Allied planes kept camp lights dimmed, making it easier for us to walk unseen over the frozen, pitted ground. Hanneli led us to the fence in the thick shadow of a building. A couple of people milled around on the other side. We waited.

"Hanneli?"

"Over here, Anne!" Hanneli whispered loudly.

I made out Anne's silhouette in the dark; gone was the lively girl that Hanneli talked about. She was draped in a dark blanket like I imagined woman of centuries, if not a millennium, past. She seemed swallowed by the cloth.

"Oh Hanneli, you're here," Anne said.

"We've brought what we could."

The old friends stood there, sharing a moment in time. I had last seen them together in Amsterdam, on a sunlit, clean street, the wind teasing their dark hair. They had been twelve—younger than I was that January night—but they had seemed so much more mature, talking about boys and high school. I rested my hand on the fence, careful not to cut my hand on the barbs.

"Hi, Anne. It's Reni."

"Hi, Reni."

"Hanneli told me about the attic, and your family. I'm sorry about your parents and Margot."

"Yeah. Thanks. Margot is pretty sick. Were you able to get anything?"

"Yes," said Hanneli. "I'm sorry it's not more."

"It's okay. It all helps."

Hanneli grabbed the wrapped parcel, and on the count of three, swung it high over the barbed wire so it wouldn't snag. I heard it hit the ground. Anne turned around and disappeared into the dark. Suddenly, there was a shuffle in the shadows.

"No! Stop!" Anne's voice cracked in the chill.

I instinctively looked around me to see if there were guards coming, but seeing none I turned back to glimpse a figure scuttle away. What happened? Then, the vacuum of silence, lightly peppered with the background of camp sounds—murmurs from buildings, the breeze by my ear, and heavy breathing—settled back.

Anne emerged at the fence again, her voice heaving.

"She took it! I can't believe it. Somebody just took the bundle!"

"Anne, Anne, we'll find more. We'll find more," Hanneli said with both hands on the fence. "Tomorrow if we are lucky, or the next night. We'll find more."

"You promise?" Anne asked.

"Yes, um, give us a couple of days, two nights from now," Hanneli said. "I promise."

It would not be easy pulling together another bundle of clothes. Helping and donating were becoming less popular. Desperation had hardened all of us.

30

Camp Bergen-Belsen, Germany

January 20, 1945 morning and afternoon

I was still savoring the food of my dreams as I awoke to the barracks' rustlings, murmurings, and groans. My eyes blinked open: I stared up at the wooden slats of the bunk above me with their familiar wavy grain and swirls. Many of the knots were like eyes. One had three dark dots at one end, resembling an owl. The smell of sleep, sweat, and sawdust hung in the air. I was about to roll over to look at Mutti, when she cleared her throat. Then I heard my brother stirring below and looked at the empty wall peg—Pappi's jacket was gone. He had left for work. A long, soft sigh swept my lips. My family was alive. Dawn had become the worst time of day. Each morning I feared waking to someone having died. *Thank you*, I said, looking back up at the knot owl.

Mutti would always say that every day in Bergen-Belsen was a question mark. Werner would say something clever like every day in life was a question mark. Pappi would say it depended on where you put the question marks. Did we let the unknown feed our fear? Or was it a chance for hope? Hope alone wouldn't keep us alive in Bergen-Belsen, but, he said, miracles did happen.

My family had more than our share of miracles. We had been saved from Camp Auschwitz, twice. At the theater in Amsterdam and at Westerbork. We had mysteriously received our Ecuadorian passports, even after we'd been deported. Lastly, we had stayed together as a family, which seemed more remarkable every day. Anne had no idea about her parents. If that were me, it would destroy me.

Mutti moaned, and I rolled over. We silently stared at one another. She looked so much older.

"So, so blue," she whispered. "My Reni, your pretty, pretty eyes. Like they hold a piece of the sky."

The door thudded against the wooden wall, followed by the sounds of heavy, stamping boots and a call to attention. It must have been time to march outside for roll call. *Appell.*

"Everyone holding a North American or South American passport must report immediately to the chief doctor to determine your fitness for exchange."

I raised myself on my elbow and peered over Mutti. The *Kapo* repeated the news, louder that time since there was now a flurry of movement and questions from everywhere. But the *Kapo* waved them off, saying that was all he knew and that he had to move along to the other barracks in the Star Camp. We would know more soon. The tip of a short rubber hose poked out of his pocket. The *Kapos* were carrying them more often for handing out punishments. I hadn't been hit, but I had heard they were painful and could be deadly. The hoses were easy to carry, quick to strike with, and left few marks. The *Kapos* would let the ends dangle as a reminder that they could be used at any moment.

There was no mention of *Appell* for the first time in a year.

The chatter intensified. This was what we had prayed for and feared. Was it real? Would the Germans follow through, and what exactly would they follow through with? We needed to talk with Pappi, but would have to wait until he returned. Werner stood, watching, and listening. He was slowly, almost absent mindedly, tucking in his shirt and smoothing the creases. With a pull, he cinched his belt in another notch and fitted the long end into the loops. Then, like Moses dividing the Red Sea, he waved his fingers through his hair just once, and it dutifully parted.

"What do we do?" I asked.

"I'm thinking," he said, leaning on his good foot. "I'm not sure Mutti can walk, but if we can't get her up and to the doctor, we may not be able to go. We have no choice. Get her dressed. I'll help."

"Your foot."

"I said, 'I'll help.'"

We propped up Mutti, helped swing her legs over the edge of the bed, and with great effort she stood, swayed, and stayed up. We explained the situation, but I wasn't convinced she was listening. She only stood if she had to use the pot next to our bed.

"So brown," I said, trying to encourage her, "your beautiful eyes."

Your tired, far away eyes, I said to myself.

"We have you, Mutti," Werner said.

She leaned into Werner, who got his balance, and I wrapped her with a blanket before getting on the other side of her. We started to shuffle. Her shoes looked huge at the ends of her skinny legs. When had she replaced her old shoes with these big ugly things with great rounded toes and wire for laces?

Mutti suddenly collapsed.

Werner stumbled on his infected foot and groaned.

We carried Mutti back to the bunk and covered her. Breathing heavily, Werner and I sat on the bed with her. Werner leaned forward, shaking his hair back into place.

"There's no way we can carry her," he said. "Too weak."

"Should we report to the doctor anyway?"

"Yes. Staying here isn't going to get us anywhere."

"I don't like leaving her alone."

"She'll be fine. For a little bit."

Mutti didn't seem to notice as I covered her with my pink blanket in addition to hers, even pulling them up under her chin. I glanced at my brother's tidiness and said that I needed a few minutes to get ready. Pulling frigid water from the sink outside the barracks, I rinsed and rubbed my face, and then brushed some dirt off my coat.

"Let's go," I said.

"Hasenbergs," Werner said. "Let's go, Hasenbergs. That's what Pappi would say."

Werner limped. Side-by-side, we headed to the reporting station, a temporary set-up in one of the other barracks. Each person stood in front of the medical director, the *Stabsarzt*, whose first question was if they understood what was happening and if they wanted to partake in the exchange. If their answer was yes, they were examined. Ahead of us in line, a man with a cap pulled low over his eyes murmured that only the Nazis would make prisoners verify that they wanted to leave hell. He propped up an old man whose head kept bobbing forward. The back of the old man's neck was covered in scabs as rough as caked mud.

"Next," said the *Stabsarzt*.

The doctor had a hooked nose and an overbite, with kind eyes belying a bad reputation. The capped man struggled with the old man, coming to a stop in front of the *Stabsarzt* and his assistant, both in white coats. The medical team sat behind a small table and chairs, their stiff pens making smart checks and etching paths across sheets of typed paper and cards stamped with blue circles.

"Names," said the *Stabsarzt*, looking pleasant.

The capped man gave their names.

"Are you sick? He looks sick," said the *Stabsarzt*, pointing at the old man.

"He is a little sick, that's all."

The assistant got up and examined the old man. The assistant's hair was patchy like a dog with mange, and his eyes seemed impossibly close to each other. His white coat was splattered with too many stains. He scratched the back of his own neck before tilting the old man's head up by the chin and looking at him from different angles. He let the head drop and fingered around the neck. The capped man adjusted his grip on the old man's belt. Looking back at the doctor, the assistant shook his head back and forth.

"Please, he can go, I will take care of him," the capped man pleaded.

"*You* can go. He can't."

"Please, Herr Doktor."

"No. Next," said the *Stabsarzt*, eyes twinkling.

They looked at Werner and then to me, saying nothing. I licked my bottom lip and my mouth settled into a tight line.

"Names," said the *Stabsarzt*.

Werner spoke for us.

"Are you sick?" the *Stabsarzt* asked, while continuing to shuffle through the papers and scan the list. His partner on the right looked us up and down. I realized I was trying to stand a little taller. The assistant asked me to lean forward. At the same time I felt a nervous cough coming on and slowly swallowed, before shaking my head back and forth: *No*. Werner said we were fine. The doctor looked more closely at me, deciding for himself.

"*Ja*, next."

His partner made two X's on the paper, wrote on two stamped cards, and handed them to his superior, who thanked him. We stepped to the side, lingering only long enough to make sure they were truly done with us. They were, and we slid away. They didn't ask about our parents.

"We are so lucky Mutti didn't come," said Werner on our way back. I squeezed his hand, then held it as we walked.

As soon as Pappi came through the door that afternoon, we launched ourselves at him. Werner did the talking, explaining the rapid developments and the need for him and Mutti to report, and how important it was that Mutti looked healthy, or at least healthier than she was. A couple of times I tried to jump in with details, but backed off, until I finally blurted:

"Pappi, it's true! It's true! We can go!"

But Pappi was silent, slouched over on the bed. I stopped, then looked back and forth between Werner and Pappi, and I studied my father. He was pale and was shaking all over, like the time when he had pneumonia. *Oh no, not now*, I thought. *How could he suddenly be so sick?*

"Pappi, please," begged Werner.

"No. I must rest," he whispered.

As our parents slept, Werner and I fretted, mulling over the options. Then Mr. Roseboom came over with his son Lex. Mr. Roseboom was tall and big, and seemed completely unaffected by the food rations. Lex, a few years older than me, shared only his dad's height. They were exchange Jews, too. Healthy ones. Easy X's for the doctor to make.

"How's your father?" Mr. Roseboom asked, his forehead rippled.

"We're afraid he's sick again," Werner said.

"He's not sick." Mr. Roseboom paused.

I looked at Lex, who held my gaze.

"Your father was beaten today…by a *Kapo*."

"How bad?" asked Werner.

Mr. Roseboom didn't say anything, which was the answer we didn't want.

"Why?" Werner pressed.

"I don't know. I didn't witness it myself, and your father didn't say."

"We heard the news about the exchange at work," said Lex, "Maybe the *Kapo* was jealous."

"What do we do?" I asked Lex. I had barely traded words with him, but now he and his father seemed important.

"Let your father rest for now," said Mr. Roseboom. "We'll check back in an hour."

"What if he needs a doctor?" I asked.

"We can't," Werner said. "Not now."

"He's right," said Lex.

They left.

"Pappi," I said, and put my face next to his. His breath was weak and cool. "You have to report. We can only be exchanged if we're healthy. You can't look too sick. Please, for all of us."

He nodded in agreement and looked at me with glassy eyes.

"Reni…you're right."

"Can you make it?" I asked.

"Yes."

"I can help," Werner offered.

"No," Pappi said. "Not good. For your foot."

"I'll go with you," I said.

Werner stayed with Mutti. We decided to let her rest more before taking her to be examined, praying the extra time would help. With short steps, Pappi made it outside and walked a few meters before bending over, hands on knees, swaying. Instinctively, I wrapped my arm across his back and tried to support him. He pushed himself up while leaning into me. I smelled the sweat and dirt on his clothes and skin, and something else cold and metallic.

"I've got you," I said, hoping I did.

He fell into me a little more. I could hardly support him against my bony frame, and I felt we might topple. I kept taking deep breaths and adjusting my posture. I was always hungry, but I now craved anything in my belly that would fuel my efforts. I summoned whispers of energy, knowing I had to get my father in front of the *Stabsarzt*.

If it was this hard with Pappi, I knew it would be impossible for Mutti. I imagined being trapped in Bergen-Belsen weeks from now, listening to the rumors of those who had made it out. Or worse, we would be split up like Anne and her family, with Mutti and Pappi left behind and Werner and me forced to go on. I couldn't bear that, I couldn't. I could handle a lot, and I had, but not that. How could we have come through so much only to risk losing it all at the last hour? I steeled myself, preparing to plead with the *Stabsarzt* on Mutti's behalf.

The line had dwindled.

Soon we were again facing the men behind the small table. This time, a guard, an older man in a uniform meant for someone bigger, stood behind them. A taut leather strap crossed from the guard's right hip up to his left shoulder, hugging a heavy rifle against his back. The *Stabsarzt* looked up at me, his expression indifferent as if he had never seen me before. Again, he searched my face. *My God*, I thought, *what would he see when he looked at Pappi?*

Pappi gave his name when asked by the *Stabsarzt*.

"Are you sick?"

Pappi shook his head no.

With his right hand the guard pulled on the strap holding his weapon. He lifted it above his helmeted head, and let it rest on his other shoulder. He then shifted his weight and stood back at attention.

With a flick, the official on the left made two marks that bled into the paper.

"Herr Doctor," asked Pappi, "A question?"

The doctor didn't say no.

"Our passports?" asked Pappi.

"We have them," said the doctor. "Your children, Werner and Irene, have already been here. Be ready early tomorrow morning, all of you."

A flash of confusion crossed Pappi's face before he glanced at the list and then slowly nodded.

I was baffled. What did he mean by "your children?" Pappi took my hand, thanked them, and guided me toward the door. Outside, and with a little space between us and the officials and guard, he groaned and fell on my shoulder.

"That was luck," Pappi said, "or something."

"For you, yes, but what about Mutti? You barely made it. How will she?"

"She doesn't have to."

"Why?"

"They thought you were Mutti."

"Me?"

He nodded yes.

Did I look that old? Were Mutti and I that much alike?

Back at the barracks, Pappi crawled into bed. Werner and I had to pack, but with so little, it didn't take much time. We decided to leave almost everything behind, and packing smaller things like Pappi's razor kit, our two brown pots, forks, knifes, and spoons. The only thing I wanted to hold on to was my soft, pink blanket. Everything else was filthy and threadbare. I told Werner what had happened with the doctor.

"Maybe they were confused. Maybe they were just being nice. Maybe they just checked off our names anyhow," I said.

"Does it matter, Reni?"

Werner was right. Asking for an answer wasn't important. Why fret over another miracle?

31

Camp Bergen-Belsen, Germany

January 20, 1945 evening

The news of our departure was the talk of the camp. Maybe I just imagined it, but it seemed as if everybody was looking at us. Prisoners from other camp sections peered through the barbed wire, pointing in our direction with their heads close together in talk. The guards who normally ignored us, except to hit or yell, looked at us like we were the newest animals in the zoo. We were called the *glück*, or lucky. What a change. I was used to *dreck*, filth. A word we heard every day. The guards used it at us. The prisoners used it. Even the kids used it between themselves, though never in front of adults. It was not a nice word, but it fit Bergen-Belsen. On the other hand, *glück* was the most rare, and the sweetest, of words. I rolled it around my mouth like a piece of hard Danish candy.

There was milling and fussing—more activity than we had seen in a long time. Parents told their kids to pack. Kids responded there was nothing to pack. They just had what they wore. Couples debated what to bring: some string, a torn jacket, or a dented water cup. Some friends and family offered to help. They cared, and they knew they might benefit from whatever was left behind. Most of those staying, though, offered only steely glances.

"Imagine if we were the ones staying behind," said Werner as we sat on his bunk.

"I don't want to," I said.

"Everybody knows we're going and yet they walk past us, frowning and not looking up, like we have already gone. All our time together and it's like we don't exist."

"Not everybody is like that," I said.

Still, how generous would I feel if I were seeing a few "lucky" ones leave? It made the people helping us all the more special. They had nothing to gain, except maybe a bit of stale bread or threadbare socks to help protect them against a place where life was fading away faster and faster. Maybe they looked at us as we had looked at the group that had left for Palestine months earlier: we were now the reminder that escape happened.

With Pappi and Mutti so sick, some of our barracks' friends approached Werner about getting our parents to the train by carrying them on a makeshift stretcher. Pappi tried to say something.

"What, John?" asked Mr. Roseboom, his son Lex behind him.

"Too risky," Pappi said, adding, "They could decide we are too sick to leave. The Germans need to exchange Jews who are living. Just because we passed the initial test doesn't mean they won't be looking for any sign of weakness."

The men looked at one another.

"We'll walk," Pappi repeated.

"Okay," the small council agreed.

"And Werner," Pappi said, "give them the powdered milk, sugar cubes, and jam."

Pappi was talking about what had come in the second, and recent, care package, which we had been rationing. The daily, single spoonful of jam was amazing, and my entire body and soul didn't want to part with the treat.

"All of it?" I asked. "Can't we at least keep the jam? I mean, just in case we need it?"

"Reni, I know you like it, " Pappi said, "but freedom will be much sweeter."

True, I thought, but I still didn't see why we couldn't bring the jam.

"Understand?" Pappi quietly asked.

Not really, but I knew the right thing was to agree.

"So," said Mr. Roseboom, "that's why they let us have the care packages."

"To fatten us up for the trade," finished his son.

The council of friends agreed that we would hand over the food in the morning, after we had had some for breakfast. They promised to divide it equally. One by one they shook hands with Pappi, including Lex, who also stuck out his hand to Werner and then me. It felt so oddly grown up.

We talked about leaving the rest of our belongings, but there was always the chance we might end up in another camp, and it was winter. With everything either packed in our one suitcase or wrapped up in blankets, and Pappi and Mutti asleep, I went in search of Hanneli. I knew she wasn't on the exchange list. She was lying in her bunk.

"All our food talk is finally going to come true for you," she said.

"I know. I can't believe it," I said. "I'll think of you with every bite."

"I'm so happy for you. For your family. Your mother needs real help. The Red Cross will take care of her."

"My Pappi isn't well either. He was hit. He seems really hurt."

"I'm sorry."

"Please tell the others good-bye. Including Anne. I'm sorry I can't help again."

Hanneli nodded. She shrugged. We sat together. Two bunks over, some adults made hushed talk. We could hear them. Just barely.

"No train has ever left here for a better place. It's another Nazi lie."

"I agree. Commandant Kramer and all the Nazis would rather we rot here. It will be a train to more hell, I'm sure of it."

"Poor folks. They think it's what they've been waiting for, and it's just a trick."

Trick or not, I thought, what difference did it make? Like Werner said, this was at least a chance—the best we'd had since we'd arrived here. Sticking around Bergen-Belsen didn't look good with the increasing numbers of prisoners and dead, but I didn't say any of that to Hanneli.

32

Camp Bergen-Belsen, Germany

January 21, 1945 morning

awoke early the next day and stared up again at the bottom of the bunk above me. It seemed to press down like the lid of a coffin. I shifted my gaze to the rows of bunks and bodies around me, to the rafters above, and to the roof above that. Beyond that was a waiting train, cold, clouds, blue sky, and…who knew? Leaving this camp alive was everybody's hope and anybody's guess.

The squeal and shudder of hinges opening stopped my musings. The door thudded against the wooden wall, followed by heavy boots stomping. I sat up in my bunk. Two *Kapos*, looking as self-important and well-fed as always, stood, dripping water and snow.

"It is seven o'clock," one of them said. "Everybody who is leaving on the train must report to the disinfection center and bath house for cleaning and delousing."

He repeated himself, then added that we should bring everything, including our baggage. We had two hours to get ready. He clapped his hands twice for emphasis. With another slam of the door, the two *Kapos* were gone, leaving behind small clumps of mud and wet boot prints that I wouldn't have to clean up anymore.

Pappi, however, didn't seem any better than the day before; in fact, he moved more slowly than I could remember. His pale face was stretched, and his thin hair was matted. Mutti didn't move at all, and I felt a flash of terror until I saw her arm drift to her chin.

"We have to get going Mutti," Werner said.

Mutti didn't respond.

Werner tried again.

Mutti muttered something.

"What?" Werner asked.

"Too tired," she managed.

"Pappi," I said, "please help with Mutti."

Werner and I exchanged concerned looks as Pappi edged to her side and whispered to her: "Trudi, *liebling*. Trudi, muster. This is our chance. Our one chance."

"Eat something," I added. "You will feel better."

She stirred. We all ate extra helpings of Red Cross jam, then fastened all our buttons and pulled our coats tight. Werner and I tested the strings used to tie together our bundled knapsacks, and slung them over our shoulders. Somebody took our suitcase. Friends carried Mutti. Our final good-byes were small nods and looks, though Hanneli ran up with a quick hug, and Vogeltje made a point of making sure we were snugly dressed and asked if we had everything. Satisfied with her work, she stood back and hummed.

The day was as cold as the rest of the month had been, and a thin frosting of new snow covered everything so that the barracks, fencing, and people stood out like a painter's first strokes on a fresh canvas. The gray sky was as thick and inviting as a new wool scarf. We were marched to the bathhouse building where Mutti and I were separated from Pappi and Werner. The men and boys were instructed to undress. We looked away. Then they filed through the door to the large shower room. We heard the pipes rumble and we heard a sputtering spray, followed by shocked voices that reminded us the water was not heated. There were sharp shrill commands from the guard at the doorway.

"Scrub harder!"

"Get in the crevasses! Ha, especially those crevasses you *Dreck*!"

"Get behind your ears!"

"No amount of water will get swine like you clean."

About ten minutes later the water shut off. Dripping tailed off.

"Stay! Don't move. Your filthy clothes are being cleaned. You will remain here until they are done."

We heard feet moving, and shaky, meek voices requesting to borrow something to dry off with. To wrap around.

"Stay!"

I thought of a watch on a guard's wrist, and its slow sweep. Minutes. A half hour.

"Ha, yes, hug each other. That's a child's way to stay warm!"

I could feel the shivering from the other side of the wall. Meanwhile, I dared not move.

"No sitting!"

A half hour. Slow sweep. An hour.

"What, you think we enjoy this? Watching you naked?"

"Swine have never looked so skinny."

"I said, '*Stand!*'"

A slap.

Was that Pappi's tired skin being struck? I could only imagine that some others were helping to keep him up. *Kapos* arrived, dumping piles of damp clothes on the ground around us. We turned away as the men and boys came out, found theirs, and dressed. A tap on my shoulder; I looked up at Werner.

"We'll s-see you s-s-soon," he said through chattering teeth. "It, it's rather ch-chilly."

My brother and Pappi filed out with the others, Werner limping more than usual, the ends of dark socks poking from his toeless shoes. Two men were on either side of Pappi. He was not being carried, but he was not walking on his own either.

Mutti and I undressed while sitting on long benches, handing our clothing and bags to female guards who took them away to be steamed, holding them at arm's length. Mutti sighed, leaning more on me as we walked into the large showering room. The walls were brick. Triangular, metal-tubed structures that reminded me of swing sets were scattered about. Each had six showerheads, one on each end and two off each side, and two soap bowls that dangled in the middle from rusty chains. Mutti was able to hold a leg of one shower structure while I helped her clean.

I didn't want to look at her or at the other women, but I couldn't help it. Everybody was so thin, especially their arms and ribs. Shoulder blades and hips pushed against the whitest of skin. The water took away my breath, and I shifted a little so it only hit me on one side.

"Mutti, will you be okay for a moment?" I asked.

She nodded.

I dipped my head under the water, wetting my hair, which was too thick and stiff to easily run my hands through. I tried frothing it up a thin wedge of soap, but the wedge stayed hard and sticky no matter how much I rubbed it. Three times I ran what soap I could over my head. In the end, my hair still felt waxy. Mutti was shivering more. Just as I thought she would faint from the cold, the water died with a snap of vibrating metal. Mutti's shivering worsened. My embarrassment of touching her disappeared in my need to get her as dry as possible as fast as possible. I swept my flat open hands down over Mutti's hair and down her limbs and body to get the water off her as fast as I could. My hands moved like the relentless tongue of a cat. Her face stayed taut, her eyes closed. Two other women came over and we huddled together in a group, not talking, breathing hard, and staring at our curled feet on the concrete. I wanted long arms to wrap what little warmth I had around Mutti. I kept a hand on her elbow as she clung to the pole. Numbness spread over my fingers and toes.

Stiffly and slowly, as if walking for the first time, we exited when instructed. We found our clothes damp, but supposedly free of lice, and we dressed with fumbling fingers. I helped Mutti dress first. Many women just draped what they could around their shoulders.

"I need to lie down," Mutti said, her teeth chattering, body shaking.

As I turned to her, she collapsed onto the wooden bench against the wall. A woman scrambled out of the way. I gasped and leaned into her so she would not fall on the floor, and eased her onto her side. Her head lay on her long thin arm. I hadn't even had a chance to pull down her dress so her hipbone jutted up like a large shell.

"What's wrong here?"

I looked up at a Nazi guard, suddenly very aware of my nakedness. She was as solid as a mountain in her thick wool uniform. Her young face was hard, her eyes as barren as a mountain peak, and blonde hair as smooth as ice-covered snow. I was suddenly and terribly conscious of my nakedness, so I looked down at the hefty buttons on her coat, avoiding her eyes.

"I…she…."

"She looks as if she's dying," the guard delivered the verdict. "I don't think you are fit to go."

Mutti's hand cast about, feeling for a grip.

"Oh, it's just my stomach," Mutti said, pushing herself up. "I think… um…I must have eaten something…something didn't agree with me."

Another guard walked over. She was just as sturdy, but had dark hair, and her eyes and mouth clustered close to her nose. She took off her overcoat, wiped her brow.

"What's going on here, Helga?" she asked.

"Says something didn't agree with her," said Helga, sizing up Mutti who now leaned on my naked torso to keep herself upright.

"Hmm, it looks like a lot of Bergen-Belsen hasn't agreed with her."

"She's getting up," I said.

"She'd better, or she will be staying down for a long time," Helga said.

Helga smiled at the joke, and the two walked off together. I finished getting us ready and, with Mutti still using me for support, we walked outside, where we were guided to large idling trucks that looked black against the fresh lily snow. They reminded me of the delivery trucks in Amsterdam, except for the German black and white crosses on the doors.

"Men and boys in those trucks, and women and girls in the others," a guard yelled to the crowd. "Move."

"You will see each other at the train," added a *Kapo*.

Women clambered up and into the tarped backs of the vehicles. I didn't want Mutti to have to move more than needed, so we waited until a truck was almost full. Then several of us had to get Mutti up and in, where we sandwiched her between another woman and me. I shivered, still damp. Nobody spoke. We hugged our belongings and watched our breath rather than look at one another. The smell of gas fumes filled the space between us. After ten minutes the tailgate was flipped up and the large canvas flaps over it were flopped down.

I stole glances outside through wavering fabric as the truck jerked forward. I was at the end of the bench so there was nothing between me and everything we were leaving behind. There were other trucks behind us, but I kept my eyes on the changing scene and landscape. Bergen-Belsen reached out in all directions, as far as I could see: low gray buildings, slow moving people, distant shouts, the musty smell of canvas and wool, and ribbons of smoke unrolling up into the clouds. I saw the main camp's center road fade away behind us and then the camp's closing gates, like a predator's mouth inches from missed prey. We turned left, the truck hit a bump, and I almost fell over Mutti. The high camp fence was on the right; a corner watchtower was at the end, perched on impossibly thin supports, its windows closed. A few prisoners watched. Their eyes on us, two skeletal figures walked into one another, took no notice of each other, and drifted on.

Our road was packed snow with strips of dirty tire ruts. It was straight and flat through the scrubbed, bony trees. Their branches were so intertwined it was impossible to know where one ended and another began, a frozen mass of veins waiting to thaw. I supposed that within a couple of months, the sweet smell of running sap would carry on the wind.

Three kilometers separated the camp from the train station. Eleven months before we had been hustled from the train by barking guards and snapping dogs, and had half-marched, half-run to Bergen-Belsen in the morning. Now, we were being delivered. You would think we'd all be ecstatic, but everyone was numb. I heard a crow and then others. A wooden fence, so simple it could be climbed in a moment, flashed by. Then a barn and a house…a home! Inside, I was sure, a family was sharing a large breakfast.

We turned right. Forest fell away to fields and the ride ended. I sat on the back edge of the truck and lowered myself, careful not to slip on the well-packed snow. The station was crowded, but felt lonely. It was on the outskirts of town, and marked with a tall tower. The black train that huffed on the track made me nervous. Trains had brought nothing but pain and fear, taking us to places that were worse than before.

"Reni, this is good," Mutti whispered after I helped her down. "No cattle cars. See those markings all over the train? The white squares with the red crosses? That's the Red Cross. The same people who sent us the care packages. No swastikas."

"Mutti, you stay here," I said and bundled our belongings around her on the ground. "I'll look for Pappi and Werner."

33

At the Train, Camp Bergen-Belsen

January 21, 1945 afternoon and evening

A group of Nazi officers looked over clipboards, heads down. One had rolled up papers he used to tap against his palm. Soldiers stood around the officers with their arms behind their backs, at the ready for the next order. Others milled in groups with stiff rifles slung over their shoulders. An officer's German Shepherd sniffed the ground, sniffed a soldier's rear, sniffed hands, and wagged its tail. I kept my distance.

I walked up and down alongside the six cars of the train, peering up into the windows, and even peeking into the kitchen car. At the back of the train I walked up the other side. Pappi and Werner weren't there. I started walking more quickly, panic beginning to take hold as I could not find the rest of my family. I started up the other side for the second time, and, not looking in front of myself, I bumped into somebody.

"Oh, slow down. Are you okay?"

I looked up at a thin and ill-clothed man. One of us.

"Help me. I can't find my father and brother anywhere," I said.

"Have you looked through the whole train?"

"Yes, in every window. They have to be here."

"I'm sure they are. Let's go inside and ask."

I thought of Mutti waiting outside, but I let the man guide me up the steel steps where snow fell off my shoes. It was so warm inside that I couldn't catch my breath. He stopped several people, asking questions, and weaving me through the passageways between settling passengers and unsettled guards. We stopped next to a compartment.

Werner looked up and smiled. Pappi was asleep with his head against the window. Pappi could not have been more visible from the outside, but I had not recognized him. I then realized how pale and gaunt he looked. Werner agreed to come with me to get Mutti. My helper was gone before I could thank him.

Mutti ended up having to be carried to the compartment by several fellow prisoners where she was gently placed on one bench, her head on my blanket. Werner and I sat on the other side, next to Pappi. Our belongings were on the floor, under the window, between the two benches. We were together. I hadn't realized how much I took that for granted, especially now, as we were heading out of Bergen-Belsen.

Werner reached under his sleeves and scratched.

"So much for the delousing," he said.

He was right. I felt itchy and reached behind to scratch my lower back.

"No matter how hard they try, the Reich can't defeat lice."

"I like that," I said, "Knowing they can't kill off something so small."

"Like us," Werner said, reading my mind.

A guard glanced in, the front of his cap as high as a salute. Another guard trailed behind him, and a train attendant after him. Like a beast, the train engine panted, its hot breath puffing through the small pipes and valves that ran the length of its giant boiler, then steaming from its stack. Within a half hour inside I was actually getting hot, but couldn't bring myself to shed my jacket. What if we were suddenly told to get off again, but take nothing? I couldn't shake the fear that this might be fake, that I would awaken back in my bunk to a cold room and a day filled with gray and brown—floors, ground, sky, food. How could this be possible? Here we were, the four of us, barely alive, but sitting in a train and about to leave this…hell. It really was, or had been, hell.

"Is this real?" I asked, my face turned to the windowpane.

"Feels like a dream," Werner said.

We held each other's gaze for a moment. Then the huge engine revved, the powerful chug-chug of the train began, and the whistle blew. Fear chilled me for a moment, but then I let myself sink into the warmth, and I allowed a sliver of the nightmare to break away. My

Mutti was in a deep sleep, her mouth open, oblivious to the departure. The same was true of my Pappi. They were missing the moment.

"They need help," Werner said.

My brother lifted up his hurt foot, carefully taking off his shoe and sock. His toes were perfectly white with black patches on the end. They smelled like sour fruit and I wrinkled my nose.

"Stinks," I said.

"Yeah, thanks," he said. He winced as he touched his toes.

"Werner, I think you need help, too." I hadn't realized just how bad his foot was. It was like the warmth was awakening all our senses. What else had the cold made me miss?

"Nah, once my toes warm up I'll be fine," he said.

We traveled on, no one telling us where we were going and what was to happen next. A Red Cross woman knocked and entered. She wore dark clothes except for a brilliantly white cap.

"You don't need those anymore," she said pointing at the Star of David on my jacket.

Werner and I didn't move. I thought of the German soldiers with the dog. What if she was wrong? What if somebody more important than her saw us without our stars?

"I'm just saying that you can take them off if you want. And food will be here soon," she added before moving on.

Werner pinched at his star, so I picked loose a thread and firmly pulled at each corner until the Star of David was free in my right hand. Then I pulled out the unruly threads and padded away the holes. Lastly, I shoved the star deep into my pocket. Just in case.

More Red Cross people arrived, bringing us four bowls of thick, hot stew with bread fresher than I had tasted in…in…I couldn't remember. Eighteen months, I guessed. The stew's scent was like new life: a rich, buttery life beyond anything I'd imagined. Mutti and Pappi sat up for a few bites before falling back asleep. Werner and I ate greedily, barely breathing as we shoveled it in. It reminded me of Mutti's cooking and eating meals at our sunny dining room table before the war.

Werner asked if we could have more. "In a little bit," we were told, and then they actually gave us more!

My eyes rolled. I burped.

"That was the best soup of my life!" I said. " I'm going to remember everything that was in it—beef, onions, potatoes, carrots—so I can make it when we get home. Look at my belly! I think I may have a soup baby!"

I deliberately pushed my stomach forward in exaggeration, and rubbed it. "And I will name her…Soupling! Lil' Soupling will grow up and make me proud. What do you think?"

My brother belched into the back of this hand, pondered it for a moment, and followed it up with another. And another. He finished with a smile.

"That. That's what I think."

"Some example you are as an uncle," I said.

I continued rubbing my stomach. I was amazed by its size. Maybe I really would gain back my lost weight. I snuggled into my pink blanket, which hugged me in return, and I napped.

In my dreams I was a dog again. The table had been abandoned and I was on the chair, lapping at the plates and butterdish, until I had to go to the bathroom. My stomach hurt. I awoke—the pain was real. My belly seemed twice the size as earlier. Werner looked equally ill and turned to belch, which steamed up the window for a moment.

"Ummm, I don't feel well," I said. "Was the food bad? Did they poison us?"

"Don't know."

We stopped a Red Cross woman as she passed in the corridor. Yes, she explained, many others felt the same. It was because we had eaten so little for so long, and the food was more than our bodies could handle. She added that our "digestive systems were compromised" and were in a "delicate condition." "Delicate" didn't seem a word related to Bergen-Belsen in any way. She told us we might get sick. We were to eat slowly, as hard as that was. She continued on, seemingly surprised by this sudden task of having to tell starving people to slow down eating. I looked at Mutti and Pappi to see their reaction, but they were still fast asleep. They hardly moved that evening and into the night. The chugging of the train lulled me into sleep.

Freedom and Loss

Switzerland and France

1945

34

Train Rails South of Camp Bergen-Belsen

January 22–23, 1945

The next day after breakfast Werner learned we were on our way to Switzerland for the exchange. No one knew how many days it would take to get there because most of the railroad tracks in Germany were damaged or destroyed. The train crept along, often stopping for hours. Our parents continued to sleep, only getting up a couple of times to take a little food and have us walk them to the toilet. They took up most of the benches in our compartment so that Werner and I sat and leaned against the windows. We ate more slowly and in smaller quantities, which helped our bellies, but now our legs and feet began to swell. The Red Cross woman came by again to say this too was normal considering our "delicate condition." My shoes hurt, but Werner told me to keep them on. If I took them off, I might be like him and not be able to get them back on again.

"Reni."

Did I hear my name?

"Reni."

It was Pappi. I turned away from looking out the window and at the stars.

"You're awake! Do you want some bread or drink?"

"Reni," he said, "Help me to the toilet."

"Food afterwards?"

He shook his head, his chin low, his head wobbly. Pappi braced himself against the wall with a shaking arm, and fell onto me as I grabbed him around the waist. His steps were small, and our shuffling to the bathroom slow. He was inside the toilet so long that I almost went for help just as the latch clicked open. Our trip back to the compartment was even slower; his breath sagged and the train lurched. After a sigh, he was quiet as he settled back onto the bench.

"Are you sure you don't want a little soup?" I asked.

"No…no more."

"We are close to Switzerland, Pappi," I said, "very close. It has been stop and go, but we've heard that we will soon be out of Germany. We really did it. The exchange. The passports. The…."

A faint "Yes."

I calmed.

"We heard there is a real hospital there. For Mutti. For Werner's foot, and for you."

"Reni…I'm sorry."

"It's okay Pappi. You're hurt. I know you need help. I don't mind."

"Not that," he said as he looked at Mutti and Werner, sleeping. "I'm not going to make it."

"What?" I said, unsure if I really made a noise.

"I'm not going to make it." Pappi leaned against me and closed his eyes.

"Yes you will. We're almost free," I reminded him. "We're so close."

"I know," he said. "I know. Free."

My hands wrapped his coat more tightly around him. His weight sank into me. My eyes welled, unable to quite spill over, but enough to blur the world. I didn't dare move, afraid that the slightest movement would do something horrible like tip Pappi away from us. My shoulder began to ache, demanding a shift. I gently shook Pappi. He didn't respond. I pushed a little harder. Nothing. I eased him down until he was lying on the bunk. Then I reached over and woke Werner, repeating Pappi's words.

Werner sat up and told me to get help.

I walked quickly down the passageway, steadying myself against the walls, and interrupted a nurse chatting with two men. She was young and said her name was Betty. I blurted out what Pappi said, and Betty excused herself. I grabbed her hand and pulled her back to our compartment where she listened to Pappi's breathing and took his pulse. She adjusted her fingers. She closed her eyes and cocked her head.

"He's very weak," she said.

"He was beaten badly back at the camp, just before we left," Werner explained.

"There may be other injuries we can't see. Did he say he was hurt anywhere specific?"

Werner and I looked at one another, hoping the other could say something helpful.

"No."

"No."

Betty felt along his neck and head and reached under his jacket, pressing around his belly. Pappi didn't move. His face was gray and stubbly.

"Mr. Hasenberg," she called, "Mr. Hasenberg, I'm Betty, Betty Ischenhauser, a nurse. Do you hear me?"

Nothing.

Betty repeated herself. She asked if he felt anything.

"When was the last time he was awake?" she asked.

I explained about going to the latrine about fifteen minutes earlier.

"There's nothing obviously broken or swollen," she said. "I can't really tell since he isn't saying anything. There's not much more I can do. I'll check in again soon after I've seen some others. Find me if anything changes."

Then there was only the rhythmic sound of steel wheels rolling along the fixed track below us. Pappi seemed so small, so much smaller than my strong Pappi who had once so easily lifted me into the air. Only his large hands, resting on his legs, hinted at his past, yet even they looked spent, as worn as a damp washrag. There was a gap between his wedding ring and finger. His skin looked too big for him. Werner and I crowded into our father, touching and holding him.

At some point in the night, Mutti shifted and sighed. We told her about Pappi. She kept her eyes open longer than she had before, only to sink away again. Her face wasn't as gray as Pappi's.

I couldn't get comfortable. Hot and cold, I took off and put back on clothes. The seat was too soft, the window too hard. Werner's foot smelled like a dead animal in a gutter, followed by the waft of dirty food bowls, and our too-long lived-in clothes. Fidgeting, I rubbed my face and scratched my scalp. It was dark in the compartment except for a couple of dim yellow lights shifting the scene into deep browns and mustards, like the newly turned soil in my grandfather's fingers from a hundred years ago in Berlin.

Twice Betty returned. She checked Mutti and nodded. She readjusted the makeshift coat pillow, then felt Pappi's wrist, which I had checked on a half-dozen times already. The third time she returned, the clouds sitting on the horizon were beginning to glow from the rising sun. Her hand stayed on our father's wrist longer than usual. She felt his neck, and bent down to listen to his breathing. She repeated her actions.

"I'm sorry," Betty said softly, "but he's de…gone. He's gone."

No, he's not, I thought. I stared at Pappi. He looked the same as he had over a minute before, an hour before. How did I miss the difference between alive and not alive? How long had he been gone? Werner shook Mutti awake, tried to talk, and choked on the message.

Betty told her.

Then Betty tidied some things, tucked in Pappi as if for a nap, and left. I wasn't sure what to say or do. If I spoke, I didn't know what sound would come out, or if it would ever stop. Realizing my hunger, I picked the food tray off the floor and mindlessly, methodically, started putting hard bread and cold soup into my mouth. Werner joined in. Mutti's eyes were closed again, so I didn't offer her any. I rocked and stared at Pappi.

It wasn't long before people started coming by to pay respects. A few friends stayed longer, praying and reciting psalms under their breath. Amens. Mutti was awake now more than ever with the comings and goings. She nodded instead of talked, keeping her eyes on Pappi as if expecting him to join in.

"Werner. Irene."

I looked up at Mr. Abraham, and his wife Gerda, friends of my parents, from Amsterdam, Westerbork, and Bergen-Belsen. Their boy, Hans, a few years younger than me, and their daughter, little Ruth, stood behind them, their hair falling over their eyes.

"Your father just died," Mr. Abraham said with eyes boring into my brother and me, before shifting down to the tray. "How can you be eating?"

I put down my spoon. Werner wiped his hands on a napkin. Was it bad manners to eat around death? Was it bad for us to eat when we were hungry?

35

Biberach, Germany

January 24, 1945

People came and went. Our window brightened blue as the sun rose. The train stopped. A guard came by and told us that we had arrived in the town of Biberach. There was a German internment camp here with mostly British and a few American prisoners. They were taking off the dead and very sick—those who might not live long enough to make it to Switzerland for the exchange—and welcoming onboard healthy British and American prisoners. I overheard that the Germans had promised a certain number of exchange prisoners and they needed to deliver.

Could the sickest include Mutti, or maybe even Werner? Nazi officers, their eyes peering from under sloped caps, looked in on us.

"That one's dead," one said with a gesture from his chin.

Mutti nodded, trying to sit up higher.

"Remove him," said the other officer. "We can leave the body at the station."

I hadn't thought about it: what would become of Pappi now?

Two men in overalls appeared behind the officers in the doorway.

"Can't we take him to Switzerland?" Werner asked. "To be buried… properly?"

The men in overalls said they were taking the body. We could follow them outdoors to say what we needed to.

"*Bitte*, please, officers," Mutti said. "I can't go outside. Give us a few minutes alone."

By "us" she meant her and Pappi.

Werner and I helped move Mutti to the bench next to our father, and nestled her in. I saw his death clearly then, his white skin holding no color or hints of motion. His hearty hands that had held our family together for so long were at rest.

"Go," she said, "I'll be okay."

We waited outside the compartment in the hallway, with the men in overalls. After a few minutes Werner looked in. Mutti was asleep, curled over Pappi. We entered. I wiped her face with the sleeves of my coat. Werner and I each gently took one of Mutti's arms, lifted her away from Pappi and placed her back on the opposite bench.

I buttoned Pappi's tattered winter coat under his chin, and felt the cool stiffness of his neck. I gulped down my tears as Werner told the men to enter. I turned up his collar and straightened his coat as best I could. One man gathered his body just under the arms, and the other man picked up his feet. They lifted Pappi's likeness with ease and angled it out the door. We followed.

The dry, bitter cold battered my face and shoulders; I started shivering. How easy it was to get used to warmth. Dozens of passengers—some sick and some past sickness—were carried and guided off our train. How the Germans decided who should stay was a mystery. Nearby, healthy, clean prisoners waited, bags in hands and eyes on us, to board. Suddenly I was afraid it was a lie, and we would all be forced to stay here with Mutti, traveling on alone. I calmed my breathing, grabbed Werner's hand, and focused on moving my feet.

Snow filled the space between the tracks and ties. The sweet scent of tobacco drifted and blew away. The Biberach station was as simple and plain as a wooden casket. The men asked Werner for Pappi's name. They placed Pappi on a bench by the door to the station, and pinned a note to his coat: *John Hasenberg. Died January 23, 1945.* Then they backed away. Everyone backed away. It was just the three of us.

Only last night Pappi and I had talked. Before that we had eaten together, slept in the same place, and stood by each other for hours. He had hugged me. He had comforted me. He had always played with me. He had leaned in close when people took photos of us. He had been so strong for so long. How would I live without him? I collapsed into Werner. He braced himself with his good foot.

"He knew we were okay," Werner said. "He'd taken us this far. It was far enough."

I wanted to protest, but I was dazed, expecting my soul to flee from the pain, to kill me.

And now Pappi was to be left alone in a place we didn't know, and we had no idea what would happen to him. The wind hurt my eyes. And the line of people waiting for the train was growing shorter. I straightened the note pinned to his coat, making sure it was secure, patted his rumpled coat, lightly kissed his forehead.

You sweet little one,
you belong to me,
you belong to me,
you are the most lovable.

We climbed back onboard and into our compartment. I wanted to crawl into a dark hole. I found my way to the corner of the bench where he had just been and hid under my blanket. Was his death my fault? I squeezed my eyes shut. If I had paid attention earlier, if I had seen that he was hurt. How had he hidden his injuries? Even Betty hadn't found anything. If the camps had taught me anything, it was how to provide comfort. But that wasn't enough. I knew that no matter what else happened or where we ended up or how I would grow up or how old I would become, I would forever remember this time, this absence.

My next fear was Mutti. Her survival now seemed as fragile as a dying flower's last petal. With one parent gone, I clung to the other. Werner wasn't getting any better, either. His toes had not only begun to swell, they were turning brown, the smell of rot was stronger. It wouldn't be long before Mutti and Werner couldn't walk alone to the bathroom. I wept more heavily into my blanket when Werner and Mutti were asleep so that I could hide my mounting fear.

36

St. Gallen, Switzerland

January 25, 1945

For two years our journeys across Europe had not been our choice. My family's trips were free, courtesy of Hitler and his Nazis, yet had cost so much. Each trip had taken us to a worse place, as we lost more and more: our freedom, health, dignity, and now Pappi.

We reached the Swiss town of Kreutzlingen, just over the border from Konstanz, Germany. Our train parked next to another that faced the opposite direction on neighboring tracks. German and Swiss officers and guards tramped about outside and inside. German guards looked ornate—badges, pins, piping, eagles, skulls—yet scraggly compared to the Swiss soldiers whose uniforms were simple and well-pressed, their faces unlined, saved from years of war.

"The Swiss even *look* neutral," Werner said.

This was it, the exchange, that we had dreamed about. The Germans ordered us off the train that would soon be heading back into Germany, and the Swiss ordered us onto the other train that would take us farther into their country. In the snow and cold between the two tracks, we passed the newly freed German civilian prisoners. These people were what we were worth. One of them equaled one of us. I looked at their clean coats, full suitcases, shiny shoes, plump hands, and full faces. Like us, they may have recently been prisoners, but it was obvious that the Allies hadn't treated them the way we had been treated. A few dizzy, brilliant snowflakes freckled the air as the Germans passed us and boarded the cars we had just occupied.

"*Heil Hitler! Heil Hitler! Heil Hitler!*"

Their joy merged into a chant. They were going home.

I was born in Germany, like my parents and their parents and their parents before them, but we had been forced to leave almost ten years before. We weren't going home to anything. Maybe Amsterdam at some point, but it felt as if we didn't have a home anywhere. The Americans in our group started their own chant.

"USA! USA! USA!"

We boarded our new train and began our journey into Switzerland, the country I had dreamed of for a decade, as I'd traveled with my heroine, Heidi. Heidi was the star of her own adventures, and I wanted the same. But *adventure* wasn't the word I would use for my life. More like perils or whatever…not adventure. In the book, Heidi's parents died, so she returned to Switzerland to live with her grandfather. My grandfather, grandmother, uncles, aunts, and friends were all dead. And now, my Pappi was dead too. Heidi and I had things in common that I never had wanted in common.

After two days, our Swiss train finally halted. I opened my eyes, groggy and full from my body's rhythmic napping, eating, and napping again. Outside, steam floated by like clouds, the shapes of spires, buildings, and mountaintops formed and disappeared in the mist. Where were we? I knew one thing: Bergen-Belsen was now far behind us.

I rubbed the sleep off my face and watched as dark-uniformed men and women trudged by outside, then climbed aboard with a blast of cold. They poked their heads into our compartment. I stiffened under my pink blanket, the one I had carried through everything, bracing for a yell, a raised baton, or a lunging German shepherd.

"Time to de-board!" a woman bellowed in an odd German accent. She walked up and down the aisle, yelling it over and over. "Time to de-board, please!"

Please? When had I last heard that?

My mother, Mutti, didn't budge or look up. She was curled on the bench just like my father had been two days before. She was wrapped in her ragged gray dress and threadbare stockings, her head heavy in the folds of a coat bunched into a pillow. I gently cupped her face in my hands.

"Mutti, Mutti, wake up, wake up," I said.

"Reni," she said, pushing her bangs out of her eyes. She wore her hair short, especially because of the lice, but she kept the front long. She widened her storm-gray eyes, trying to awake. I loved her big, pretty eyes, even when she was so ill.

"I'm here," I said.

One bony hand alighted on the back of my head. I hugged her close, but not hard. Then I turned toward Werner, asleep on the other bench. I tapped his good leg.

"Werner. Wake up."

People shuffled by in the aisle.

"What's all the ruckus?" Werner asked, shaking his head so his bangs fell into place. His eyes were so much like Pappi's, I thought, always a little puffy.

"We've stopped," I said. "I think we're really free."

"Well, that's good news," he said, grimacing and looking down. There was no way he was going to put his shoe back on. His injured foot was balloon-swollen.

He gathered his coat and one small bag, favoring his good shoed foot.

"Reni, help me up," Mutti whispered.

I tilted her small body up off the bench, my arms seeming to sink into nothing but her clothes. She was as frail as a dry leaf. I leaned her against the door frame and gathered our belongings: two knapsacks with clothes, Pappi's shaving kit, some papers and photos, a couple of brown pots, and a few utensils. Back in Amsterdam our dining room table had had more on it than we now owned. Gone were the smooth white coffee pitcher, the slight silverware, the crystal sugar bowl with the silver top, the china with little cups just for eggs. Little cups crafted for only one pleasant purpose. I grabbed my blanket and my knapsack, and helped my brother. The dent in the leather bench that Werner left behind slowly rose as if a spirit was trying to join us, and all I could think of was Pappi. I could feel Pappi's hug. I could feel his hand on my shoulder.

Neither Mutti nor Werner could walk alone, and I couldn't carry them. Forcing my eyes open, I headed out into the aisle, bumping into the large belly of a man dressed in night blue wool. He was with two nurses in white.

"We need help," I said.

Nobody replied, but their eyes said everything. A nurse took a breath and a step back. Her makeup looked loud on her pale features. Her clothes were pristine, not a thread out of place, and not a stain anywhere. How was that possible? How must we look? For the first time I saw our weakness, our sickness, and our filth. Mutti and Werner looked so old, their eye sockets deep as buckets. Even my beloved blanket suddenly looked tired, and more gray than pink.

Gloved men carried off Mutti and Werner in narrow, sagging stretchers, instructing each other to be careful around corners. I followed. At the last step before the concrete platform, I was taken by the elbow as if I were being courted. On the platform, our belongings surrounded us like beach debris after a storm. I stared at the train door we had just exited, and out of habit, expected Pappi to walk through it.

The sky was as blue and thick as a baby's quilt. The bitter wind slapped my cheeks. Toward the center of town, pastel buildings with crimson roofs stood shoulder-to-shoulder like sentinels in front of steeples, and a clock tower jabbed up at the sparse clouds. In the other direction a few houses speckled the hill that rolled up to violet mountains that hemmed the horizon. I had never seen anything so tall, as if the peaks were scratching at the doors to heaven. The train station was a palace: five stories of great, curved stone. Nothing was smeared, nothing was broken, and nothing was makeshift. If we seemed unreal to the people here to help us, this place was unreal to me, like a page ripped from a fairy tale.

Important-looking people glanced at us from behind clipboards, sometimes pointing, sometimes making little marks, and sometimes asking questions. A doctor with a wire-thin mustache gave Werner's foot a close look, bending it back and forth as Werner swallowed and grimaced, before moving over to Mutti, travelling her wrist with his fingers. After finding what he was looking for, he closed his eyes and moved his lips...one, pause, two, pause, three, pause. Then he spent time looking her up and down: in her mouth, ears, and eyes. Mutti reminded me of a baby bird fallen from its nest.

"This one," the doctor directed men with a nod toward Werner. "Werner Hasenberg. Sixteen. To the hospital. The foot is bad. I'm concerned about gangrene."

"And for this one…" he said, pointing at Mutti, "Gertrude Hasenberg…." He stopped and whispered to a nurse who looked at me before walking off.

Werner was carried off before I could say anything to him. I returned to Mutti. A balding man with in a hefty overcoat knelt by her. Deep grooves divided the space between his eyebrows, and lines ran from his nose to the corners of his mouth.

"Who are you?" I asked.

"He's the priest," a nurse said.

"Can he help Mutti?"

"He's giving last rites."

"Last…what? Dying rites? Oh, no, no…."

The world blurred.

"Excuse me, Father," someone said behind me.

I turned to find Mr. Wolf, the dwarf, standing next to me, straightening the glasses on his nose. Mr. Wolf's wife was in a nearby stretcher, with their two children next to her. The priest finished a sentence and looked up, his hand still on Mutti's forehead. He didn't have to look very high. "In the Jewish faith we give traditional death prayers—the *kaddish*—after the person has died." Mr. Wolf stretched his back while keeping both hands on his cane. "Not before."

"Jewish?" The priest repeated. "All of you?"

"Most. Probably all."

"I was told there were refugees, some dying."

"We're both. Is there a rabbi here?" asked Mr. Wolf.

"No."

"Then bless you for helping. But don't bless Trudi yet," he said. He turned to me and added, "I'm so sorry, Reni."

The priest told a nurse that he would return. Then he left with a look in my direction, but not quite at me.

"Your mother is very, very sick. Do you understand?" the nurse said. "We will do our best."

I knelt down and held Mutti's hand, trying not to wring it too hard. I looked at her face. She was asleep. Her eyes were shut and still. *She can't die*, I told myself, *not after everything we have been through. Not after Pappi.* I rose, still grasping her hand as the orderlies picked her up. The nurse stood in front of me and put a hand on my shoulder. I looked up at her. I felt a slight squeeze.

"You have to stay here. The hospital is full with the sickest. You aren't that sick."

"But I need to go with her! She's my mother, and my brother is gone already," I said and grabbed the nurse's hand hard and felt the bones grind together.

The nurse didn't flinch. I tried to move, but she held firm. The thought of being alone, even for a short time, was too much. I tried going around her, but her hand stayed on my shoulder and then one grasped my other shoulder. The space between Mutti and me got longer. Mutti and the orderlies were lost in a sea of people and noise. Suddenly weak, I had no energy to fight. Even my head seemed heavy.

Scraps of conversations drifted around me.

"…so…broken."

"…never seen anything like this…"

"…barely alive…"

"You'll see them again."

"What?" I said.

"You'll see them again," the nurse repeated.

I surrendered to directions and orders, and got into a line, moving behind a large man to block the wind. We were told that we would be taken to a place to rest and eat. After climbing into the back of yet another large gray truck full of people like me, somebody piped, "Welcome to Switzerland." With elbows on knees, I let my head droop and roll with the bumps in the road.

"Welcome. Make your bed anywhere along the wall there," said a guard at the entrance of a huge barn, by a table. He thrust out two neatly folded dark gray blankets sandwiched between his hands. Behind him another soldier was preparing two more blankets, and behind him another was straightening a bench of blankets. I took mine.

The late afternoon sunlight pouring in from high-curved windows striped the inner walls as white as the outside snow. The lower halves of the walls were painted brown, dented and chipped, and the floor was made of packed dirt. All around the walls, a thick layer of hay cushioned the ground. A row of wooden tables ran down the center of the building, end-to-end. Carefully, I watched the guards, their rifles slung across their shoulders and draping down their backs. They were Swiss, I repeated to myself, not German.

"Let me help you with your things," said a voice behind me as a hand took one of my bags. I dropped my blankets, and grabbed my bag back in one motion.

"Okay, okay," a guard said, putting his hands in the air, black leather-gloved palms up. He had on a stiff round cap with a black visor, and he wore knee-high boots—the sign of an officer. He had a long face shaped like an inverted triangle. His eyes and mouth were small.

"They looked heavy for such a girl," he said. "I didn't mean to scare you."

The knapsacks *were* heavy, but what if he *had* wanted to scare me? What if this was some kind of trick? I turned, and, with my eyes to the ground and hunching back, I walked away. I found a space near a man who was already asleep, his head on the still folded blankets and his coat over his legs. Gray stubble ran over his chin, up his cheeks, and over his head. His nose and thin mouth reminded me of Pappi.

It was warm for an unheated barn. As we settled in, the guards told us we were not to leave and not to talk with any Swiss people, even if we had friends or relatives in the area. They said it was for our own good that we were being quarantined. We might be infectious and we wouldn't want to spread disease.

I lay down atop my straw and wool nest and put my pink blanket to my face until we were called to eat. The food arrived in large, perfectly white, heavy, unbroken porcelain bowls with matching saucers. The soup was even better than what we'd had on the train. I drained two bowls of the rich, meat-filled broth, huffing on each spoonful twice before shoveling it in. And then they brought the sandwiches. Dark rye bread with cheese and salami. I stared at the layers and fondled the crust between my thumb and fingers. Two soft, fresh slices all to myself. I ate until I licked my fingers clean.

The food gave me courage. I tracked down the officer in the tall boots and round cap who had tried to help me with my bags, who was watching over people eating. A woman in dark pants and a bulky sweater that was tucked in was talking to him about the need for more food. He nodded as she talked, keeping his eyes on the eaters. She left, adjusting the sweater in her pants.

"My mother and brother," I said to the officer, "are Gertrude and Werner Hasenberg. They are in the hospital. How can I find out about them and their health?"

"Don't worry *Fraülein*, they'll be fine."

"I'd like to see them, I mean, I *need* to see them."

And then he said a bunch of other stuff like: "They're being well cared for. A lot of work went into bringing you here. You should be happy to be here at all. We'll get you in touch with your mother and brother as soon as we can."

I felt it was a lie. I retreated, scared.

37

St. Gallen, Switzerland

January 26-29, 1945

The next day, I talked to the same officer several times. He told me again and again not to worry, and finally that I *needed* to stop worrying. That afternoon we were driven back toward the center of town to a school that had been made into a temporary hospital. It was a big building, with many roofs and walls pointing and swooping in all directions, and a little brick entrance that fed into a long hall lined with doors. Beyond each door each room had rows upon rows of thin metal-framed beds, on which the ill, hurt, and weary were tucked under crisp white sheets and smothering blankets. The heads of the beds could move up and down, and most were angled up a little. Everybody looked at us, and we looked at all of them. Hair was combed back, faces clean. We were filthy, with hay in our hair. We were all looking for somebody we knew. At the foot of each bed was a chair for the person's clothing, with unchipped porcelain bedpans underneath.

Did I hear my name?

"Reni! Reni!"

Werner! I turned to the left and right.

"Over here, near the window."

His face! I started toward him, bumped into a woman, apologized, and ran to his smile. I squeezed him hard.

"Wow, careful, I'm an invalid!"

I didn't let go. Oh, how good it felt to see him.

"It's okay, Reni. What's wrong?"

I cried from relief, the tears flowing down my face and onto his shirt. He was alive, and I wasn't alone. I kept his hand in mine while I told him about the barn and my first night alone, ever.

"Don't get me wrong," I added feeling ungrateful, "I'm glad we're here. It just isn't how I expected."

"No," he agreed.

"What about you?" I asked.

"I guess I'll be okay. I mean, I can't walk. I might lose the toe, but I'm okay."

"What about Mutti?" I asked, almost afraid I had.

"She's in a real hospital, not a makeshift one like this one. I haven't seen her. Hey, don't squeeze my hand so hard."

I heard his heartbeat as I pressed my head against his chest.

"Your hair needs cleaning."

I ran my hand over my hair and felt the mats in it, then I felt his. "You showered!"

"Yeah, there are showers in the locker rooms."

"You smell like lavender."

"No, its edelweiss. The soap is edelweiss."

He was right.

"Wait, you might lose your toe?"

"It's okay. Nothing, really, compared to everything else."

"Like Mutti...." I said. I was going to also say, "and Pappi," but I couldn't bring myself to say his name. It would hurt just to say it, so I decided to be more like Heidi and lighten the situation. "Well, if you're okay with it, I will be too, I guess. I'll just have to give you a nickname like 'Old Four-toed Werner.'"

"Nine. Nine-toed Werner."

Werner was right again.

That night, I had my first hot shower in over a year. It felt like magic. I soaped up and watched the dirt swirl down the drain until I, too, only smelled of edelweiss. Two nurses sandwiched a new bed into the space next to Werner for me. A real bed—right next to Werner's. Hearing Werner's familiar noises that night made me feel much better. Before finally falling asleep, I imagined that our family, all four of us, were high in the Alps, at a fancy hotel as upright and clean as everything else in

Switzerland. We went sledding, and even tried skiing. We played until we ate, and we ate until we rested, and started all over again.

The next few days passed in a blur of sleep and warmth and food. One evening, just after wolfing down our dinner, a Swiss official quieted us, getting to his point quickly and loudly.

"Tomorrow, you will leave by train, for the port of Marseilles. In France. From there, ships are heading to the United States and elsewhere. Please pack your bags. We leave by nine a.m."

"Elsewhere? Where's that?"

"I don't know," Werner said. "Ask."

Tugging the sleeve of a tall official who walked by, I explained our situation. "Can we stay in Switzerland? It is closer to the Netherlands and our home. And we don't speak English."

He looked directly down at me and slowed down his way of speaking German.

"You are displaced persons, and Switzerland is not your country."

"We are Germans living in Amsterdam. I mean we lived in Amsterdam," said Werner.

"Both under Nazi control. You can't go to either place: Germany or Holland."

"What about Ecuador?" I asked. "We have Ecuadorian passports."

"Your Ecuadorian passports aren't valid," the tall official said. "They got you out of the camps, but they aren't good for passage to South America."

"Well, if we don't have anywhere to go, then I don't understand why we can't just stay."

"Young lady, there are too many refugees, and more are coming. You must go."

"What about our mother? She's very sick."

He told us he would check on her condition. Then he was called away. He didn't come back. I asked another nurse. She said she would check, though it was getting late. I didn't see the nurse after that, but a man in wire-rimmed glasses came after the lights were dimmed.

"Your mother is Gertrude Hasenberg?" he asked.

Werner and I nodded.

"She is very sick, and in critical care. That's all I know. We'll see in the morning." He left.

"Too bad we couldn't just use the Henki Express," I said. "You could make us tickets to anywhere."

"Pappi liked the Henki Express," he said. "He said it was important to get to know other people in other places. That if we do that, it was a sure way to have more friends and fewer enemies. I'm not sure I agree anymore."

We seemed to have a lot of enemies, and they had looked us right in the face.

"Maybe it's still true," I said. "The Nazis never bothered to get to know us."

"They hated everything they saw."

"I don't think they really saw us at all."

38

St. Gallen, Switzerland

January 30, 1945

n the morning, everyone who could walk was directed outside to a truck. I told Werner I'd see him at the train. The station platform was littered with the displaced, some in stretchers and wheelchairs. The mountain breeze tightened my face. Spirits seemed hopeful—smiles on faces, quickened steps, and hugs and touches between people—yet I couldn't stop worrying about Mutti. I hoisted the knapsack straps across my shoulders.

After waiting what seemed like too long a time for Mutti and Werner, I decided to search, weaving like a needle through the crowd until I stitched a path from the engine to the rear of the back train, with no luck. Panic pricked at me. I shifted the weight of my knapsack. I scanned the faces of the officials, approaching one with big cheeks and soft eyes who was talking with three people. I waited my turn.

He listened to me and said, "If I were you I'd just stay right here so you can watch for them. When did you lose sight of them?"

When I told him I hadn't lost sight of them—I hadn't seen them here at all—he directed me to a man with a clipboard. After letting me spill a few sentences, the clipboard man held up a hand.

"Wait a minute. Name?" he asked a man who approached him.

"Schlamm," a man said.

He made three check marks on his sheet, and three people boarded. He looked at me.

"Name?"

"Hasenberg," I said. "Irene. And Gertrude and Werner, my mother and brother. All Hasenbergs."

He made one check mark. Then a couple came up behind me and pushed forward.

"Name?"

"I just said Hasenberg."

"No, not you. This couple."

"Levy," the man said.

He made two check marks and nodded. "There is only one of you leaving," he said to me. "Only one Hasenberg: Irene."

"That's not right."

"That's what I have. Now get on board."

"Werner isn't on the list? Gertrude?" I asked. I tried to see the writing on his clipboard.

"No," he said. "Now...."

"Come on young lady, let's go," said a man behind me. He shoved his luggage up into the car just as the train whistled.

"Now *go*," said the official. "Your family is right behind you. Not on this train, but on another, I'm sure. Go."

I couldn't speak, but my head started shaking slowly back and forth.

"Name?"

"No...no...no, no, NO!" my voice rose. "I can't leave without them. I can't! They need me!"

"Calm down...."

"They need me!"

"Calm down."

"I need to ask my brother something! I need to say good-bye!" I panted. "I need *them!*"

Voices told me to calm down. I looked along the train, the steam, and the white light glinting off a distant, high window. I needed something to hold my gaze. Everything was a blur. I could barely swallow. I was lifted up and in. Placed on a bench. The train chugged to life. The station rolled away behind us.

My numbness collected in the corners of my eyes, the tears welling and dripping through the day and into the night. Food and drink came, sat uneaten, and was taken away. We travelled west toward France, stretching out the distance between my family and me until I felt I'd snap. I begged anybody who looked important to let me return to my family. One said, "We'll see what we can do," but did nothing. They began ignoring me.

My legs twitched so I wandered the train. Families and groups hunkered about. My feet pulled me from car to car. Eventually, I found myself at the very back of the train leaning my forehead against the frigid glass, watching the rails disappear into a point on the horizon. The trees, snow-blotched fields, telephone lines, and red-roofed village buildings passed and changed, but not the rails. They always seemed to converge at the same spot, the places and the people I had left behind.

The Swiss had done what the Nazis hadn't been able to: tear apart my family. For two years and despite the thickening threat of death, we had stayed together through the camps, although I had heard the terms "concentration" and "extermination" camps now used. The four of us were finally free, but broken apart by death, sickness, and rules.

I looked over a cliff of loneliness that felt emptier than even the hunger I had felt in the camps. I had nothing and no one. I was disowned by my birth country of Germany, and couldn't return to my adopted country of Holland. I wasn't even a prisoner anymore. In its own way, Camp Bergen-Belsen had been my last place of belonging for the simple reason it was the last place the four of us had lived together. It was a place of darkness that I was trying to shove into the shadowed corners of my mind, but I could already tell my heart wouldn't allow it, not fully. I clung to that last memory of home.

39

Train Rails through Switzerland and France

January 30–February 8, 1945

"Hello, are you okay?" came a voice.

I turned around and looked up into a round face grooved with worry: a woman about Mutti's age, but well-fed and well-dressed. Not fat or fancy, but definitely not from Bergen-Belsen.

"Yes," I said. She looked kind enough to ignore. I turned back to watching the railroad ties flash by.

"Mmm. I'm Mrs. Eisenberg. What's your name?"

"Irene Hasenberg."

"You're from Bergen-Belsen."

I nodded.

"Oh my," she sighed behind me. "I'm from New York. I've spent the last two years trapped in Germany, in Biberach. I do so hope 1945 will be a better year than the ones before it. The month of January always does give one hope. Where's your family?"

"Not here."

"I'm sorry. I shouldn't have assumed. I mean with so much loss...."

"We left my father, I mean his body, in Biberach...."

"I am so sorry. Where you are headed?"

"Don't know. My mother is back in Switzerland...she is very sick, she has been sick for so long and nobody really knows what it is; she might die like my father...my brother...."

And then I blurted my story, still unfolding, my words scattering everywhere as if I had spilled something.

"Irene, I'm alone, too," she said. "I can take care of you."

My eyes felt very heavy.

"I can take you to America. I promise."

Taking my hand, she brought me back to her compartment, where she pulled me onto her lap and held me. A knock on the door delivered more Red Cross rations. I pulled aside the strings that held the brown box together. Small tin cans and a small can opener fell out. I opened and ate pudding, rice, and fish. I stared at the chocolate bar. Was the old Droste still hidden atop our cupboard back in Amsterdam, collecting dust? Then I just stared into the corner.

At some point in the afternoon, Mrs. Eisenberg left. She returned after a brief period, dabbing her eyes. She sat down next to me and held both my hands in hers.

"Irene, I am so sorry," she said. "I can't take you to America. Without a US passport or other documents, they aren't letting people in. I should not have promised. I did find out that you are going to Africa."

The next few days felt torn from somebody else's tale, and from a book I couldn't follow because I couldn't concentrate, my thoughts ricocheting down anguished corridors of dread.

We arrived in Marseilles, and somehow ended up at the port. The largest ship was a white passenger ship held fast to the wharf ropes as thick as tree trunks. The sides were painted in tall letters spelling "Gripsholm" and "Sverige," and with the Swedish flag. Gold and blue stripes ran up and down the ship. The *Gripsholm* was preparing to take Mrs. Eisenberg and others back to America.

We spent two days on a floating hospital ship before being split into two groups. I found myself in the smaller one. The bigger group was, like Mrs. Eisenberg, going to depart on the *Gripsholm*. She hugged me and then made her way up the gangplank with a wave.

My group walked to another wharf and onto the *Citta di Alessandria*, a dumpy, dirty Italian freighter. I ran my hand up the railing as we boarded, my palm turning red with rust. A man in a stained white uniform told us we were heading to Algeria, but not a word was said about why, what for, or for how long.

Beds lined the walls of the long room, their sheets and blankets tucked taut, their mattresses encased within low wooden walls, which, according to the pantomime of an Italian sailor, would keep us from falling out in rough seas. With his hands in a fist under his tilted head, the sailor rocked his body back and forth, then twirled his hands in the air, lower and lower until he spread out his fingers near the floor. *Splat.* He repeated the gestures until I nodded that I understood. With a satisfied smile, he tapped his white cap before backing away.

"Wait," I called. "When do we eat?" I pretended to put something in my mouth, then pointed to his watch, which he held up in front of my face, pointing to the twelve with his right finger. Noon.

"Now? Can I eat now?" I poked at the nine and the six on his watch face, the current time.

He shook his head while making a pout and departing with a shrug.

So I sat on a top bunk, my belongings a small mountain on the floor. The room was stuffy and smelled musty with a far-off whiff of oil. My eyes fluttered. I fell back on the gray blanket, leaning to one side so I didn't hit my head against the wall.

My stomach growled. I was already famished, though it had not been very long since breakfast. I could hear people mulling about. I kept my eyes closed. I should do something, I thought faintly.

You're waiting for lunch. That's good enough.

I didn't want to move. Not for a thousand years, unless it was to join Mutti and Werner, or to eat. My heart and soul had thrown everything else off the lifeboat, so to speak.

Long ago when I had gone to school, Miss Pino had taught my class that the heart is a muscle. She had flexed her fist for emphasis. She had talked about the importance of exercise, of building strong muscles including the heart, but not to overdo it and pull something. My heart was pulled, ripped. It was trapped now, beating on my ribs like a hurt and frightened animal. Thump. Thump. Thump.

I heard a familiar voice and opened my eyes.

It was stout Mrs. Abraham, her smooth, dark hair pulled back from her high forehead. I hadn't seen her since we had left Pappi's wrapped body on the train station platform, when Werner and I were eating, and her husband chastised us: *How can you eat when your father has just died?* I turned my head to see if Mr. Abraham was here too, but there were only her two children, Hans and Ruth, behind her, and the pantomiming sailor. Behind them more people who must have been prisoners like me—judging by their clothes and skinny bodies—found their bunks and collapsed onto them.

I greeted Mrs. Abraham, but I didn't want to talk. She looked at me like I was something she had lost a long time ago and had just found.

She had the same look that Mrs. Eisenberg had had: concerned. Was she going to make promises, too, that she couldn't keep?

"We need to tidy up," she directed at no one in particular.

When I didn't move, she repeated herself two more times. Finally, I descended, hung my jacket on the hook on the door, and put my bag under the bunk. I climbed back up and balanced a photo of my parents on my bunk shelf—Mutti was as tall as Pappi in her heels. Then I opened Pappi's razor kit with its long-gone scent of sandalwood shaving soap. As if in a trance, I folded my pink blanket and placed it at the foot of the bunk, flattening out all the folds and picking out slivers of straw nestled in the fibers—remnants of Bergen-Belsen.

Mrs. Abraham murmured something to her kids and left.

My hand continued flowing over my blanket; I mindlessly smoothed out every imperfection.

As I slipped between the taut, cold sheets, someone loosened the porthole window, swinging it open. I fell asleep to the sounds of seagulls, a distant laugh, the sea smell, a breeze across my neck, and finally the image of Pappi in his gray pinstripe suit. He was reclining in a large green-and-white striped beach chair with a drooping hood that offered protection from sand and sun. He was smiling, his hair parted like a fold and slicked back, his right leg thrown over the left. He had come directly from the office to see us, not even bothering to change into his bathing suit. He wanted to be with us that badly. In my dream, I started to come up from the surf where I was playing, but was bogged down by swirling sands that buried my feet. The hem of my short dress was wet and heavy, my legs were tugged forward and backward by the currents, my feet locked in the sand. A force so much bigger than me was pushing me around in every direction except toward Pappi.

I awoke startled and panting, my emptiness and hunger having returned. And I was shivering. I closed the porthole window and descended to the lower decks and followed some people to dinner.

We sat at wooden tables that had raised edges to keep the sliding dishes from flying off. *Splat*. As Mr. Abraham sat next to me, I stiffened, waiting for a rebuke of some sort. The kitchen door swung open with a bang—I jolted—as sailors strolled in with platters of hamburgers. I gazed at the pile of greasy miracles in the center of our table. Even the rolls glistened. I only started eating after Mr. Abraham took his first bite.

I tried to make Mutti proud and eat slowly, but I couldn't. Like a wolf, I pushed in the food, taking messy bites before I had gulped the last, juices streaming down my chin that I didn't bother wiping until the sandwich was gone. I inhaled water to force down the last choking chunk before grabbing another burger, and then the empty platter was swept off and another full one took its place.

"This'll put fat on your bones," Mr. Abraham said, and commanded, "Keep eating!"

As when we were on the train leaving Bergen-Belsen, my stomach was suddenly so big I couldn't breathe. Barely excusing myself, I bolted topside, my hand holding my belly as if it were a dike trying to hold back a spring flood. On deck, I stretched out, my back to a wall, and looked at Marseilles and the silhouette of the church on the hill backlit by a deepening purple sky.

Light fell across the deck as a door opened and a cook came outside, his white apron stained brown, a cigarette clinging lightly to his lips. He carried a large steel bucket that pulled his body to one side.

"*Buonasera*," he greeted me, making his cigarette bob.

At the railing, he lifted the bucket with a grunt and let dozens upon dozens of hamburgers splash into the sea. More meat than I had seen in two years. Enough to keep all of us healthy; enough to have saved Pappi. All that cooking, wasted. I got up and ran to the railing. This time I threw up over the side. The cook laughed, his cigarette falling to the deck where he ground out the orange glow with his heel.

"You sick already? The ship still in port. No big waves yet!"

Late the next morning I awoke to thrumming engines. The sea was glass-smooth. It was almost February, but it was warm, and I freed myself from my brown, frayed sweater once I was on deck. It hung in my hand looking filthy and grotesque, like a dead animal. I wanted to hurl it overboard, but knew better, because I didn't know where I would end up.

"Hi, Reni." It was Lex Roseboom. "Warm, huh?"

"Yeah."

"I mean, I saw you take off your sweater."

"It's gross."

"It's not so bad."

I didn't say anything, so he cleared his throat and went on. "I'm sorry about your father. He was a great man. I mean, my dad says he was."

I fingered my sweater, continuing my silence.

Lex said, "Look, I just wanted to say that. That I'm sorry."

"Okay." I managed to say.

"That's it. See you around."

My mood didn't change. At lunch I kept my head down, creating the shortest distance between the food and my mouth. Even after three helpings of potatoes, I was scraping the empty platter with my spoon.

The crewman collecting the platters tapped my shoulder. "If you come to the kitchen, there is more," he said in simple German. He had a pointy nose and chin, and heavy eyebrows.

"My name is Francesco."

"Reni."

I followed him. The relative calm of the dining hall disappeared in the din of the kitchen where men in white pants, t-shirts, coats, and hats were pivoting and maneuvering around each other, all the while swinging plates, cleavers, boiling pots, and huge sides of meat. Every movement seemed a preamble to disaster, only to be averted by inches. It was as smooth as a Shirley Temple dance scene. Francesco guided me to trays and trays of cut meats, eggs, fried potatoes, and loaves of bread.

"Eat."

I hesitated, remembering back to the camp. Food was power. What if he wanted something from me in return, like some of the guards at Bergen-Belsen wanted from girls?

"I'm full," I said, "I need to go."

"Really? But you look so hungry? It's okay," Francesco said, "nobody will hurt you. You eat what you want and we go back."

A jacketed, high-capped cook came over, looking at Francesco from over the top of his glasses. They talked, hands moving until the cook smiled, nodded, and extended his open hand to the feast. Once I started eating I couldn't stop. He started to ask questions, but I wasn't sure if he was directing them at me since he seemed to be talking to himself. How did I get so skinny? Where was I from? I didn't respond because I didn't want to. I met his eyes after each question, but kept chewing, the food devouring my thoughts and feelings.

Rebirth

Camp Jeanne d'Arc, Algeria

1945

40

Philippeville, Algeria

February, 1945

For the next two days, that was my routine: eat, sleep, and worry about my Mutti and Werner. Then someone on deck called out that he saw land. For the next few hours I watched the smudged horizon grow into hills, white buildings with orange roofs, and trees with sweeping trunks and brushy tops as if ready to paint the sky. This was the northern coast of Africa, then it was Algeria, and finally, the port of Philippeville. A small tugboat glided out and led the *Citta di Alessandria* through the maze of harbored ships until we hugged a pier, and we were tied in place. It was dinnertime, too late, we were told, to leave the ship.

The next morning we ate and packed. Sun-reddened British soldiers in caps and rolled-up khaki pants, and bronzed Algerian men in robes with their heads wrapped in long white scarves, swarmed the jetty. With yells, commands, and laughs they brought our belongings ashore in their hard hands and on their broad backs. The Algerians' voices and words were deep-throated and fast as if they were singing along with a tune I couldn't hear. The air was heavy with the smell of engines, fish, new spices, and fires. I merged into the throng of people walking down a bobbing gangplank that was so steep I had to watch every step. I steadied myself as I crossed the swaying wooden plank, suspended above the sea, and onto the continent of Africa.

Soldiers guided us toward a string of cars and military ambulances. I'd never seen land like this except on muted postcards. We passed rows of palm trees that lined the road as if at attention. Our route through the city began by passing densely packed, white-arched buildings, then moved on to jumbles of earth-colored houses outside the city center. The flat, gray town roads turned to tracks of red gravel. On our right a never-ending beach swept up the coast, running between the turquoise water with endless whitecaps and growing cliffs. Our driver slowed for cattle, goats, and men on weaving bicycles. The heat was intense even with all the windows open, and I blinked in the dust.

The hills grew and became steeper. We headed higher. Once we veered and stopped to let a convoy of trucks pass. A group of people were coming down a hillside trail, their faces and bodies covered in long, faded robes, edged in red dust. As they got closer, I saw they were women, with scarves encircling their foreheads and faces. How could they stand being so covered up in the sun, I wondered. Their bare toes poked out of their flowing garments with each step forward. I saw the tiny toes on tiny feet before I saw the children gathered within the folds of the group. Eyes stared at me as they went by. How I longed to be among them, to be a child, protected.

We turned at a small, white metal sign that read "Camp Jeanne d'Arc." Above the name was an arrow, pointing further up a hill speckled with scrubby bushes and lonely trees. Long, rounded metal huts lined the dry landscape. Parts of the curved buildings had been bent up, windows open. One hut had a hospital cross on it, which is where the ambulances stopped. There were no fences and no barbed wire anywhere.

We squinted in the sunlight as we left the bus and grouped in what shade we could find. I opted to be alone, settling under a tree that had a large, twisted, and ropey trunk. Leaning back against it, I felt the roots. I looked up and saw little green fruits among the thin leaves that leapt at even the lightest touch of wind. Nearby, dirty sheep with their heads down nibbled at grassy patches. Jeanne d'Arc had been burned at the stake in her teens; that used to seem far-fetched, dying so young in such a horrid way.

There were guards in the gray-green color of German uniforms, but with small caps that looked delicately perched on their slicked hair. They all had little mustaches, as if sketched in with a soft lead pencil.

We were called to the hospital. I stood in line and listened as adults shared information. I learned that the soldiers were Yugoslavian.

The French people who lived in Algeria were facing uprisings by the Algerian people, which was to say the guards were not there to keep us in as much as to keep possible trouble out. The camp was a "displaced persons" camp and was run by the UNRRA, the United Nations Relief and Rehabilitation Administration. One woman said that the UNRRA was a new and improved League of Nations. One man said that the League had failed miserably and was responsible for starting the war. It was all so confusing and made me feel small.

Inside, a young doctor, his hair tossed, poked and prodded and listened to my heart and lungs and peered into my ears and mouth. He had me step up on a scale. A nurse followed our every move, and silently handed the doctor things and took things away.

"How can someone who has survived so much, and is so malnourished, have such thick hair?" the doctor asked, though it wasn't clear if he was asking me a question, so I didn't respond, and he didn't repeat himself.

I glanced at my face in the small mirror above the sink. He was right. My hair was as unruly and big as ever, making my face look thin. Shadows under my eyes made my blue eyes look like shards of clear sky. I wasn't sure I liked that. I didn't want to stand out.

"You're here without your parents," said the doctor, peering into both ears and slowly combing through my hair. "Is there anybody else I should talk to about your health?"

I ignored him, asking, "Am I okay?"

"Well, you are malnourished, but otherwise okay. Have any questions?"

"Are my eyes okay?"

"Are you having trouble seeing?"

"No, it is just that they seem more blue than I remember."

He grabbed something that looked like a big pen and put it near my eye. I flinched.

"It's okay. This is called an ophthalmoscope. That's a mouthful, yes? Or an 'eyeful' in this case. Keep your eyes open and relax." He peered into the scope. "You're fine," he remarked. "Nothing wrong."

"How does my heart sound?"

"Sound?"

"I mean, is it okay?"

"Your heart is fine. Very strong."

"I was worried it could just, I don't know, stop."

"It's not going to stop. Not for a long time."

I was assigned to a barracks for children whose parents were too sick to care for them, or who didn't have parents. The nearby bathhouse smelled of fresh paint, and there were showers with hot and cold water. I turned the knob until it was steaming. I closed my eyes as I washed my hair over and over, and then I just felt the water flow over me until a voice yelled for me to get out and leave some water for others.

At the dining hall I approached a large bench lined with other children without adults. Bowls of peanuts and large prune-like things sat in the center. I sat down next to a small girl a few years younger than me. Her straight hair was wet and hanging almost onto her plate.

She looked at me, smiled, and said, "I washed it four times. It was wonderful! I'm Mieke," she said. "Mieke Wolf. My brother is Jaap. Our dad's the dwarf. That's how people remember us."

"I know," I said.

"Hi, Reni," said a boy, Werner's age. Thin. "I'm Jaap. You should try these. They're soooo good."

"I think they're bugs without legs," said Bob Joski, another kid from Bergen-Belsen who was about my age. He had dark brown food caught in his teeth.

"Gross, Bob!" said Mieke.

"Great-tasting bugs," said Bob.

A voice from the neighboring table yelled over, "They're called dates!"

I took one of the dates and it clung to my fingers. I sniffed it and it smelled like molasses and spice. I popped it in my mouth. It tasted like heaven. I added the pit to the small heap of them in the middle of the table. I learned that Bob's parents and older sister Ellen were in the hospital. Mieke and Jaap were staying in the kids' barracks because Mr. Wolf spent all his time caring for their mom, who had cancer. We had goat meat soup with carrots and potatoes, and hot tea. Once the food and plates were cleared, we were given a care package of toilet paper, toothpaste, a pencil, paper, and soap.

"What we really need are toothpicks," Bob said while using his finger to pry out gooey date.

Back at the barracks, Mieke and I moved our beds next to each other.

I awoke in the dark to the dream of an air raid siren, before realizing it was a scream.

"What's that?" I whispered, my voice shaking.

"Vitek," Mieke said, "the little five-year-old Polish boy who sleeps in the corner. I heard he lost his entire family—murdered right in front of him. Only a month ago. They almost made it out alive."

Almost made it. I curled into my pink blanket and covered my ears from the sound of so much pain. Vitek sobbed, *Mama, Tata, Mama, Tataaaaa,* until sleep won.

It was not the last nightmare. We all had them from time to time. Bob talked about how his sister, Ellen, often woke up in the hospital in terror. But of everybody, Vitek had them the most. His shrills ran through my ears. His was the sound of a mind pushed to the brink of a cliff. He terrified me because I knew I was like him. Even though my belly was filling, my heart was cracking open, ready to fail. The pebbles under my feet were crumbling and falling over the edge.

41

Camp Jeanne d'Arc, Algeria

February–March, 1945

For those of us without parents, we had a "house mother," a Spanish woman who only spoke Spanish and looked after the children's hut. She smiled a lot as she swept the floors and tidied up. In the evening, she drank straight from a bottle of wine and sang songs to herself, and at night she would sometimes, just sometimes, shush away our nightmares. Mostly she slept and snored through all the terrors.

Every day, an administrator walked around the camp to deliver mail and telegrams, precious handwritten letters and typed strips of paper that said who was alive, dead, or missing back in Europe. They foretold futures, revealing who could go home, or who had to find a new one. Going back to Germany didn't look promising even when the Nazis were close to being defeated. Other countries, like the Netherlands, were in shambles. People cherished the letters and telegrams as if they were chocolate, savoring each one in small bites. Each word and phrase was repeatedly tasted and chewed, and swallowed slowly to make sure nothing was missed. Each sentence from a loved one far away was thoroughly licked clean before moving on. The words held life.

I wrote to Mutti and Werner in Switzerland. I wrote about food—eggs, oranges, apples, meat, breads, coffee, and juices—and signed off with a thousand kisses, reminding them that I thought of them all the time. With each day of eating and sleeping, I felt a bit stronger. My fingers didn't tremble any longer from hunger, but I also worried because I heard nothing back. Every day I asked the administrator if there was anything that had come for me, and every day he shook his head.

"No news is good news," said Mrs. Abraham.

My thoughts would seem clear only to fall back into the abyss of bad dreams and nightmares. How would I survive as an orphan? Had I been wrong about miracles? They seemed hollow. We had escaped death for years only to lose Pappi in the space between release and freedom. I thought back to Mieke's words: Vitek's family had almost made it out alive. I knew that didn't guarantee a thing. My whole family made it out alive only to be torn apart. The long road of hope was petering out at the end of a dirt path in a foreign country in the middle of nowhere. The end was dust.

I stayed out of the hut as much as possible, away from the others and away from Vitek, until I was instructed to go in and go to bed.

"Reni! Telegram!" came a shout one morning.

What?

The paper was dated March 2, 1945. My name was written in blue ink. For a scant second I hesitated, afraid of what would spill out, of how it would shape my future. I held it to the light of window and ripped open the end, careful not to tear what was inside.

Mutti and Werner were better, but they were still in the hospital. Werner would keep his toe.

My eyes darted back and forth several times to make sure I didn't miss something. Mutti and Werner were *ALIVE!* I cried, and then I danced around my bunk and hugged the paper to me. I even hugged the startled housemother who was changing a bed. "*ALIVE!*," I said to her. She smiled and raised an imaginary toast. There was no word about us reuniting, but they were alive, and that meant we would be together at some point in some place.

Later that day I was introduced to a tall woman named Madame Benatar. Although from Morocco, she spoke English so it was hard for me to understand her, but an officer translated. She was a lawyer helping reunite families. She said that the camp administration had also received a telegram from family in the United States who could sponsor us to move there. They were already in touch with Mutti and Werner, and had tracked me here. This wasn't a guarantee, Mme. Benatar explained, but a good sign that we might go to America.

The sun was dropping. The hills seemed to be both advancing and retreating, aglow in golden light and purpled in deep shadows, and looked more beautiful than ever. I imagined Werner with his Henki Express map in his hands, trying to figure out the trains, buses, and ships that would bring us back together. I blew one thousand kisses into the wind to lead the way.

The next day, I received a letter from Werner. Instead of giving any details about his or Mutti's health, he wanted to know all about the camp. I figured he must be feeling better to ask so many annoying questions. I did my best to answer: there were 400 people in our camp; 200 Jews; lots of Yugoslavian soldiers; I didn't know how big it was; yes, I had eaten delicious oranges; and yes, I would try to get him Algerian stamps.

The kids' barracks began to empty as parents got healthy enough to take care of their children. Mr. Wolf came for Mieke and Jaap after Mrs. Wolf died of her cancer. Mrs. Joski took Bob. Ellen left the hospital with their father, Dr. Joski. Mrs. Joski had light brown hair, glasses, and eyes that were kind and open. Ellen, at twenty-one, had the wide smile, blonde hair, blue eyes, and figure of a movie star. Then there was Bob. The impish boy who had thought dates were bugs.

"Please celebrate Passover with us," Mrs. Joski said.

"Okay," I said.

"Don't agree too fast," said Ellen. "Mom's matzot is thick and dry and pretty awful."

"Okay," I said. Homemade matzot. It had been a long time.

"Wonderful, it's decided," said Mrs. Joski.

"Reni," Bob said, "a group of us friends are going to walk on the beach later. Want to come?"

Friends? Friends! That sounded good.

"Okay!" I said.

I joined a group of teens around my age—a group I hadn't really known existed in the camp. My isolation melted like butter in the sun. I hadn't realized how much I missed being with people my own age. We usually met up after breakfast, took English and French lessons from Mr. Wolf, and figured out what to do in the hot afternoons. The group waxed and waned depending on the day and the planned activities, but it usually consisted of about six to eight of us, including Lex Roseboom.

Lex was nineteen. Tall with a lean face and body, for which he almost seemed apologetic whenever he stooped over to talk to others who were almost always shorter than him. Lex could appear stern when he was listening, but he could also light up with a full, teeth-showing smile in an instant when he thought of something funny, like Mrs. Bing and her singing.

Mrs. Bing was a short, plump woman who loved to sing, most notably on a full belly. The instant she left the dining hall after a meal, she'd break into an off-key tune for all to hear. With the cafeteria door barely closed behind her, Lex leapt up, put one hand on his heart and the other high in the air and began to mouth her words. His lumbering gait and wide-open eyes were a perfect imitation, and everybody bent over their empty plates with laughter. His straight brown hair stayed neatly parted on the side throughout his antics, which reminded me of Werner. He sat down next to me on the bench when it was done and cocked his head at me for approval.

I surrendered a small smile.

42

Camp Jeanne d'Arc, Algeria

April 1945

The day came when I was the last girl and Vitek was the last boy in the children's barracks. One night, I dreamed of Pappi out in the water at the beach. I screamed for his attention. He stopped and turned. His mouth moved, as if he were telling me something, but I couldn't hear him as the surf got louder and louder until I jolted upright in bed.

"Mama! Tata!"

It was Vitek. Where was the housemother? I waited for her as I watched the small window curtain gently wave and felt a breeze wash over my face. The curtain parted again to reveal far off stars like the torches of a million souls looking for each other. She wasn't coming.

"Mama! Tataaaaa!" Vitek wailed for his dead parents.

Mutti. Pappi.

I peeled back my coverings, draped my pink blanket over my shoulders, and went to Vitek. Sinking onto the edge of his mattress, I hushed and shushed him as if I were the hut mother. It didn't help, so I sang him the Dutch lullaby *Twee emmertjes water halen*…the same lullaby that had quieted the hungry babies in the Hollandsche Schouwburg theater. As he calmed, I lay down beside him, pulling his head onto my chest, and wrapped my pink blanket around him, allowing it to soften the stony weight of all his sadness.

Each night I rocked Vitek back to sleep, and after a few days I coaxed him outside into the morning rays. Like a chick imprinted with a new mother, he suddenly wanted to be with me all the time. He startled less often. His terrors subsided, though they didn't go away entirely.

One day, while we walked across the camp hand in hand, Vitek and I nearly bumped into the singing Mrs. Bing as we rounded a barracks' corner, her lilting voice ringing off the metal building with alarming intensity.

"Good morning, Reni!" She serenaded my name and shook an open letter. "I just found out that my son is alive! My beautiful boy is alive and well!"

She repeated "alive and well" several times as if she were a drunken sailor; she was not to be contained, and I was afraid she would scare Vitek so I held his hand tightly, ready to pick him up. To my surprise he looked up at me, pointed to Mrs. Bing, and laughed.

As I got to know the other kids better, they invited me to do more, and I participated more, especially going to the beach and wading in the shallows. We were warned not to go out further, even though it was getting hotter. The locals warned the camp director that the undertow was strong enough to pull you out too far, too fast, with little chance of swimming back. There was talk of swimming lessons, which led to talk of marking off a swimming area. With the rising temperature there would be no keeping the kids from the sea.

Mostly, though, I tended to Vitek. He needed me. Vitek still had a reputation, and my new friends were leery about him being around. He wasn't yelling as much, but that didn't mean he seemed normal. The wildness in his eyes mirrored the war that we were all trying to forget. What I didn't say was how much I needed Vitek. Other kids wouldn't understand because they had families. Maybe the two of us could stay together, and maybe he could join our family.

"I promise to take care of you," I said into his hair as we settled for bed, though I knew he couldn't understand my words.

Then I remembered Mrs. Eisenberg and her same promise to me—the one she couldn't keep. Part of me knew this wouldn't be forever. I would take care of Vitek for as long as I could, but then somebody with a clipboard would tell us what was really going to happen. Tears slid down my cheeks, but I wiped them before they landed on Vitek.

The next week, Mme. Benatar arrived with an administrator and a woman I hadn't met. Vitek and I were outside in the shade, flipping through a worn magazine. The new woman had a large face and a tentative grin that revealed missing teeth. She wore a headscarf. Mme. Benatar explained that she was the mother of a newly arrived Polish family. Vitek and I were looking up, squinting into the bright sky when the mother began speaking in what I assumed was Polish. Vitek looked confused, glancing between her and me and back at her. Suddenly, he spoke a few words in a rusty little voice that I had never heard. Then he started rattling off in a way that felt how miracles were supposed to feel. Full.

Mme. Benatar went on, saying that the mother and father had a little boy; they would take Vitek when they returned to Poland, to help him try to find his relatives, or take care of him themselves. Vitek was to join them now. I took Vitek's hand.

Mme. Benatar: "It's okay, Reni. You will still have time to see each other."

I held his hand tighter.

"Reni...."

I knew what she was going to say: I had to let him go. But I didn't.

It was Vitek who pulled his hand from mine. He took me into the barracks, and as the others followed, he rummaged around the edge of his suitcase, took something out, and placed it into my palm. It was a tiny photo of a beautiful Vitek, his eyes wide, but relaxed. His cheeks and lips full. It was pre-war Vitek, as he should have been. As he, hopefully, would be again.

That night I sat on the beach alone, watching the sky darken, and stars seemingly search for each other over the sea.

43

Camp Jeanne d'Arc, Algeria

May 1945

"We heard that Vitek has a new home," said Dr. Joski. "We are hoping that you can come live with us."

"We asked and got written permission from the camp directors to take care of you," said Mrs. Joski. "If you agree, we will just need to get written permission from your mother."

"Which we are sure she will give," added Dr. Joski.

"Unless you want that entire hut to yourself," Ellen said, "and Lex," she added with a whisper meant just for me.

Ellen had been teasing me for the past week about Lex. At first I had assumed it was because she was interested in Lex, but in a sing-songy voice she repeated the claim. When I told her I was too fat, Ellen told me I was shapely and womanly. When I said all the men looked only at her, Ellen admitted it was mostly true, but that Lex 'only had eyes for me.' *Me? Womanly? I guess so.*

"I never liked the idea of you being on your own," said Mrs. Joski. "It has been a thorn in my side. What a stupid rule that children have to live on their own. It's good that Vitek has a home, and now you can have one too."

So I moved in, sharing a room with Ellen, which we decorated with flowers. I even put up a picture of Mutti and Pappi.

The next week as Mieke and I were having breakfast in the dining hall, a chatter rippled between everybody, but I wasn't listening as we had recently gotten a kilo of oatmeal each because we were "children under the age of 15," and I was busy stirring jam and milk into our porridge. Mieke was quiet, like she had been since her mother died. Lex ran to the table.

"Hitler's dead. He's really dead!" He hugged me. I felt the heat of him as I squeezed back. I didn't expect Hitler's demise to feel *this* good.

The next week had even better news: the Germans had surrendered.

The camp burst with jubilant yells. The Yugoslavian guard jumped up and clicked his heels together. Players took to the piano with upbeat tunes. We hugged, we danced. Even Mieke started to brighten. Ellen, Mrs. Joski, and I swung each other around by the arms in a circle, faster and faster. Dr. Joksi swung Bob by the arms, Bob's feet flung out to the side like a crazy bird trying to take flight.

For the first time, people could think about returning home or going to new ones. I felt sure now that Mutti and Werner would be able to leave Switzerland, now that the threads of evil had been snipped, the web's strands blowing away.

Later that day there was a spider on my bed. I hated spiders; I rolled a magazine to swat it off the blanket and onto the floor where I could finish it. Mieke took one look at my weapon and commanded me to stop.

"Don't kill it. Spiders are good luck if you find them in your home."

"Really? Ugh."

"Just promise me you'll not kill it. Please."

"Okay," I said, my fingers crossed within the folds of the magazine in an attempt to get around my obligation.

"It's good luck, Reni. Like 'you'll get some time alone with Lex' type of good luck."

I opened my mouth, but couldn't find the words.

"Everybody knows he likes you," she said.

"I thought only Ellen knew."

"Sure, Ellen. Ellen and *everybody else*."

I could only blush.

"You know what else everybody knows?"

I shook my head.

"That you like him back."

I liked to sit at the table of our barracks' section to write and read my letters while Mrs. Joski chopped vegetables and cooked on the small stove. A cup of flowers stood on the windowsill, the pedals pointing in all directions. I wiggled back and forth, pulling on my skirt that had become tight and uncomfortable.

"You're big," said Mrs. Joski.

"Big?"

"I mean you've gained weight. Grown, I mean you've grown."

"I know, but I don't have any other clothing."

"Do you still have some of your mom's things?"

"Yes."

"Maybe we can adjust something of hers for you."

Maybe. But Mutti's clothes weren't better than mine. Oh, I so wanted new clothes. And that didn't include the fact I only had two pair of underwear. I was constantly washing.

The administrator came by with mail. There was an airmail letter for me from the United States. The postage stamp had a little plane on it, which I would save for Werner. Cousins of my mother's had invited us to live with them in New York. Moving suddenly felt real.

I started asking Mrs. Joski questions she couldn't answer: How would we get there? When? What was New York City like? How would I fit in? Learn English? What about Mutti and Werner?

She waited for a pause, said she didn't know, but it was cause to celebrate with pudding. She said to have patience, as no one knew what the order of things would be, but that no matter what, she felt certain I would be reunited with them, together again. She handed me the pot so I could scrape the thick layer of chocolate off the bottom. As I cradled the familiar brown pot, I remembered licking off and savoring drops of cold turnip broth in Bergen-Belsen. Now it was full of warm chocolate. I ate every last bit off the bottom.

Thanks to Mieke, I would never again kill a spider, but that didn't mean I liked bugs. Grasshoppers swarmed in response to the thickening heat. They were everywhere, flying through the camp, bumping into buildings and trucks, and tangling in my sweaty hair. I tried not to crunch them on the ground.

Then Mrs. Roseboom, Lex's mom, decided it was time for swim lessons.

"There are fewer locusts near the water," she said, wiping her brow. "Besides, it's dangerous to live so close to the ocean and not know how to swim."

"We've been living near the ocean for months," I whispered to Lex. "Isn't she a little late?"

"Yeah, but it'll be fun," he said.

"Promise?" I asked, looking up, into his brown eyes.

My past experience with water consisted of skating on ice, paddling in the shallows, and drinking it, but I'd never been in over my head. How would I float? Step by step I waded in, pausing to let the waves rise over my ankles, knees, and waist. None of us had swimming suits. I discovered that shirts and cutoff pants were like an anchor.

Mieke stayed behind, skeptically watching my progress. "I've always been told to keep my clothes dry and now I am supposed to get them wet!" she said, laughing.

"C'mon. Let's go," I urged.

"I'm going to sink!"

The water was cool as I submerged up to my stomach and felt the push-pull of the waves. I squelched the panic that rose up, and concentrated on Mrs. Roseboom's lessons.

"The salt water will keep you afloat," she said.

I lowered myself, leaning back, hoping the water would hold me high like a new mattress. Water splashed into my face. I stumbled to standing and wiped my wide eyes.

"Wow, you're really good," Mieke laughed.

"Try it again, on your back. Just float," Mrs. Roseboom encouraged.

I took a deep breath, tilted my head back and relaxed, feeling the pulse of the waves and learning when it was safe to catch some air and when to hold. It worked. The water rushed into my ears, and I could hear my breath. I slowed it down. Then I opened my eyes. A bleached white gull floated overhead against a sky as blue as my eyes. I lowered my gaze to see green hills dotted with pink-blossom bushes like blotches of spilled paint. I was suspended between earth and sky.

Walking back to the beach to dry off, I marveled, feeling clean and new in a way I didn't know was possible.

"I can't wait to go again," I said.

I swam every day. I couldn't stay away. I never got my chance to sled and ski in Switzerland, but I didn't care. I couldn't imagine it could be better than this.

"You're a natural," said Mrs. Roseboom.

"You're a torpedo!" said Lex.

I moved through the swells, back and forth, back and forth along the shore, the backstroke and the breaststroke being my favorite. My mind focused on my movement in rhythm with the sea, and nothing else. The trains, Westerbork, Bergen-Belsen sank below me like stones. Despite the heat, my swimming clothes were constantly wet.

"We can't buy bathing suits?" asked Mieke.

"I don't think they have any here," Lex said.

Mrs. Roseboom was now on a mission. She tracked down an old sweater from a friend. We unraveled the yellow and brown knitting and she helped me re-knit a bathing suit out of it. She took me to the nurse's station where there was a full-length mirror. I tried it on.

"Lean forward."

I did. And I felt exposed.

Mrs. Roseboom pursed her lips, muttering, "We will definitely have to fix that."

"How's it going?" Lex asked from the other room.

"Fine, honey. Stay there," his mother said.

Then she had me move this way and that, while pulling at the edges.

"It looks like I am wearing a blanket," I said without thinking.

"You don't like it?"

"I mean, it's wonderful. Thank you."

Mrs. Roseboom cocked her head. "Well, you know what I think?"

I shook my head expecting to be told she thought that I was spoiled.

"I think it's going to look like a really nice blanket," she said.

I looked past the "blanket," marveling at my new shape. Just three months ago the suit would have hung off me like a flag on a windless day. Now, I had curves. Was this really me?

Mutti had recently written asking if I had menstruated. She told me that menstruation would involve bleeding in my private place for a few days at the same time every month. It was normal, she wrote, and had to do with getting older and my body changing. Normal or not, it sounded horrible. Still, I pondered as I turned in front of the mirror, if I looked like this, maybe it wouldn't be so bad.

"Can we take it in a little more at the waist. Make it tighter?" I asked.

"It's tight enough dear," Mrs. Roseboom said. She stretched the suit out across my belly and tucked the excess fabric into the folds around my hips. With a final pinch in the back and tightening at the waist, she announced that she was done for now.

"Swimming will be easier," she proclaimed, and it was. I felt fast and strong. I imagined swimming all the way across the ocean to America or Italy or wherever. Maybe the same water that washed over me had touched the shores of my future home.

After several laps back and forth near the outer rope marker, I stopped and treaded water. *Ha,* I thought, Werner would never believe that I could do this. He didn't know how to swim! I glared at the open ocean, feeling gloriously dwarfed. It never ended, never culminated in a pinpoint like single-minded trains on tracks. It went off in every direction—any direction that it wanted. Any direction that *I* wanted. I suddenly felt a snag on my leg. Lex's face shot up on my right side.

"Ha, ha, got you!" he gurgled.

"How did you…?" I blurted.

"'The shark has its way, especially when you are looking away.'"

"I'm gonna get you back," I yelled and tried to dunk his face back in the water, but all I did was tap his shoulder and plunk my own face down.

"Just cuz you're getting good at swimming doesn't mean you can catch me,'" he taunted, darting out of reach. "You may be a torpedo, but I'm a natural! I'm 'the shark!'"

I grabbed at him, but he slipped under the waves again. I spun around to make sure he didn't sneak up on me when he surfaced right in front of me, and after a fast shake of his head we found ourselves looking into each other's eyes.

"So you came to get me?" I asked.

"I think I got you."

"Yes, you did."

He moved closer and then we were kissing, our weight pulling us under. My ears popped. All I could think of was the feeling of holding him until I finally had to breathe. We surfaced, laughing.

"Wow," he said. "Just, wow."

"So you came to get me?" I repeated, adding, "Now, I think I'm going to get you."

I expected him to move towards me again, but instead his serious eyebrows shot up. Lex spun around and dove, swimming, hands going over his head toward the shore. I took a deep breath and ducked. Like a frog, I pulled myself through the water, following his cloud of bubbles. The dark blue below me lightened to green as the sand rose from the depths. Lex's long legs kicked above me while I continued to glide like a fin underneath, my lungs beginning to tighten. His feet flashed in the foam, and I grabbed his right foot with my right hand, swinging sideways to avoid being kicked by his left. As I pulled him to a stop I rose, gasping for breath. I was a little light-headed, and thrilled.

"Wow, you are fast," he gasped and tried to splash me away. "Of course, I let you catch me."

"Oh, so 'the shark' is nice?"

"'The shark' is weak in the face of beauty."

The sand found our feet and we pulled up and out of the water. My legs were shaking. I had not swum that long before. He wrapped his towel around himself and then his arm around my waist. We walked like that arm in arm, sandy and warm, to join our friends.

"We saw that!" Ellen yelled.

44

Camp Jeanne d'Arc, Philippeville, Algeria

June 1945

The camp was heavy with impatience. There was talk about countries I'd never heard of, like Uruguay. Mme. Benatar still had not received any affidavits from my family in America, which were sent months ago. No affidavits meant no visa, and no visa meant no leaving. In her letters, Mutti worried how long it would be before we saw each other. I wrote to Mutti, suggesting we consider some other country if the United States didn't work out. Maybe we could return to Holland first and get some of our belongings. Who knew?

We made excursions into Phillippeville, wandering the market to pass the time. Ellen held hands with her boyfriend, one of the Yugoslavian guards; they were only brave enough to show their affection outside the camp. Mieke and I looked at bracelets.

"Can I have one of those?" Lex asked, coming up between us, draping his long arms over our shoulders.

"No. These are for girls only," I teased.

He smiled his perfect smile and gave me a wink.

We were excited about going to see a movie after hearing the town had a cinema. None of us had seen a movie in years. *Misunderstood* was showing. It was based on a book I had actually read before the camps.

"In we go," said Lex.

As we walked up the steps and Lex gave his few coins to the turbaned man behind the glass counter, memories flooded in. It all felt so normal, but new in a way I couldn't take for granted. A theater could be for movies, or it could be for rounding up people to kill.

"Are you alright?" he asked.

"Yeah, just remembering, you know?"

We all settled in. The newsreel blinked on, and talked about how Japan was still fighting, and suddenly I was back in Bergen-Belsen. The pictures were blurred in black and white, but I knew every building. The voice talked about the atrocities at Bergen-Belsen. Every close-up of a face could have been somebody I knew. Every dead face. Then the commentator explained how the British decided it was best to burn the buildings. Tractors moved in front of our barracks, belching and throwing flame over all that we had known. The next clips showed smoke billowing over the camp.

Lex gripped my hand harder, and I wept into his warm shoulder. I didn't remember the movie starting, but at some point I dried out.

"Sorry, I think I made a mess of your shirt," I whispered.

"It's okay," he replied. "Now you can get on with the rest of the movie."

After the credits we walked back out into the warm evening and to the truck waiting to take us back to Jeanne d'Arc.

"We've got to start thinking about the future, Reni," he said. "Holland is liberated! Life is going to get back to normal in, I don't know, probably a few months."

"I want Mutti and Werner to come here," I said. "To Jeanne d'Arc. That is what I want more than anything. Then we can go from there."

"Think bigger, Reni. I mean the real future—years from now—far away from this place, and far from Bergen-Belsen." He flung his right arm out with a punch. "I'm going to return to Amsterdam, find our house, and if it's been destroyed, rebuild it. I'll find out what happened to my father's business—he made burlap sacks, you know—and get it going again."

I looked up at him, admiring his determination. I wanted that clarity, but I couldn't think beyond reuniting with Mutti and Werner.

Over the next few days, I felt out of sorts. My skin, limbs, and changing body felt ready to burst. My stomach hurt, so I stayed back at the Joskis. I awoke from a nap, something damp between my legs. It didn't feel hot enough to sweat, I thought, as I made my way to the bathroom. It was blood. I changed my clothes and put the dirty ones in a small pile under my bed. I decided to find Mrs. Joski. I went into the kitchen, into her room, and called, but no one came. I went outside and into the front yard and called again. I began to walk back toward the cafeteria.

"Hey, Reni," said Dr. Joski. "Aren't you supposed to be in class?"

"Umm, yes," I said. "I was just looking for Mrs. Joski."

"She's at the nursing station visiting a friend," he said, and looked me up and down. "Are you alright?"

"I don't think so," I said, holding back tears.

"What's wrong? Are you sick?"

"I don't know," I said pulling my arm away.

"Does something hurt?" he said.

"Yes, my whole belly hurts and, well," I said, "and there is blood…I mean, I think I may have…." I looked up at him, at a loss for words.

He searched my eyes.

"Oh, my dear child," he said and put his hands up to his mouth in a prayer, and putting his hand on my shoulder. "Come. It's a sign that you're healthy, not that you're sick."

At the nursing station, Dr. Joski whispered in his wife's ear; she rose up and hugged me. She told her friend she needed to tend to me, and the friend said her good-byes.

"Oh, Reni," she said in warm tones, "normally, a mother talks with her daughter…."

I explained Mutti's letter asking if I had menstruated.

"Well, she's not here, but I am. So," she said, with a swat of her hand across each cheek, "Mazel Tov! You're a woman!"

I must have looked surprised.

"It's a tradition, slapping the cheek of a girl with her first period—that's what most women call it. It's a way to shock you out of childhood, but you've already been forced into adulthood, yes? So, just a good tap for you."

She got the nurse who brought supplies and showed me how to use them. They both hugged me again and smiled.

"Your Mutti will be proud of you," Mrs. Joski added.

I walked outside to go back to our hut. Did I look different? I tried to hold my head high and walk straight, even though my belly hurt so much. A woman? I felt the same. I didn't feel ready, but Mrs. Joski was right, I had seen a lot and I had done a lot of grown-up things. Despite taking lessons, I couldn't speak English or French very well, and I didn't truly know if I'd be off to America or elsewhere, or when. I still wanted to curl up and be taken care of by Mutti. To feel her next to me, putting my hair behind my ear, or feeling my forehead, or making a favorite dish to cheer me up. I still wanted Pappi for protection and safety. Why did becoming a woman mean so much loss and unknown?

45

Camp Jeanne d'Arc, Philippeville, Algeria

June–July 1945

A few days later I was eager to swim again. A few of us even ventured beyond the ropes. We giggled nervously, vigilant for the slightest tug of current that would warn us to head back. There was none. Afterward, we lay on the beach, tanning. Mutti and Werner would never recognize me now—I was curvy and brown.

"I love swimming," I said while lying on my back, my arm thrown over my eyes. "I love it."

"You're really good at it," Mieke said. "Probably the best of us, and you just started!"

"Yeah. You know, this is the first time I've ever been good at something. I've never been better than the rest of my family at anything. Everybody is older than me, and just better at everything." I felt guilty. I hoped it was okay to feel so good.

"You *are* the baby of the family, just like me," said Mieke. "But we're not babies anymore."

The news from Bergen-Belsen, in the papers and in the newsreels, was more and more terrible. The photos in the papers that now arrived in camp were familiar and gruesome. Bodies tumbling over bodies as British bulldozers plowed the dead into great pits. There was very little hope for our friends. We hadn't heard from any of them. I thanked God that he had taken Pappi out of that horrible place, even if I didn't know where he was. At the same time I was sad that Pappi was not allowed to experience where I was—the blazing beach and soothing sea he so loved.

As much as I shuddered at the images of the mass graves at Bergen-Belsen and was forever thankful for my escape, the camp continued to haunt, no, to beckon, me. I stared at the gritty newspaper photos for a familiar angle, building, or face, trying to eke out what I could from the empty spaces between the tiny printed dots on newsprint. I longed to be back because I ached to be with my family. I would forever be pulled to that place if only to see again where my father had last had a life: the unforgiving wood pallets, floors, walls, and tables; the clothing riddled with lice and holes; the mud, wind, and dirt; and standing side by side for hours on end with the people I loved the most. *Let's go, Hasenbergs,* Pappi's voice called. And we always did. It seemed we went everywhere together until the journey became mine alone.

Letters flew back and forth almost daily. Affidavits and paperwork were in motion, and it was looking more and more like Mutti, Werner, and I would end up in America, though probably at different times. I got letters from Vera, my dear old friend Vera, and others from Amsterdam who suggested we not return there. The war was over, but who knew how long it would take to heal. Food was rationed, and jobs were impossible to find. If there was ever a time to start over, it was now. At the same time, the first camp group received permission to leave. They were to return to the Netherlands, and it included Lex's family.

"Come with us," Lex said. We sat watching the sun set over the hills after dinner. The dry grass felt scratchy and little flies buzzed around the flowers.

"Come back to Holland. It's your home. Your Mutti and Werner can join you there. It's so much closer than America. No need for sailing across a big, bad ocean…."

"I can't, Lex," I said.

I looked into his sad brown eyes.

"You know that. Everything's in motion. I have to be with my family again. There's nothing left for me in Holland: no family, no home."

"But I'd be there," he said.

"I want to be with you," I said. "But I need to be with Mutti and Werner."

He looked out over the ocean to the buzz of insects and the breeze-bent grass. Distant ships crawled over the ocean. Then, as if to explain myself, I told him about the miracles that had saved me and most of my family: the passports mysteriously arriving at Westerbork, being saved from the train to Auschwitz, and being confused for my mother. Pappi's work to save our family from the camps had worked. Now I had to make sure the dream came true. The three of us had to be together.

"You never know" Lex said. "America might not work out. Your English isn't so great. You could still end up in Holland."

"True."

"Promise me we'll always be friends and that some day, somewhere, we'll see each other again."

"I promise," I said, and meant it.

We sat there until darkness seeped into the grass and sea. Lights flickered on across Phillippeville far below us and pinpointed the crawling ships. And the stars glimmered.

Lex and I said a tearful good-bye the next day. I hugged him, trying to burn a snapshot of him in my mind, as I had no photo. I vowed to think of him when I thought of the ocean, and the motion that was always there and alive.

46

Camp Jeanne d'Arc Algeria

September–October 1945

Mutti sent photos of her and Werner: it was the first time I'd seen them in half a year. I scrutinized them for any and all details. Werner looked terrific, his hair flawless. People who knew Mutti agreed that she looked exactly the way she used to look, and those people who never met her were amazed how young she looked considering how sick she had been. I wrote back saying I needed to lose weight. I needed a diet.

The camp kept emptying. People packed, boarded buses, and disappeared down the road. The last we saw were hands waving out windows. Moving to America took the most paperwork, so those of us who were bound for the United States would soon move to Algiers and wait for available ships.

Just before the Abrahams left, they hugged me by the bus. Mr. Abraham reached his hand out to me, and I saw it held 200 francs.

"Go on. Take it. It is out of friendship for your father."

"Mr. Abraham. Thank you."

Saying good-bye to the Joskis and the other kids was hardest. I'd never done so much hugging in my life. Mrs. Joski reminded me that I was wonderful. Dr. Joski and Ellen joined in, while Bob reminded me to clean my teeth after eating dates if I ever hoped to keep a boy.

The Wolf family, including Mieke, would be going to Algiers with me, though leaving Jeanne d'Arc was hard for her. This was where her mother had died. This was the last place her family had been whole.

My dreams of Pappi at the beach changed. He wasn't in his suit on the beach, or in trunks swimming away. He was between worlds, standing in the shallows, the hem of his white, thick bathrobe, catching the tips of small waves. I had to squint against the blinding glare of the sun, sky, and reflection, not able to look at him directly as much as just knowing it was him, and knowing he was smiling. *Let's go, Hasenbergs,* he ushered to me. *I will, Pappi,* I said, *but not today. I'll catch up with you later.* When he did turn away I wasn't scared or sad. I felt warm, even as he walked into or across the water—I couldn't tell which. Did it matter? He was happy, so I felt happy, too.

I would always be his sweet little one and most lovable, no matter how old I got. I would always belong to him, and him to me.

Pappi had saved our family. Luck had been part of it, but not all of it. Mutti, Werner, and I would not be alive and seeking each other if he had not fought so hard to put miracles in motion. If anybody proved that one person can make a difference, it was Pappi. I decided I would best honor Pappi by always fighting for what was right, no matter if that fight seemed impossibly small or impossibly big. Small like soothing Vitek's screams, or big like crossing an ocean to be with my family.

I walked through the flowers and around stones to the beach, and waded into the surf. Nobody was there. The ropes and markers had been pulled, but I wanted to go out one more time. The waves fought me, but it didn't matter. They had always pushed and pulled, long before I arrived on shore and would continue long after. I dove under, re-emerging with strong strokes that cut into the water with ease. I didn't know when I would see Mutti and Werner again, but I knew I would. I didn't know what would happen tomorrow, but I could make it. I was fourteen, and would swim through any waters.

Postscript

ecember 2017. I'm looking back across more than seventy years to December 1945. I should have expected that my journey from the shores of Algeria to the shores of the United States would not be simple.

After Camp Jeanne d'Arc was closed in late summer of 1945, I spent three months in Algiers, the beautiful, whitewashed capitol of Algeria, waiting for a ship bound for America. It was hard to find ships that had room for passengers. Following the war's end, the United States government had a new mission: get hundreds of thousands of soldiers back home by the holidays. When word arrived that a ship had room, it was 150 miles away in the port of Bougie. It would be leaving the next day.

I, along with other female refugees from Poland, climbed into a taxi and a small truck and headed across the mountains and desert. Clouds of dust, kicked up by our churning tires, billowed around us as we raced over the ragged and sandy roads. At times, we could barely see, and it was at one of those times on a steep turn on the high road that our taxi crashed into the small truck. Our belongings flew everywhere. Some of the women broke bones, but I was only bruised. We were in the middle of nowhere, but lucky to be alive. We waited in the heat, treating our wounds, as our drivers tried to fix the taxi, which refused to start back up again. Hours ticked by. Finally the engine sputtered back to life, and we were once again speeding to the ocean. We made our ship, the *SS Cleveland Forbes*, with just moments to spare.

You'd think my adventure ended there, but it didn't. I crossed the Atlantic Ocean in a Liberty Ship, a military cargo ship meant to carry supplies and not people. The ship had tall turrets, large guns, and many layers of decks that creaked and moaned over the waves. It was three weeks of dark gray water, light gray sky, and bracing white spray—so different from the calm, aqua blue Mediterranean Sea where I had learned to swim. Another passenger on board, a doctor, told me that the American Liberty ships were so quickly and poorly built that some broke in half during large storms and only the half with the engine made it to land. I know now he was kidding, but at the time I was terrified. There were frequent storms, and I didn't want to be too far away from the engine room. During the worst tempests, all of us refugees were instructed to sleep on benches in the dining room, which was closer to the decks and lifeboats than our sleeping quarters. One night, silverware crashed to the floor when the roiling sea opened an unsecured drawer. I stayed awake, listening for the sound of the ship splitting in half as the forks and spoons rattled back and forth across the floor.

Days later, under a brittle, blue clear sky, we carved our way into Baltimore harbor, slicing through frozen ocean until we couldn't go any further. I climbed into a lifeboat that was lowered into the watery space between ice floes, and stepped ashore: it was December 25, 1945. I was a fifteen-year-old refugee with a sixth grade education, broken English, and a small knapsack of belongings.

My journey, up until that point in my life, had been by command and not by choice. Pappi and Mutti hadn't chosen to move to Amsterdam; they were forced to. We didn't choose to be hurled through the camps, we were forced to. I didn't choose to live in Algeria alone; I was forced to. But finally, in America, I had choices and could exercise my free will. There were no restrictions. No yellow stars on clothing. No men with guns stopping people to see papers. My distant relatives and the beautiful city of New York welcomed me with open arms.

Six months after I landed, Mutti and Werner arrived. I will never forget Werner's hug. Over the year and a half since we had last seen each other in Switzerland, he had grown taller and bigger. Our hold was full, solid, and strong, and not just bone against bone. We were healthy, and we were together.

We lived with the Kaplans, Mutti's cousins, and there was only one rule: we must start over. This meant no talking of the past, especially about the war. No ruminating, and no whining. Beginning fresh necessitated forgetting.

Werner and I entered high school. It was hard because I had been out of school for three years, but exciting to be in a classroom and learning again! Compared to the camps, high school was a piece of cake. Mutti took a job as a factory worker. She had a much harder time recovering. She had gone from being a wealthy banker's wife in Berlin to a widow and a low-paid cashier. I privately reminisced about Pappi daily, but she missed him to the core of her being.

Mieke and Jaap Wolf ended up in New York as well. Early on, we saw each other a few times and then fell out of touch. You'd think we would have clung to each other, given what we'd gone through, but we embraced forgetting, and forgetting was easier without reminders. Even Lex and I lost touch. We wrote a few letters, and he sent me a photo of himself in Amsterdam, inviting me to come, saying the city had changed and I would be welcome. But I didn't respond. I had a new life, of my own making.

After high school, Werner and I attended Queens College while continuing to live at home. Werner worked in an insurance company by day and took classes at night, while I was on the opposite schedule, attending classes during the day and working two evening jobs, as a sales clerk in a department store and in a local bakery. I majored in economics, as I loved understanding how the world worked. I also loved philosophy and art history. I wanted to keep studying, keep learning, as if I had a lifetime to make up for. I applied to graduate schools and was accepted at Duke University and found myself the only female in a PhD program in economics, earning my doctorate in 1960.

It was also where I met my husband. Charlie was a fellow PhD student, studying neuroscience. He was brilliant and kind, moral, and dapper. Pappi would have loved him. I returned to Amsterdam to do my thesis work, and it was there that Charlie and I married in 1957. I saw Lex during that time: he was married and had started a family.

Charlie and I spent our careers as professors at the University of Michigan in Ann Arbor, Michigan, Charlie in Neuroscience, and me in Public Health. I taught the economics of healthcare and women's health, and conducted research on the "brain drain" of doctors. Charlie and I had two children, our daughter, Ella, and our son, Noah, both adults now. We lived a life filled with art, especially modern art, music, and laughter. Werner married, too, had a son and daughter and settled in Washington, D.C.

I very rarely spoke about the past. It was buried under my job, family, and activities, but sometimes I experienced a shiver. Like when I walked Jubilee, our yellow lab, along the Huron River, and a train passed: the whistle, the steel wheels passing from rail to rail. I froze until the beast rounded the corner while poor Jubilee pulled on the leash to keep going. Or the time I was served turnip soup at a friend's house and couldn't lift the spoon to my lips. Or when my kids left food on their plate and I saved it as leftovers, even when it was the smallest of crusts. When something about the Holocaust came up on TV or in the news, I quickly changed the topic.

In 1986, I was asked to serve on a panel about Anne Frank at the Detroit Holocaust Center. My friends in the Jewish community had pieced together enough of my story to suggest my participation. It was a turning point. During the panel question-and-answer period it dawned on me that Anne wasn't here to tell her story, but I was. Yes, there was her Diary, but Anne and six million others had been forced into silence. I was fifty-six years old and had chosen to stay silent.

I had survived. Why? Was there a message attached to my survival? Was I supposed to do something great? My life was so good. My career and marriage were successful, and my children, healthy. How could I pay back for this privilege of being alive? I knew I must bear witness to suffering and use my experiences to lessen the burden of others. I decided that I didn't want to identify with being a victim, but a survivor with the responsibility to put my strength and privilege to good use. Elie Wiesel, the famous Holocaust survivor, wrote:

"If you were there, if you breathed the air and heard the silence of the dead, you must continue to bear witness...to prevent the dead from dying again."

My silence had helped others to forget the Holocaust, and silence meant that the dead would have died in vain. But action was hard. I was still locked in the habit of keeping quiet, and I was also scared of revisiting my past too closely—some memories cut to my soul. Yet I knew that silence about what happened to me during the Holocaust was no longer an option. I thought of my parents, especially my Pappi, and all they had sacrificed for me. I had to exhibit that kind of courage and be the voice that others were denied.

So I began to speak, and I haven't been quiet since. What surprised me most was that students who were the same age as me when I lived through the Holocaust were interested in my story! At first I was afraid to speak about my personal history in front of hundreds of middle school and high school students. Looking back, I was most afraid of being laughed at, of being judged, being misunderstood, or facing an auditorium of yawns and blank stares. But the unexpected happened. Not only did students listen and ask good, hard questions, but also they wrote me afterwards to share reflections on my story and share their own stories. They wrote me of losing a loved one and of being bullied, of having someone stick up for them and of sticking up for someone else, and of feeling discriminated against and not letting it get them down.

From inner city high schools in Detroit, schools in Ann Arbor, and rural middle schools in Dexter, students in what has become my home state of Michigan are ready to hear a message about standing up against hatred, bullying, oppression, and discrimination. They seem naturally disposed to wanting to stand in the shoes of others, with compassion. Their writings, drawings, and poems hearten me, and give me the motivation to push through the pain and keep talking and sharing.

"I love how much hope you have and that you kept reaching for your goal. I hope to be like you some day."
—*Cora, 7th grade, Discovery Middle School, Canton, MI*

I can no longer remember my childhood in Germany or the Netherlands without students' words dancing along the canals of Amsterdam, or their drawings floating down from the grey sky over Bergen-Belsen. They recognize that all of us are responsible for each other, regardless of our color, religion, or race. We are all hungry for stories of hope and triumph over tragedy.

> "Your story changed my view of the world we live in. Your lesson that we must protect each other and accept each other's differences made a deep impression on us."
> —*Anthony, 11ᵗʰ grade, Henry Ford Academy, School for Creative Studies, Detroit*

The idea of "never a bystander," of standing up for others even when they aren't members of your "tribe" is a strong theme in my life's work. With this idea in mind, I helped found The Wallenberg Lecture Series at the University of Michigan. Raoul Wallenberg was a Swede—not a Jew—who risked his life, and lost it, in order to save tens of thousands of Hungarian Jews at the end of 1944. He is one of the greatest heroes of the war. Each year since 1990, The Wallenberg Lecture brings an outstanding humanitarian hero to give a lecture, receive a medal, and inspire students and all of us to serve. The Lecture's motto is "One Person Can Make A Difference In Building A Better World." With that motto, I remember Pappi's contact and the Swedish man who helped get our Ecuadorian passports. I may never know them, and the Swede was not Raoul Wallenberg, but they were people who took a risk to help when they had plenty of excuses to do otherwise.

I also co-founded a women's group called Zeitouna, named for the olive tree, a symbol of peace. It's a way of building a bridge between two peoples that normally do not connect with one another. Zeitouna is a group of six Arab and six Jewish women. We refuse to be enemies; we find common language, common ground, and have even traveled to Israel and Palestine to experience our homeland together.

I am now eighty-seven, and, like many women of my tender age, I find deep joy in my grandchildren. My granddaughters were born in Israel to a Jewish mother—my daughter—and a Palestinian father. This hasn't always been easy for them. But I've learned that the surest path to peace may be when the "other" becomes your own. My grandson, born in San Francisco, is ten years old and the youngest of the bunch. In a few years, he'll be the age I was when I entered the camps. He looks at the world with eyes full of wonder, and feet always ready to explore. I talk about my past for him. He is Pappi's great-grandson, after all. The family courses through his veins. I also do it for his classmates, for Vitek's grandchildren (for I think surely he must have them), and for young people everywhere. They give me hope that we will lay aside our differences and build a better world, together. One world, one family.

Character Biographies

Abraham Family
Siegfried (1899–1974): father
Gerda (1911–2000): mother
Hans (1933–2006): son
Ruth (b. 1938): daughter

The Abrahams were neighborhood friends from Amsterdam. Siegfried was also a business friend of Pappi. Like my family, they were deported from Amsterdam to Westerbork in 1943 and to Bergen-Belsen eight months later in 1944. They became part of the prisoner exchange transport to Switzerland in January 1945 and finally to the United Nations Relief and Rehabilitation Administration (UNRRA) Camp Jeanne d'Arc in Philippeville (now Skikda), Algeria. They immigrated to New York City in 1946.

Helene Cazes Benatar (1898–1979)
Madame Benatar was director of repatriation and emigration at the UNRRA Camp Jeanne d'Arc. She was a Moroccan-born female lawyer and a Zionist. During the war, she was the Northern Africa representative for the American Jewish Joint Distribution Committee (JDC), a relief organization based in New York City, where she tirelessly oversaw the JDC's aid activities for Jewish refugees from Nazi-occupied Europe.

Gerda Bosch Schotanus (b. 1937)
Though I was seven years older than Gerda, I loved playing with this little blonde girl, fixing different hairdos with her long curls. Her parents owned a dairy store on my block where my family often shopped. The family was not Jewish, but they continued to be friends and be supportive even under Nazi occupation. Greetje, Gerda's older sister, often shopped for us when Jews had limited access. One night Mr. and Mrs. Bosch allowed Pappi to sleep at their house when there was a rumor he might be arrested. Gerda contacted me through the Internet five or six

years ago, and we have renewed our friendship. I visited her in Holland in 2017.

Stien Bremekamp (?–1980s) and Max Wulf (?–1980s) and their tenant Ri Ritsema (?)

Stien Bremekamp and her partner, Max Wulf, lived in the apartment one floor above ours in Amsterdam. They were close friends of my family. Max Wulf was a singer, especially of Schubert songs, and we often attended his concerts. Ri was a photographer. These kind people hid some of our most treasured possessions before we were deported, including my Poesie book, jewelry, some china, and some of the photos you see here in this book. Mutti and Werner brought these few things to the U.S. with them when they arrived as refugees in early 1946. We visited Stien and Max a couple of times after the war, and I fondly recall the heartwarming reunions with them.

Leo Buschoff (1883–1944)

Leo was my father's best friend from World War I, where both were Jewish-German officers. He was in Westerbork at the same time we were and, according to my parents, he was the one who was responsible for keeping our names off the list of prisoners bound for Auschwitz. He ended up being deported and sent to Auschwitz, where he and his wife Else (1885–1944) were murdered.

Mrs. Eisenberg

I have no information other than my brief interaction with her on the train from Switzerland to Marseilles.

Anne Frank (1929–1945)

Anne remains the most revered and the most frequently read young author in the entire world. Anne was born in Frankfurt, Germany, and moved to the Netherlands to escape the Nazis. Our families lived in the same neighborhood in Amsterdam, but did not have close contact. Her family went into hiding in 1942, was discovered, and sent to Westerbork in August 1944. The next month they were transported to Auschwitz concentration camp on the last transport to ever leave

Westerbork. In October, the Franks became separated. Anne and her sister, Margot, were sent to Bergen-Belsen where Hanneli and I met up with Anne. The sisters died in February or March. Only their father Otto survived. I am often asked to speak about Anne because of our similar backgrounds and experiences.

Hanneli Goslar (b. 1928)
Hanneli was born in Berlin where her father, a high-level government official, was forced to resign when Hitler came to power in 1933. Subsequently, the Goslars moved to Amsterdam and Hanneli attended the same Montessori School as Anne Frank where the two became best friends. Hanneli's family was deported to Westerbork and Bergen-Belsen in 1943–44, where we lived in the same barracks. Hanneli's mother died during the birth of her third child, so Hanneli raised her younger sister, Gabriela, or "Gigi." Hanneli and I became friends and at times shared the task of childcare. Mr. Goslar died in Bergen-Belsen. Hanneli and Gigi immigrated to Israel after the war, and Hanneli and I met again in Jerusalem in the 1980s.

Hasenbergs
John (1892–1945): father
Gertrude "Trudi" Mayer (1903–1988): mother
Werner (1928–2012): son
Irene (b. 1930): daughter

My parents were married in 1927 in Berlin. After the war, and as a widow, Mutti was courageous and adaptive as a single parent and provider. But as the wife of a banker, she had not worked outside the home or attended college, so making a living as a factory worker and a cashier was tough for her. She found solace in music, art, and nature, passing on that love to her children and grandchildren.

Werner and I shared a lot of joy and a lot of hardship early in our lives. We always stuck together and supported each other. Werner was always my big brother and I depended on him for guidance because he grasped the circumstances far better than I did. After Mutti, Werner, and I arrived in the United States and shared an apartment, Werner

---

took on the role of head of household. He studied economics and was employed at the U.S. Department of Commerce in Washington D.C., for most of his career. Werner married Geraldine Barkan, and they had two children, a girl and a boy.

Pappi was a German officer during World War I, and was a highly respected banker and citizen. It is to Pappi that the three of us owe our survival. I think about that, and him, every day.

After we left his body at the train station in Biberach, Germany, he was buried in a small Jewish cemetery in the nearby town of Laupheim, which I found out years later. I have since visited his grave a number of times, becoming friends with the wonderful local caretakers. The cemetery was restored in 1970 and the town takes great pride in preserving it. Descendents of Jews who are buried there are welcomed with open arms. Students are invited to help clean the grounds and are educated about the Holocaust. It is a source of great comfort to know that Pappi is resting in a place of dignity.

On my last visit there I was the guest of Michael Schick and his family, who are deeply involved in care of the cemetery and also in remembrance of local Jewish life and culture before the Holocaust. Michael's invitation to tell my story to Laupheim high school students prompted me to re-embrace my mother tongue after decades of refusal to hear or speak the German language. This experience became an opportunity for reconciliation.

Betty "Fanny" Ischenhauser (1923–?)
Betty and her mother Ada (1892–?) survived Bergen-Belsen. Although Betty couldn't finish her training because of their deportation, she still served as a nurse in the so-called hospital in Bergen-Belsen and on the train in January 1945 where she was called to our compartment and certified that Pappi had died. After Algeria, Betty immigrated to Palestine; her mother returned to Holland. Betty married, had a family, and stayed there for the rest of her life. Despite a bout of polio, she finished her studies in nursing and had an extensive career. We met in Jerusalem a few years before she passed away.

Joski Family
Siegfried (1899–1970): father
Hilde (1899–1993): mother
Ellen (1924–2000): daughter
Bob (1931–2014): son
The Joskis came from Berlin. They were deported to Bergen-Belsen where mother, Hilde, and daughter, Ellen, were housed in the same barracks as Mutti and me. The moms became friends. The Joskis were my main source of support during our time together in camp Jeanne d'Arc, taking me in when I was the only child there from Bergen-Belsen without a family. Hilde looked after me with tender loving care and wrote letters to Mutti in Switzerland, reporting about my well-being. Siegfried, Hilde, and Ellen returned to Germany after the war, and Bob moved to the United States and settled near Seattle, married, and had a family. Sadly, the Joskis and I did not reconnect after we parted in Algiers late 1945. I owe them much gratitude.

Vera Kan (b. 1930)
Vera was born in Indonesia on the isle of Java, and was my best friend in Amsterdam after her family returned to Holland in 1940. During the German occupation, we were not allowed to visit each other's homes since her family was not Jewish, so we spent a lot of time together outdoors. War separated us, but Vera tracked me down when I was in Algeria and wrote to me. In 1947, she sent me the first edition of Anne Frank's Diary in Dutch, *Het Achterhuis*. With her husband, Vera spent most of her life in Aruba, raised three children, and returned to Holland later in life. During the last decade it has been thrilling for us to reconnect and see each other.

The Loewenbergs
The Loewenbergs were friends of my parents in Amsterdam before the deportation. We shared a compartment with Lucie (1885–?) and her husband (?–1944) on the train from Westerbork to Bergen-Belsen. Mr. Loewenberg died at Bergen-Belsen, and Lucie ended up in Camp Jeanne d'Arc. She immigrated to South Africa after the war.

Mrs. Mandel
Mrs. Mandel is a pseudonym. Mrs. Mandel was one of my first lessons in understanding and forgiveness. I honor that by giving her and her descendants anonymity.

Tante Alice Mayer (1902–1943) and **Oom Paul Ullendorff** (1898–1943)
Aunt Alice, Mutti's only sibling, was married to Uncle Paul. They moved from Berlin to Amsterdam some time before we did. Uncle Paul had joined a pharmaceutical company, and they lived along one of the Amsterdam canals where Werner and I loved to bike. Early in 1943, they were deported to Westerbork. Soon after our arrival they were deported to the Sobibor concentration camp and murdered shortly thereafter.

Opa Julius Mayer (1863–1942) and **Omi Pauline Mayer** (1879–1942)
My maternal grandfather, Opa, owned a bank in Berlin, where Pappi was a partner. When Hitler came to power, the bank was taken away from the family. Opa and my father had to stop working. Pappi eventually found employment in Amsterdam. Opa and Omi were not allowed to emigrate from Germany to Holland with us. They were deported to the Theresienstadt concentration camp and were murdered. Thanks to Gunter Demnig, a German sculptor who invented the Stolpersteine (stumbling stones), there are two named stones placed in front of their house in Berlin. These stones mark the homes of those who died in the Holocaust and help us remember that they once lived. It pleases me that they continue to have a place and an identity in this city.

Miss Pino and Mr. Pinto
Miss Pino and Mr. Pinto were my two favorite teachers in elementary school in Amsterdam: Miss Pino from grades one through three; Mr. Pinto in grades four and five. Both made a deep impression, and my Poesie book includes verses from both of them, giving me purposeful guidance.

"To fly high without wings
let that not be your path
no one becomes smart by doing nothing,
without effort nothing is gained."

—*Miss Pino, 1941*

"Sometimes there will be rain and darkness
when everything seems black and grey
be brave, be a blessing; things will soon lift again.
Go through life strong and fair
Dear child, this is your teacher's advice for you."

—*Mr. Pinto, 1942*

Roseboom Family

Abraham (1898–1947): father
Karoline (1900–?): mother
Alexander "Lex" (1928–1998): son

Abraham, the father, was very tall, husky, and bright with the personality of an "official," which enabled him to deal with the Nazis in Bergen-Belsen and allowed him to get the less arduous or more popular jobs for himself and his family, like a kitchen job for his wife. Karoline was my swimming teacher in Algiers. Lex was a tall, handsome guy, and my boyfriend in Algeria. The Rosebooms returned to Holland in the fall of 1945 where Lex helped his father revive the family's burlap sack business in Amsterdam. Lex married a classmate of mine from elementary school, and they had three children. Somehow, Lex ended up being the last to write in my Poesie book in February 1946, probably before it was mailed to me in the States. It includes a photo of him looking dapper in tie, suit, and hat, and with a cigarette poised in his left hand. Around the photo he wrote in English "Do Not Forget Me!" and in Dutch:

"When we sat on the beach or walked along the waterfront of this beautiful sea, we forgot the sadness of BB [Bergen-Belsen]."

Rudi Berg(?) (circa 1929–?)
Sadly, I don't remember Rudi's surname and know nothing of his fate, other than he and his family were sent to Auschwitz.

Omi Silten (circa 1878–1944)
Omi Silten was the grandmother of my distant cousin Gabriele "Gabi" Silten, the daughter of Ilse and Fritz Silten. Gabi, her parents, and Omi lived in our neighborhood in Amsterdam and were deported at the same time we were on June 20, 1943. Omi Silten was a very warm, outgoing person, and in some sense Werner and I related to her as our Omi. She struggled with the conditions at Westerbork, and when the family was notified that Omi would be deported to Auschwitz, she begged her son Fritz, a pharmacist, to help her commit suicide. Through this act, Fritz saved his mother from being murdered by the Nazis. Gabi and her parents were sent to Theresienstadt concentration camp in January 1944. The three Siltens survived and moved to England after the war. We met on several occasions before Gabi settled in the United States and we had more contact.

Sussman Family
Friedrich (1900–1990): father
Margaret (1896–1988): mother
Peter (1928–1995): son
The Sussmans, originally from Germany, were also deported to Westerbork from Amsterdam. The father, Friedrich, worked in the book trade; the mother, Margaret, was a social worker; and son, Peter, was Werner's classmate. Our paths paralleled through Westerbork, Bergen-Belsen, and Camp Jeanne d'Arc. Peter and his father traveled to America late in 1945 on a ship restricted to males, while Margaret and I followed about a month later aboard a ship for women. After New York, they moved to Switzerland, but Peter ended up in Colorado and became a successful attorney, married Genifer, and together they had three children. The Sussmans and I remained friends for many years.

Vitek
I have no other information than our time together at the UNRRA Camp Jeanne d'Arc in Algeria.

Vogeltje, or "Little Bird"
I think this may be Vogeltje Groen-Knoop (1874–1944) who died in Bergen-Belsen, and who was married to Abraham Groen (1873–1940).

Wolf Family
Henri (1898–1974): father
Sara "Lien" Swaab (circa 1906–1945): mother
Jacob "Jack" or "Jaap" (1929–2014): son
Marie "Mieke" (1933–2009): daughter
We lived very close to the Wolfs in our neighborhood in Amsterdam. Werner and Jack were classmates in elementary school. Henri, the father, was a language teacher in Amsterdam. The Wolf Family and my family were deported at the same time from Amsterdam to Westerbork, to Bergen-Belsen, later to Camp Jeanne d'Arc in Algiers. Sara, the mother, died in Algiers shortly after our arrival, from cancer. Mieke and I shared the grief of having lost a parent right after liberation. Mr. Wolf became the language teacher for the young adults in Jeanne d'Arc, and with his help we made a good start at learning English and French. Both our families resettled in New York City in 1945 where Mieke, Jack, Werner, and I used to get together on weekends. Mr. Wolf took an administrative job in an office. Jack finished college and embarked on a career with the Social Security Administration where he worked until retirement. Mieke worked as an assistant to patients in a clinic. Although they have all passed, I feel fortunate to be in contact with two of Mieke's daughters, Lorrie and Patrice.

Acknowledgments

From Irene:

Thanks are due to the hundreds of students who over some thirty years have listened to me in their schools, blessed me with letters, drawings and verses, and described the relevance of my story to experiences in their own lives. The many tough questions students asked have not only lent depth to my memories but have inspired me to write this book. Of course I am also thankful to the many teachers who have invited me to speak in their classes to interact with their students in the United States, Germany, and Israel. Teachers whose classes I visited repeatedly include Jon Berger, Suzanne Hopkins, Ton Broos, Annemarie Toebosch, June Griffenhagen, and Hank Greenspan. They enabled me to reach out to new generations of students for which I am grateful.

I feel fortunate to have a number of close friends who are familiar with navigating the writers' world. Louise Borden, a well-known author of books for children of all ages, has given me valuable insights during our long friendship about the writing process as well as persistent encouragement for staying on track. Penny Schreiber, writer and editor, generously spent many hours helping me shape a frame for the book in its early stages. Mary Bisbee, my publicist friend, provided a different perspective on the complicated world of writers and publishers. With Leslie Stainton and Michelle Segar, also writer friends, I have enjoyed fruitful conversations about the various steps and stages required to carry out a plan so that it becomes a book. Jan Jarbou Russell clarified an important segment of my journey that I had not been aware of before she interviewed me for one part of her book, *The Train to Crystal City*. All of these friends have assured me that my story merits publication and I am most thankful to them.

Most of all Kris Holloway and John Bidwell deserve huge recognition for helping develop the main characters and voices in the dialogues of *Shores Beyond Shores*. During the countless hours we have spent together visiting, Skyping, or on the telephone they succeeded in reviving, enlivening, and deepening memories that were solidly buried in my past. Without their unrelenting dedication to the relevance, freshness, and intensity of my journey the book would not be what it has become. They transformed the account of an amateur writer into an engaging book. My gratitude to Kris and John is beyond words.

Members of Kris's writers group also deserve credit: Jacqueline Sheehan, Ellen Meeropol, Marianne Banks, Lydia Kann, Pat Riggs, Kari Ridge, Celia Jeffries, and Brenda Marsian. A number of the group's meetings were devoted to chapters that Kris presented for review and critique. The group provided constructive feedback regarding organization, elaboration of details, delving into feelings, etc. The opportunity to receive suggestions from a group of professional writers has been most valuable.

Last but not least is the role of my family. My husband Charlie supported me from beginning to end by giving me all the space and time needed for writing, even when it led to neglect of other aspects of our lives, for several years. My children, Ella and Noah, have taught me many valuable lessons during my post-Holocaust journey. Ella as a young child was the first one ever to insist that I tell my story to her. Noah has had a big impact on my life by introducing me to Buddhism and mindfulness. Both helped me understand what it is like to grow up as a child of a Holocaust survivor, and made me aware of the importance of breaking the silence. I have been blessed with many gifts.

If there is anyone who has been omitted unintentionally, my thanks to you.

Irene Butter
Ann Arbor, MI
December 2017

From John and Kris:

We first met Irene in the fall of 1992 in her role as Kris's graduate school advisor. Kris and Irene got on famously from the start. When Kris gave birth to our first son, Aidan, in 1994, Kris was the only nursing mother in her program. It was hard balancing high-powered grad school, work, and motherhood. Irene was the one professor who made it easier. She helped take care of Aidan during key events and meetings, and helped normalize motherhood in the classroom. Kris could not have completed her degree without Irene's support.

Irene attended the birth of our second son, Liam, in 1997. It was our second home birth, and Irene was the first person after John to hold Liam. As we became closer with Irene, we got to know her husband Charlie and had meals at their home in Ann Arbor. It was during our first visit that we noticed photographs on the wall of Irene and the Dalai Lama and other peacemakers, and it was then that she began telling us her story. We were dumbstruck: how could this petite, bright bundle of energy and joy have experienced such horror? We listened. This book is a product of that iterative journey. It has been one of our greatest blessings.

In addition, we want to thank:
- John's writing workshop, Writers in Progress, led by the wise Dori Ostermiller.
- Our patient friends and family members who read our words over and over, gave feedback, and many times just listened: Aidan and Liam Holloway-Bidwell, Jane and Bill Holloway, Pam Holloway, Paul Bidwell, Ginger Milord, Jim and Ruth Bidwell, Betsy and Mark Bartholomew, Darryl Caterine, Amy Russell and Michael Sanders, SuEllen Hamkins, and Michelle Segar.
- Linda Roghaar and White River Press for helping us pull all this together!

Our deepest gratitude goes to Irene and all the Irenes in the world who choose to stand and bear witness even under the most trying of times, and speak up for others even when their own skin isn't on the line.

John D. Bidwell and Kris Holloway
Florence, MA
December 2017

Authors

Irene Hasenberg Butter is a well-known peace activist, Holocaust survivor, and Professor Emerita of Public Health at the University of Michigan. She is a frequent and favored inspirational speaker, talking about her experience during World War II and stressing the importance of "never a bystander" and that "one person can make a difference." Irene is a co-founder of Zeitouna, an organization of Jewish and Arab women working for peace, and a founder of the Raoul Wallenberg Project at University of Michigan, which honors the Swedish diplomat who saved thousands of Jews with fellowships and an annual award for peace workers such as the Dalai Lama, Elie Wiesel, Desmond Tutu, and Aung San Suu Kyi. She received a PhD in Economics from Duke University.

John D. Bidwell is consulting editor of *Monique and the Mango Rains*, the critically esteemed book authored by his wife Kris Holloway that chronicles their time in the Peace Corps with the Malian midwife Monique Dembele. He is a branding and marketing executive and consultant, a frequent presenter, and has lectured and taught at the University of Michigan, University of Massachusetts, Smith College, and Marlboro College. John has his BA from McGill University.

Kris Holloway is author of the critically acclaimed *Monique and the Mango Rains: Two Years with a Midwife in Mali*, which has been called "a respectful, unsentimental portrait [and] a poignant and powerful book." (*Kirkus*, Starred Review). She has delivered hundreds of presentations, and the book remains a favorite "common read" and is used in 150+ college and university courses. Kris is President of CISabroad, a leading education abroad organization responsible for sending thousands of students to study and intern abroad worldwide. She holds a Master of Public Health from the University of Michigan.

A Call to Action

Irene has inspired thousands over the past three decades through her presentations, lectures, and film. She reminds us all of our ability to make meaningful change through seemingly small gestures, and reminds us that "refusing to be an enemy" and "never being a bystander" makes all the difference in the world. Here's what you can do:

Commit to volunteering 4 hours a month. That's it. Research social justice issues important to you in the world or in your local community. Start small. Think about what's important to you and get involved, in your local government, with nonprofits, or volunteer with national or international organizations. Just devote 1 hour a week to something you care about.

Use these resources that Irene has developed for you:
- **Download the Reading Guide:** www.irenebutter.com/book
- **Order the DVD** on Refusing to be Enemies to learn about facilitating dialogue across differences. www.irenebutter.com/zeitouna/
- **Watch the documentary film** *Never a Bystander* and join the conversation. www.irenebutter.com/neverabystander

Invite Irene to speak or to Skype into your group, book group, or classroom. www.irenebutter.com/contact

Learn about the organizations that Irene believes in deeply:
- **Raoul Wallenberg Award:** www.raoulwallenberg.org/awards
- **Zeitouna:** www.refusingtobeenemies.org
- **The Practice of Tibetan Buddhism:** pemachodronfoundation.org
- **Southern Poverty Law Center:** www.splcenter.org
- **Equal Justice Initiative:** www.eji.org

"...accept the call to action by speaking out against injustice on your own journey."

JAMES F. JOHNSON
Assistant Principal
Discovery Middle School